FAMILY LIFE UNDER ISLAM

FAMILY LIFE UNDER ISLAM

Shujaat Husain

ANMOL PUBLICATIONS PVT. LTD.
NEW DELHI - 110 002 (INDIA)

ANMOL PUBLICATIONS PVT. LTD.
4374/4B, Ansari Road, Daryaganj
New Delhi - 110 002
Ph.: 23261597, 23278000
Visit us at: www.anmolpublications.com

Family Life Under Islam

First Published, 2004
ISBN 81-261-1911-X

PRINTED IN INDIA

Published by J.L. Kumar for Anmol Publications Pvt. Ltd., New Delhi - 110 002 and Printed at Mehra Offset Press, Delhi.

Contents

Preface

Islam is the first religion in the world, which emerged on the scene as a perfect discipline. Islam, as a faith introduced a flawless code of conduct for leading the worldly life and for attaining peace and salvation, in the world hereafter. Under the same code of conduct, the divine commands have identified all that is good and all that is bad in this world for the faithful.

This study is focussed on the pattern of family life in Islamic manner. It brings to light the lesser known facts that Islam has given a very progressive design for an exemplary family and its members. The Islamic tenets explain the duties, rights, obligations and previleges, granted for the menfolk and womenfolk in order to make their life peaceful, achieving and purposeful.

Islam as a logical school of thought, has touched all the aspects of life in its fold. It has distinguished good from the evil and piety from the sin, in an unerring fashion. The followers of Islam have to abide by all rules and regulations and even a slight laxity or failure on their part may invite serious sanctioning, as the Holy book and other scriptures have injunctions for all functions—commissions and omissions.

Islam being a misunderstood religion seldom receives criticism from certain quarters for its so-called harsh laws and its non-existing oppressive measures.

This book, accomplished with a missionary zeal is an attempt for clearing the anti-Islam air and presenting the real face of the faith, so that the world could recognise the worth of real Islam and its contribution in creating a new civilization and society for the betterment of mankind.

This editor is confident that this modest effort of his would be appreciated by all concerned circles.

Editor

1

Introduction

Islamic attitude towards life has been defined by the Holy Qur'an in the following verses:

> Blessed is He in Whose hands is the kingdom and He has power over all things, Who created Death and Life-that He may try you-which of you is best in conduct. (lxvii. 1-2)
>
> And He it is Who created the heavens and the earth in six days and His throne was on water that He may try you - which of you is best in conduct. (xi. 7)
>
> Lo! He produceth creation, then reproduceth it that He may with justice recompense those who believe and do good works. (x. 4)

Life, for the individual, according to the above verses is an opportunity, provided by nature, to bring out the best and most spiritual in him by being placed within a network of human relationships which constantly put him on trial in respect of his social sympathies and sense of justice towards his fellow-men. The purpose of life, therefore, is the spiritual betterment of man. Nature secures this cud by placing individuals in a social situation where they may develop their altruistic self and restrain their-egoistic desires. The response of the individual to the requirements of this situation is a measure of his spiritual progress and an index of his success or failure in the trial spoken of by the Holy Qur'an.

It is clear from the verses quoted above that Islam does not judge civilisation by its mechanical efficiency, technical progress or productive capacity. A society may achieve phenomenal success in any or all of these aspects and still remain spiritually bankrupt, if in the distribution of material wealth and the products of technical development, it betrays an insufficient regard for social justice and human equality. On the other hand, there may be civilisations lacking in material productivity, yet marked by a high sense of fellow-feeling and greater regard for human values. The test of a civilisation, from the Quranic viewpoint, lies in the harmony of relations between its component parts, whether horizontally as affecting the different national groups which inhabit its sphere of influence or vertically as, reflected in the mutual attitude of the different economic classes whose total productive efforts sustain its material existence. That is the meaning of the Quranic statement that 'God created Death and Life in order to try which, of you is best in conduct.' The primary value of civilisation, according to this attitude, lies in the moral conduct of its individuals as reflected in their beliefs, institutions and class and sex relations, etc. Here, and not in its mechanical development and technical efficiency, should be sought the criterion of its success or failure.

That social conduct in its various manifestations is the main concern of the religious spirit, has been further emphasised by the Holy Qur'an in the following verses:

> The love of desires, of women and sons and hoarded treasures of gold and silver and well-bred horses and cattle and tilth is made to seem fair to men: this is the, provision of the life of the lower level, and Allah is He with Whom is the higher goal (of life).
>
> Say: Shall I tell you of what, is better than these? For those who guard (against evil) are Gardens with their Lord, beneath which rivers flow, to abide in them, and pure mates and Allah's pleasure: add Allah sees His servants.

> Those who say: Our Lord! surely we believe, therefore forgive us our faults and keep us from the chastisement of fire.
>
> The patient and the truthful, and the obedient, and those who spend (benevolently) - and those who ask for forgiveness in the morning times (iii. 13-16).

Here the Holy Qur'an presents two alternative ways of life. First, the-lower way, which is distinguished by the predominance of acquisitive desires, the love of sexual pleasure, the pride of family, wealth and other kinds of material acquisitions and, secondly, the life of creative social sympathies marked by the pursuit of higher ideals which call forth our powers of patience, philanthropy, and remind us of our duties to our fellow-men. The Holy Qur'an declares its preference for this latter way of life and holds out the prospect of a rich reward for those who follow it. Here again Islam emphasises, social values other than those which lead merely to greater abundance; of material goods without in any way ennobling and harmonising human relations.

Further evidence of this attitude towards human social existence is provided by the following statement:

> Permission (to fight) is given to those upon whom war is made, because they are oppressed ... those who have been expelled from their homes without a just cause ... those who, should We establish them in the land, will keep up prayer and pay the poor-due and enjoin good and forbid evil. (xxii. 39-40)

The Holy Qur'an describes here the distinctive qualities of a, party which comes into power as the result of a successful struggle against the forces of evil. What is significant is that we miss here any emphasis on purely physical valour, military preparedness, technical efficiency and mechanical skill — qualities which, by any test of fitness, are necessary for those who wish to come out successful in a military struggle. Instead, the virtues recommended by the Holy Qur'an are those which tend to, harmonise and ennoble human relations-deference to the claims of the downtrodden, humility in a state of power and success manifested in efforts to establish prayers, and an active desire to stamp out evil and injustice in all forms, at reforming zeal to encourage virtuous behaviour leading towards improved human relations. For a group engaged in a life-and-death struggle for survival, these qualities seem rather inappropriate, since a state of struggle calls for just the opposite qualities of physical valour, mechanical efficiency and technical superiority. The only explanation for this seeming paradox is that, according to the Holy Qur'an, the latter virtues are the necessary but secondary products of a struggle whose inspiration comes exclusively from a spiritual vision of life. The main object of human existence is the continuing improvement of human relationships. But this object requires for its successful accomplishment the secondary qualities of material strength and mechanical efficiency, etc. A civilisation which inverts this natural order and sets up material progress and technical skill, etc., as ends in themselves runs the grave risk of disintegration from within by social conflicts arising from the deteriorating relations of its component parts.

In passing judgment on Islamic teachings with regard to sex relations and the ideal of sex equality, it is necessary to keep in mind this aspect of the matter. As against Western civilisation which regards the abundance of material wealth, technical skill and mechanical efficiency as of primary importance and which subordinates, as of instrumental value and secondary importance, the ideal of social justice and other spiritual values. Islam puts primary emphasis on just those qualities of the soul which lead to greater social harmony and prevent class conflicts. Material wealth and the human qualities which tend to increase it are not belittled by Islam. They are allowed only a rank of secondary importance. This difference in the two systems of values alters the perspective in which human and social problems are tackled respectively by Islam and Western civilisation. Islamic civilisation stands midway between ancient ascetic cultures, which negated life and matter and looked upon the things of this world as having a soul-degrading effect, and the materialistic culture of the modern West, which has turned material wealth and economic prosperity into objects of idolatrous worship. From the Islamic viewpoint, economic wealth and the qualities which help its furtherance are good only in so far as they subserve spiritual interests and make for greater social harmony. When raised to the level of primary importance, they become the agents of the devil.

2

Historical Background

Man is a combination of contradictions. He is an embodiment of virtue and evil, love and hatred, good and bad. He is, on the one hand, the best of the creation, the vicegerent of Allah on earth, the most exalted-personages, called prophets (peace be upon them), belonged to the human race. On the other hand, tyrants, like Haman, Shaddad, Pharaoh and Namrud, whose atrocities send a shiver through our bodies even today, were also born into this race. But The Almighty in His Infinite Mercy made the arrangement to reform humanity and eradicate sin and vice, and sent Prophet Muhammad (peace and blessings of Allah be upon him), the last of the Prophets, the mercy for the worlds among mankind and vouchsafed him the Holy Quran; the complete code and constitution for our guidance. It embraces all aspects of human life.

Almighty, the Exalted, has made sexual intercourse as a means of protection and perpetuation of the human race. He has created two sexes called man and woman having irresistible charm and attraction for one another. One sex is badly in need of the other and is a source of satisfaction for the other and vice versa. The life of one without the other is incomplete and devoid of any purpose and meaning.

This is the reason why a man as a complete man cannot do without a woman and likewise a woman, as a woman, cannot lead a peaceful and comfortable life without a man. But man is by nature rash and hasty. He has proved to be extravagant even in this respect and has transgressed the lawful limits in the satisfaction of his sexual desires. This trend is fatal for humanity and the human race.

Just as Islam does not permit man to transgress the lawful limits in other spheres, it does not allow him to deviate from a natural, balanced course in the matter of sex. A permanent moral code has, therefore, been given to us so that we may mould our lives according to it. Those who fear Allah and the Hereafter and have love and respect for His Messenger (peace and blessings of Allah be upon him) will be able to reform themselves by reading this book.

Women's Position

There is no denying the fact that when Islam promulgated the rules and regulations concerning moral conduct and behaviour, people had forgotten the real purpose and significance of marriage. The peace and happiness which conjugal life gives to the husband and wife were not enjoyed by them. The mutual love and affection which brings the two souls and their two families so near and inculcates mutual love and cooperation between them, no longer existed, nor did there remain any good and wholesome influence from such marriages. Even modesty and chastity, which are the essence of marriage, were cast to the winds. Only the custom existed, but the real spirit and purpose of marriage did not exist.

In every part of the world woman was subjected to unbearable tortures by man, who treated this weak and delicate creature like a beast of the jungle. Women were purchased and sold like cattle and household goods. Men did not hesitate to beat women to satisfy their lust. They were even compelled to prostitution. So these wretched creatures not only satisfied the lust of their husbands, but earned for their husbands through nefarious trafficking.

Before the advent of Islam woman was considered a creature between human and beast whose main function was to bear children and to serve man. Due to this very reason, the birth of female babies was considered to be disgraceful and to bury them alive at their very birth was taken as a laudable action. The information which is gleaned from the pages of the Holy Quran about this evil practice of the days of Ignorance is pathetic and heart-rending.

Cause of being Female

The Holy Quran explains how the news of the birth of a female child affected the feelings and sentiments of a father:

> When if one of them receiveth tidings of the birth of a female, his face remaineth darkened and he is wroth inwardly. He hideth himself from the folk because of the evil of that whereof he hath had tidings, (asking himself): Shall he keep it in contempt, or bury it beneath the dust.
> (16:58-59)

The Holy Quran has alluded to this incident at another place:

> And if one of them hath tidings of that which he likeneth to the Beneficent One, his countenance becometh black and he is full of inward rage. (43:17)

The Holy Quran refers to the idiosyncrasies of the people of the Days of Ignorance. On the one hand, those people called the angels the daughters of God in other words, they believed in female deities, and on the other hand, they could not bear the disgrace of being called the fathers of daughters. The Holy Quran points out this contradiction:

> Hath your Lord then distinguished you (O men of Makkah) by giving you sons, and hath chosen for Himself females from among the angels? Lo! verily, you speak an awful word! (17:40)

The Holy Quran has mentioned at another place:

> And they assign unto Allah daughters. Be He glorified! And unto themselves what they desire.
> (16:57)

Such were the feelings and sentiments of the people about those poor creatures in the Days of Ignorance. It is, therefore, easily comprehensible why people often killed their daughters to save themselves from disgrace. The Holy Quran says about these hard-hearted people:

> And when the girl-child that was buried alive is asked: For what sin she was slain. (81:8,9)

Besides the feelings of shame and disgrace attached to the birth of daughters, people committed this heinous crime due to baseless fear of poverty. The Holy Quran ordains:

> Slay not your children because of poverty-We provide for them and for you. (6:151)

> Slay not your children, fearing a fall to poverty, We shall provide them and for you. Lo! the slaying of them is great sin. (17:31)

Due to these evil practices, the number of women in the Days of Ignorance decreased and heavy amount had to be paid to purchase one.

Moral Degeneration

Some light is thrown on the status of women in the Days of Ignorance by the rules and regulations relating to moral conduct and behaviour which were enforced by the Holy Quran:

> Force not your slave-girls to whoredom that ye may seek enjoyment of the life of the world, if they would preserve their chastity. (24:33)

A Tradition in "Sahih Bukhari" reveals that women were mortgaged to men in the Days of Ignorance. Muhammad b. Musailama reported that when he went to K'ab b. al-Ashraf and asked him to lend corn, he said:

> "Mortgage your woman to me." (The borrower): "How can we do so when you are the most handsome of Arabs?"

The above incident shows the sad plight of the women of those days. How cheap was their modesty and chastity! The custom of marriage was in vogue; but the various forms in which it existed were nothing short of adultery. It is a fact that no value was attached to the modesty and chastity of women.

Marital Bonds

It has been reported by Hadrat 'A'isha (Allah be pleased with her): There were four practices of marriage in the Days of Ignorance:

1. The practice which is in vogue today.
2. The husband said to his wife: 'After menstruation when you have taken a bath, go to such and such a person and have sexual intercourse with him.' The husband remained aloof from his wife till her (his wife's) pregnancy was established. Thereafter, the husband could go to his wife if he desired; but he did not generally do so, so that the child may be of a noble descent. This marriage is called 'Nikah Istabda', -that is, 'the marriage for the sake of getting seed'.
3. The third tradition of marriage was that a number of men came to a woman to have sexual intercourse with her, but their number did not exceed ten, when she became pregnant and delivered a child, she sent for all those men through a messenger after a few days. No one could refuse. When all of them were present, she would say: You used to come to me for sexual intercourse. I have delivered a child and it belongs to you. Now you should give some name to the child as you like, so the child went to the person whom the woman identified. He could not refuse to take the child.
4. There were some women who had hoisted flags. These were prostitutes. Anyone who desired could have sexual intercourse with them. When anyone of them delivered a child, a physiognomist was called, and he judged on the authority of his knowledge, as to whom the child belonged. That person could not refuse to accept the child.

When the Holy Prophet (peace and blessings of Allah be upon him) was sent with the True Faith, he banned all such marriages of the

Days of Ignorance. He allowed only that marriage which is in vogue today.

It is clear from the above that in the Days of Ignorance, the modesty and chastity of a woman had no value in the eyes of the people. The derisive attitude of the people concerning female modesty can be judged from the fact that the husbands voluntarily sent their wives to strangers to get seed (offspring) of noble descent. This was due to the wrong notion that the husband considered his wife his personal property which he had acquired on payment of dower. After the death of her husband, she was, therefore, treated as inherited property.

Situation in other Societies

The above was the treatment of the Arabs with their womenfolk in the dark Days of Ignorance. Now let us discuss the attitude of other nations towards their women. In this connection, excerpts from the book of a famous non-Muslim scholar, Gastauli Ben, are reproduced below.

> The Greeks considered the woman as low creation. If a child was born to a woman in an unnatural position, they killed her. In Sparta, the unfortunate woman who could not give birth to a soldier was put to death. When a woman delivered a child, she was in the national interest, temporarily lent to serve another person to beget child from his seed (race). The Greeks did not respect their women even in their most civilized times, except at the time of circumambulation.

It has been mentioned in the Chapters 'Sermon' of the Old Testament.

> He who loves God must shun woman. I found one out of one thousand men whom God loves, but there is none among the women of the world whom God loves in Rome. The husband's attitude towards his wife was cruel. She enjoyed

no share in the social activities. He had every right to claim even her life. The same was the position of the Greeks.

(Arab Civilization: 372,373)

It has been mentioned in the Torah, Chapter 25, Verse 5- 10:

'If two brothers live together and one of them dies childless, the wife of the deceased should not be married to a stranger, but her husband's brother should have sexual intercourse with her in privacy, treating her to be his wife and fulfil the right of being her husband's brother as the child which will be born to her would be called the child of his deceased brother. Thus his name will not be effaced from Israel. If he refuses to act as her husband, his brother's wife should draw out shoe from her feet and spit on his face before the judges saying: "who does not care for his brother's home, deserves such treatment." His name would become notorious among Israel as being the house of one where a shoe has been drawn out.'

It has been stated in the Bible, "Woman is more bitter than death."

What protection or safeguard the Hindu Law provided for female morality can be judged from the following excerpts from *Satyarath Parkash* edited by Sawami Dayanand Sarsvati Ji Maharaj which are reproduced below:

'Marriage is of eight kinds: 1. Braham, 2. Dev, 3. Arish, 4. Parjapat, 5. Asur, 6. Gandharb, 7. Rakshash and 8. Paishaj. Their details are given below:

1. When the bride and bridegroom are pious and chaste and of excellent moral character and have been tied in wedlock on their mutual consent, the marriage is called Braham.

2. To give over the girl in gold ornaments to the bridegroom in a ceremonious way, is called Dev.

3. Where the parents receive some money before giving the hand of their daughter, it is called Arish.
4. Where the couple marry to promote the cause of faith is called Parjapat.
5. Arrangements of marriage after giving something to the bride and bridegroom is called Asur.
6. Irregular and haphazard meeting and contact of a man and woman by their mutual consent is called Gandharb.
7. Seizure of a girl by force or allotment is called Rakshash.
8. Forced sexual intercourse with a sleeping, drunk intoxicated or mad girl is called Paishaj.

The keeping of a common wife in a family or among a few brothers was also in vogue in the ancient times. An extract from *Manu Samriti* p. 59 is given below:

'Nayug is a custom among the Brahmans according to which, if the woman is childless, she can, with the permission of her grandfather, have sexual connection with her relatives or her husband's brothers to get offspring according to her desire.'

It has been mentioned in *Satyarath Parkash*: 'If the woman is barren (she does not become pregnant for eight years) or she gives birth to dead babies or she delivers female babies only, her husband should wait for eleven years. But so far as the woman who uses bad language is concerned, her husband must forsake her immediately and have Nayug (sexual intercourse) with another woman to get offspring.

Likewise if the husband is very cruel; the woman should leave him and get children by having sexual connection with the husband of another married woman, who will be his inheritors. When the husband is rendered impotent, he should give permission to his wife in the following words:

"O fortunate woman who desires children! Now seek another husband besides me as I am lacking in sufficient strength to produce children." Then that woman would have sexual union (Nayug) with another man; but serve her large-hearted husband. In the same way when the woman is rendered unfit to bear children due to illness, she should permit her husband to have sexual union with some widow to produce children

Many other practices of Nayug have been mentioned in this book. So much about marriages; now let us see what their views about women were.

According to the Hindu Law, luck, storm, death, hell, poison, poisonous snakes, none is more harmful than woman!

According to Manu Law, a woman should remain under the care of her parents, in youth under her husband and after him, under her sons. If she has no sons, she should remain under the care of her relatives, as no woman can lead an independent life.

Before the advant of Islam, ancient Indian history is full of incidents of non-reliance on woman. For instance, in order to level the charge of adultery against any woman, it was sufficient to say only that she remained with another man for the time during which an egg can be fried.

Tartaulian was the spiritual leader of the early Christians. He explains the Christian view in the following words:

> "She is a gate through which Satan enters. She allured man to the forbidden tree. She is a breaker of Divine law. She spoiled man, the image of God."

A renowned Christian leader says about woman:

> "An inevitable evil, an hallucination, a pleasant hardship, a domestic trouble, a destructed charm, a decorated scourge. (Pardah, Maududi)

Popular Sayings

The current proverbs about women throw light on the degrading view of men towards women:

> There is a Russian proverb: A horse may be good or bad, it needs beating. Similarly a woman, good or bad, cannot do without beating. There is a proverb in the Spanish: one should shun an ugly woman but one should never rely upon a beautiful face.

Other Faiths

Before the advent of Islam, the union of husband and wife was considered as harmful for morality and spirit, as it hampered their development. Sayyid Salman Nadvi in his famous book *Sirat-un-Nabi* Vol. VI has written:

'Before the advent of Islam, the relation between husband and wife was considered disastrous for morality and spiritual development. In India the followers of Buddha, Jain, Veda, Jog and Sadhus held the same view. In Christianity celibacy and abstinence from woman was regarded as the height of spiritualism.'

The above excerpts have been given so that the readers may know the derisive attitude of the followers of various religions towards women and female morality and chastity.

Islam's Entry

In this dismal darkness, the resplendent sun of Islam rose and its brilliant rays illuminated every nook and corner of the world. This trampled and downtrodden humanity was accorded due respect and honour and its status was raised in society.

Extravagance and aggression were put to an end and Islam taught the lesson of a balanced systematic life. The rights were given to their rightful owners.

Islam vehemently supported the cause of the oppressed and downtrodden women, tenaciously safeguarded their honour and chastity and prohibited all acts which led to immodesty and adultery. Rules and regulations regarding the moral conduct and behaviour of husband and wife were framed and unlicensed sexual unions were banned. Islam imposed rules for the balanced and healthy satisfaction of sex and perpetuation of the human race. It enforced stability and discipline in household life and insisted on maintaining a healthy and wholesome atmosphere. Instead of being a curse, the woman is considered to be a harbinger of blessing and prosperity. Asceticism was discouraged and instead of adopting celibacy, the necessity of leading a married life was stressed.

Position Defined

It was declared in the first Qur'anic charter determining the rights and status of women:

> "O mankind! Be careful of your duty to your Lord Who created you from a single soul and from it created its mate and from them twain hath spread abroad a multitude of men and women." (4:1)

In other words, man and woman are waters of the same spring. As regards 'humanity', differentiation between the two is based on a mere superstition or supposition and it has no reality.

The above verse repudiates the view that woman is not of the humankind and says that both man and women have the same origin and have been born from a single soul. They are not separate creatures and are like men. Due to this very reason they should respect each other and be proud of each other. The well known Qur'anic verse:

> "O mankind! Lo! We have created you male and female, and have made you nations and tribes that ye may know one another. Lo! the noblest of you, in the sight of Allah, is the best in conduct." (49:13)

Besides other things this also alludes to the fact that in the birth of man, woman has her share. When man is not born of his own accord, what right does he possess to treat man with honour and respect and degrade woman? The human body is a compound of both man and woman; but according to medical research, it is woman who creates the major part of the human structure. It is woman who bears the burden of a child during pregnancy, then delivers, suckles and rears the child.

Just think, what does man do for his child? Is it not a sheer folly on our part that we should hate the existence of a woman who gives us shape and form during pregnancy and is responsible for our existence? It is woman who reared us, trained us, enabled us to walk and speak and provided our needs at the time when we could not express. It is she who served us till the age of competency. And in spite of all this sacrifice we treat her with hatred and contempt. Woe be upon the people who entertain and express such ideas concerning woman.

The above, and other verses of the Holy Quran bear out the fact that woman is not a low creation, but she is equal to man in the matter of respect and honour. Treating women like animals and forcing them to earn through prostitution, and adultery is shameful for men and mankind.

Main Objective of Existence

Despite common 'human' elements between man and woman, there are some physical differences between the two sexes, which everyone knows. The real wisdom behind these differences is known to Allah only:

> "Unto Allah belongeth the sovereignty of the heavens and the earth. He createth what He will. He bestoweth female (offspring) upon whom He will, and bestoweth male (offspring) upon whom He will; or He mingleth them males and females, and He maketh barren whom He will. Lo! He is Knower, Powerful." (42:49,50)

There is no reason to be wroth and to feel annoyance at the birth of a female, it is sheer folly on the part of man that he considers a blessing a curse. If these female babies should not grow up and become women and you do not marry them off, wherefrom will you get hale and hearty soldiers?

When the mother of Hadrat Maryam (Mary) (peace be upon her) vowed a vow and she gave birth to a female instead of a male, she said in deep sorrow, 'My Lord! I am delivered of a female' (3:36). It has happened against my hope. I have vowed unto thee that which is in my belly as consecrated and a female is not accepted.'

> Allah heard the pathetic voice and said, "Allah knew best of what she was delivered-the male is not as the female." (3:36)

The Almighty knows better than you, and He, the All Knowing, knows that a male cannot be like this female. The reward and blessing, the honour and prestige which this girl would bring would not be brought by a male. You thought in your own human way and thinking so felt dejected. The work which Allah proposes to take from this girl is hidden from your sight.

The world knows that the birth of Mary became a blessing and means of salvation. Mary gave birth to Christ, who preached the true Faith and delivered humanity from the doom of Hell. It is strange that the followers of Christ should consider woman as the gate through which Satan enters and as an inevitable evil.

Annihilation Banned

Islam prohibited the killing of daughters, removed the unfounded fear of poverty from their hearts and inculcated the feeling of reliance on the absolute power of the Provider and Sustainer. It has been mentioned in the Holy Quran.

> "Ye slay not your children because of penury - We provide for you and for them." (6:152)

> "Slay not your children, fearing a fall to poverty. We shall provide for them and you. Lo! the slaying of them is a great sin." (17:31)

In the above verses, killing of children, male or female, is strictly prohibited. It is unlawful in the Shariah to kill anybody. It is a heinous crime.

Islam removed the unfounded fear of poverty from the hearts of people and stated that Allah is the sole Provider and Sustainer. Have you ever thought who provides your livelihood in penury? Whenever any soul comes, He provides for his sustenance beforehand. If there exists no provision in the Divine budget or decree, and God goes on multiplying His population, it would be inferred that it is not God, the Gracious, but a Nawab or Raja whose treasury is empty and cannot pay the salaries of people. When Allah has guaranteed sustenance to everyone, we should not consider ourselves to be the providers for our children.

> "And there is not a beast in the earth but the sustenance thereof depends upon Allah."
>
> (11:6)

Ancient Experience

The mankind began its journey with the union of man and woman. It also spread the human race and evolved science and art, trade and industry and civilization and culture. All other relations amongst mankind are either the outcome of the union of man and woman or are the result of external causes and circumstances in the absence of which no such relations could be evolved. A neighbour loves another neighbour, a companion embraces another companion, a traveller joins another traveller; similarly a student associates with another student and a trader cooperates with another trader, because they have mutual interest. But as soon as their interests cease, they fall apart and become strangers to each other. But this is not the case with the union of man and woman. Their union is based on the natural feeling and attraction which keep them united in spite of their range of action and interest being quite separate.

A woman, no doubt, nurtures the human race with her blood and looks after the affairs of her home, but she finds it difficult to work in the field and defend herself against the enemies, for, she has no sufficient strength to do so. Her heart is the abode of only love, sympathy and sacrifice; whereas man is hard and sturdy, therefore, his duties include hunting, farming, trade and defence.

This difference of strength between man and woman has been the matter of grace and disgrace in periods of history. Man has physical power and strength; what he can do, a woman cannot do because of natural weakness, so man was considered superior and woman inferior. Hence, the countries which were well-known for their justice, character-building and grant of human rights, considered man as superior to woman.

To some extent, detailed knowledge of the ancient, history of the Greeks and the Romans is available. Their culture, civilization and knowledge of science and arts considerably flourished, so much so that on their bases many cultures came into being. But in spite of all these, the place of woman was very low in their societies. They would regard her only a burden on human being. Her only purpose was to serve man in the house like a maid servant.

In spite of all their lofty ideas and rationalism, the Greeks had very ridiculous concepts about women. They used to say:

> "There is a cure for burning by fire and snake-bite but there is no cure for a woman's mischief."

She had to live under the subjugation of her parents in childhood, of her husband in youth and of her children in widowhood. On the other hand the rights of her male relatives were always superior. Though the law provided her with the right of divorce but practically, it was of no avail because the act of going to court of law was considered a matter of shame and disgrace in the Greek society. No doubt Plato pleaded for the equal rights for man and woman but this was no more than a theoretical preaching and was nowhere in practice. The purpose of marriage was just political, that is, to produce strong and healthy children for the defence of the country. It was laid down in the, law of Sparta that, the husbands who were not fully young or weak, should offer their young wives to healthier and stronger young men to enable them produce sturdy soldiers for the army.

The Roman Law kept the status of woman very low for a long time. The head of the family, either or husband, had full authority over his wife and children. He could turn out his wife at any time he wanted. There was no system of dowry. The father had the right to give his daughter in marriage to anybody at his sweet will. He could also break the marriage. Later on, this right was transferred to the husband who could even kill his wife if he so desired. The system of divorce was unknown for about 520 years.

In Roman society, the purpose of woman was like that of slaves. Man used to marry woman only for his own benefit. She was never considered fit for any post or even able to give evidence in any matter. She had no legal rights whatsoever; only some facilities were granted to her because of her physical weakness. Of course, the woman was given some rights by the Romans in later period, yet she was not treated equal to man.

> When if one of them receiveth tidings of the birth of a female, his face remaineth darkened, and he is wroth inwardly. (Holy Quran)

Medieval Experience

In modern world, Europe claims to have given all the rights to woman. But the same woman was the victim of man a century ago and there was no law to prevent a male from tyrannizing the woman. The husband had full right over the wealth and property of his wife. There was no law of maintenance of wife. She could not sue her husband. He could even deprive his wife of her right to property.

Woman was not free to deal in any matter whatsoever. She had no right to sign any contract. She was neither allowed to spend money earned by her nor to marry a man of her choice.

Daughters were the property of their parents. Marriage was nothing but a trade because they used to sell their daughters to whomsoever they liked.

Before the advent of Christianity, man was the master of woman. There were no rules and regulations for the control of a man. Even after Christianity, woman had no equal rights.

> At the time of nuptial she is asked to swear before the priest to remain obedient to her husband for whole of her life in all circumstances. She can do nothing without his permission. She has no right to own her property because it, automatically becomes the property of her husband. Thus her position is worse than a slave.

The woman was thought as a cause of disgrace and shame in ancient Arabia. The birth of a daughter would make the Arabs sorrowful and sad. They would feel pride in having sons but felt ashamed of having daughters. The Holy Quran has perfectly described their feelings in this regard.

> "When one of them receiveth tidings of the birth of a female (daughter), his face remaineth darkened, and he is wroth inwardly. He hideth himself from the folk because of the evil of that whereof he hath had tidings, (asking himself): Shall he keep it in contempt or bury it beneath the dust. Verily evil is their Judgment".
>
> (16:58-59)

The Holy Quran further depicts the feeling of the father of the Age of Ignorance in respect of the news of the birth of a daughter in these words:

> "And if one of them hath tidings of that which he likeneth to the Beneficent One, his countenance becometh black and he is full of inward rage." (43: 17)

Thus, before the advent of Islam, a large number of Arab fathers buried their newly born daughters alive in order to escape their whimsical and superstitious disgrace. Moreover, they had no feeling of kindness and love for woman, and they buried their daughters alive. A man related his own action during the days of ignorance to the Holy Prophet Muhammad (S.A.W.) :

> "I had a little daughter who loved me very much. Whenever I called her, she came running happily towards me. One day I called her, as usual she came running and then followed me. I took her to a nearby well and pushed her in. At that moment she cried, "Father, father." The Prophet of Islam (S.A.W.) was shocked to hear it and his eyes were filled with tears."(Sunan Darimi)

> It is stated that Qais bin 'Asim had buried alive about eight daughters during the days of Jahiliya. (Tafseer Ibn Kaseer)
>
> Even if the Arabs kept their daughters alive, they deprived them of all their rights. There was no limitation for marriage. They married as many women as they liked. When Wahal Asadi (R.A.A.) embraced Islam, he had ten wives. (Abu Dawood)
>
> Similarly Gheelan Saqfee also had ten wives at the time of his conversion to Islam. (Tirmizi)
>
> Likewise, there were no restrictions on divorce, man was free to divorce his wife any time and any number of times and reunite at will. (Mustadrak)

The wife had to serve her husband during his life-time and after his death, his heirs had full rights-over her. They were free to marry their step-mothers themselves or got her married with anyone they liked. They were also authorised to prevent her from marrying anyone. In order to misappropriate the wealth and property of the widow, they did not allow her to re-marry. If she were a minor, her marriage was delayed, so that they may marry her themselves.

Allama Abu- Bakr Jassas writes:

> "It was a common practice to marry step-mothers during the days of ignorance . (Ahkamul Quran)
>
> Whenever, an Arab happened to be the guardian of a pretty and wealthy girl, he would himself marry her and paid no dower. (Bukhari).
>
> In pre-Islamic Arabia, woman had no right of inheritance. After the Battle of Uhud, the wife of Sabit bin Qais complained to the Holy Prophet

> (S.A.W.) that her husband had been martyred and she had two daughters. But Sabit's brother had misappropriated everything. Now, how would she arrange for their marriage?"
>
> (Abu Dawood).

> When Islam granted woman the right of inheritance, the Arabs were wonder struck and asked the Prophet of Islam (S.A.W.), "O Prophet of Allah! how can a woman inherit half of the property when she cannot ride a horse nor defend herself?" (Tafseer Ibn Kaseer)

Modern Experience

Woman was victimised for a long time. When her agony reached its climax, the situation became very serious. The modern age brought revolution in every aspect of life and changed the status of woman. Formerly she was slave but now she is 'free'. The Industrial Revolution in Europe helped woman achieve her 'Freedom'. She broke the chain of 'slavery', and came in the open field. The doors of employment were opened for her which helped her to revolt against man.

Woman desired freedom not for the betterment of her lot but for vengeance. She went to such an extent in this process that she herself took the place of man. She forgot the fundamental principle that woman can't take the place of man. Both are quite different in their capabilities and characteristics. Man and woman are physically and psychologically quite different from each other.

The main difference between man and woman is of sex and this difference cannot be removed by means of education, training or environment. They differ in their very nature. What a man can do, a woman cannot do it; and what a woman can do, a man cannot do. But the West accepted the equality of man and woman not because it has proved their natural differences wrong but simply because it found it the only solution for the freedom of woman from 'man's tyranny'.

It is explicitly clear that the West has created its own standard of respectability. According to this criteria, only the characteristics and strength of man have been taken into consideration and the nature of woman has been neglected. She has been invited to bring herself to that standard if she wants to be honourable in the society. In fact, she ought to have been assigned the task according to her nature and capabilities. Then, she would have not resorted to the artificial means to acquire dignified position in the society.

The Western thinkers maintain that present concept of the nature of woman is nothing but an artificial state created by man's constant tyranny. Her talents have been suppressed. Had she been free to act, she would have achieved better position even in the fields reserved for man.

As far as intellect and reasoning are concerned, it is wrong to say that man and woman are equal in these respects. They think woman would have performed her duty better if she had been free to act. But it is also possible that she would have remained at the same position where she was before, despite her freedom to act. Hence it is false to say that she can also fulfil the responsibilities of man.

The history shows that woman had opportunities, in different periods, to struggle along with man, but she failed to achieve the status of man owing to her natural weaknesses. Besides, the modern world has provided her freedom along with man for over the last one century, but her freedom has brought no change of any sort in her feminine nature.

Another stand that Western thinkers take, is that if woman is removed from civil and social work, the advancement in the field of modernization would be reduced to fifty percent and the progress of fifty years will take one full century. This argument is absolutely false and baseless, as society is not a technical institution for the progress of one particular technique. On the contrary, it came into existence due to the association of various departments of human life. Some of these departments belong to woman also. If these departments are abolished, the whole society will suffer. Hence, evolution of society means progress of every department to achieve overall higher standard of life.

Despite all facilities, woman has not been proved as useful as expected in the assigned fields. A less qualified man has been proved more useful than a highly qualified woman. The reason is that woman wants to do the work of man but her nature does not allow her to succeed in her efforts. Her natural characteristics forbid her to follow the modern trend, This struggle has put her in such a condition that worries even the West. Now, it is a proven fact that Western way of living has failed to provide a dignified status to woman in the society, while all talk of women lib remains mere sloganeering.

Various Societies

Let us first peep through the window pane of civilisation, and see how women were treated and what rights they had, so that we may have a better perspective of how Islam dealt with this problem. Turning to the *Encyclopedia Brittannica*, we come across the following:

In Ancient India: In ancient India subjection was a cardinal principle. 'Day and night women must be kept by their protectors in a state of dependence', says Manu. The rule of inheritance was agnatic, that descent traced through males only to the exclusion of females. She wag regarded as the source of sin and moral and spiritual depravity. A wife used to call her husband: "My Lord" or even "My God", as he was regarded as her earthly god. She never ate with him. She had to follow a few yards behind him when both walked together. She was to worship her husband. She had to serve her father, be a chattel of the husband and submit to her children. A woman became a plaything for animal passion. Indians looked upon sex relations between man and woman as loathsome and evil; whether they contract legally or illegally. They used to regard a good wife as a woman whose mind, speech and body are kept in subjection, and so acquires high renown both in this world; and in the next, the same abode with her husband. So much so about India.

In Ancient Greece: Let us now see how the ancient Greek civilization, treated its women. The woman was forced to marry without her consent, as her consent was not regarded as a necessity. The parents made her submit to their wishes. She was supposed to accept a husband and lord, chosen by her parents, even though he were a complete stranger to her. She had to obey. The Greek women were always looked down upon as minors, and were to obey blindly their male kinsmen: that is to say, father, brother or to some extent their uncles. During the prime of Greek civilization a chaste woman was a precious thing. Greek women observed some sort of, Purdah. They had the Harimlek (women's apartment). Later on the house of a prostitute became the focus of attention of all classes of the Greek society, and all national decisions were taken under her influence. Her house became the place of worship as she represented Aphrodite: the goddess of love and beauty who betrayed her husband god and made love with three other gods. Women in Greece were of three types: (1) The prostitutes who were for men's satisfaction only. (2) The mistresses, and their main task was to look after the body and health of their lords, massaging, etc. (3) The third group was the wives whose duty was to bear and bring up children and look after them in the same way as nannies nowadays do. Their status never rose higher than that.

In Rome: Coming to their next door neighbours the Romans ;we find that they used to regard a wife as a babe, a minor, or award; therefore she must be looked after. She must be continuously under the protection and guardianship of her husband.

During those days if a woman married, she and her property passed into the power of her husband. Not only that, but he also exercised every right over her. When she did anything wrong it was he who had full right of passing judgement on her. He had the right of even sentencing her to death. A Roman wife was something like a purchased property of her husband's. Thus, she was like a slave acquired solely for her lord's benefit. She was not allowed to take part in any civil or public affairs: that is to say; she could not be a trustee, a witness or stand surety for another or even be a tutor. She was just like a piece of furniture to decorate a man's abode. When her husband died her sons or in laws especially brothers-in-law; had the legal right over her.

In Slavonic Tribes: If we read the history of Slavonic Tribes and go very deep we come across something very interesting about the status of their women. It suffices to read extracts of a book being published by its author Ossolineum when translated to English it becomes *The Upturned Anchor*. The extracts were published in the Fakty 76 of September 76 under the title "Jok Oni Kochali" (How they loved).

The extracts read :

> "At the beginning of the 12th Century, Kosmos, the author of the Chronicle of the Czechs wrote that a hundred years earlier it was possible for Pommarian man to marry more than two wives, and it was not a Violation of the law for a man to take another man's wife."

Nearly at the same period we come across the Polish king Bolestaw Smialy (the brave) punishing the unfaithful wives whose husbands used to spend long years away from home, because those wives were not faithful to their husbands. They had committed adultery during the absence of their husbands. A German chronicler Thietmar tells us that Slavonic wives were killed after their husbands' funeral in order to share their, fate. This type of killing a wife after the death of her husband reminds us of the Sati in India where they used to burn the wife alive together with her dead husband. Bolestaw Chroby enacted that whoever dared to seduce another man's wife he was to be taken to the market bridge and fixed to it with a nail. It is also said that Slavonic girls used to have premarital relations before they got married. It sometimes happened that a husband expelled his newly wed wife just because he found her a virgin. To preserve a woman with her honour (virginity) was regarded as a sign of the low value of the girl as nobody had wanted her before. The consequences and reactions of such a treatment of expelling a newly wed wife who was found virgin was that she used to be a prostitute; and when she grave birth to a baby girl; she generally buried her alive.

The Slavonic women were not the only ones who used to kill their daughters. We see that Prussian women killing their fatherless daughters or better still the illegitimate girls. The state of killing young girls alive made it easier for the Christian bishop to buy the girls, educate them, and using them to give chorus to Christian missionaries who used to go from place to place propagating Catholicism. Kosmos tells us also that a Czech prince, Brzetyslaw by name, used to sentence to banishment unmarried women and widows who got pregnant. He gave the following reason for his act: "None forbids them to contract legal marriage. So why on earth! do they do this thing illegally, and then they procure abortion which is worst sin of all crimes?"

In Scandinavia: Scandinavian women were under perpetual tutelage, regardless of their being married or otherwise. This state of affairs went on for a long period. No woman was to marry without first getting the çonsent of her tutor, otherwise he could use his for her property during her powers and make use lifetime if he wished so.

In China: The position and status of a woman in China was far worse than in any other part of the world.

Let us quote one example: One of the Chinese ladies said, "We women are given the lowest position in the human society. We must perform most of the tasks as our share in the society."

It is also said: What a pity! The woman is the most unlucky being. There is nothing in the world less inferior than a woman. Boys would stand in front of the doors as if they were gods fallen from high heavens. No father was happy when he was told that his wife gave birth to a baby girl. When a girl matured, then she hid herself in her room so that she might not look at anybody's face. And when she died nobody wept about her.

We quote the following from *Encyclopedia Britannica:*

> "Unmarried women were members of their natal families, but on marriage a woman moved to the family of her husband and was afterwards subject to the authority of her husband's parents and seniors. Any property brought by the bride, apart from such items as personal ornaments, was transferred to the ownership of her husband's family. The position of a bride who became a daughter-in-law, was largely weak, and she could rely on the physical protection of her natal family, only if she could risk disfavour. In practice, however, the wife's position strengthened with time more particularly after the birth of sons and performance of mourning for her husband's seniors."

> "Marriage was arranged by formal agreement between the heads of the family concerned, after negotiation usually conducted through a go-between according to the generally accepted forms."

A husband could divorce his wife on specific grounds such as adultery; provided that her parents were willing to have her back, otherwise she will go to the streets. A wife who was left by her husband might report to court asking the magistrate to look into her case.

Various Religions

In Arabia: Coming to Arabia, or better still, to Mecca, the cradle of Islam we meet with the pre-Islam Arabs burying their daughters alive.

A Jahiliyya (Pre-Islamic) Arab considered a woman as an inferior creature. When man was told that his wife had given birth to a baby girl, he was really grieved. His face darkened. What was he to do then? He ran away from people because of the shame of giving birth to a baby girl,

The Jahiliyya Arabs accepted the girl in two different ways. Many of them buried the girls alive and with them, they thought, they buried all the shame that might encounter them, had they brought up those girls. Others used to act quite differently, they brought up the girls on sufferance and contempt.

A Jahiliyya Arab wife was inherited just like chattel. Al-Bukhari narrates that when a man died his son had every right upon his wife. One of them might marry her for himself, if he wished to; or they might marry her to anyone they desired. They might even stop her from getting married. If she wanted to get married, then she had to pay them money as her ransom.

In Judaism: Some of the Jewish faith regarded a woman as a much more inferior creature than her counterpart the man. Others considered her to be even lower in grade than that of the servants. She never inherited anything from her parents, if she had a brother or brothers. Her father had every right of selling her if she were under the maturity age. When a woman got married all her possessions were transferred to her husband. He used to exercise full right over her possessions during their joint life. If a Jewish wife caught her husband in bed with another woman; she was to keep silent and not complain. This was so because he had every right over her. He could do anything he liked. If a wife complained that her husband made love with her in an immoral and unnatural way, the reply was "We cannot do anything because you are his property." In Public Prayers there should be at least ten men. If it happened that there were nine men and a lot of women, no prayers were conducted because women were looked upon as nothing and were not counted. It was not encouraged to commit adultery with a Jewish woman, and was permissible with a non-Jewish. The heaviest burden for maintaining the daily requirements of the Mosaic dietary laws falls on the woman, as she is much inferior to man. She is to see that meat and other daily foods are not mixed with forbidden things. She is not to touch pickles, wine or meat soup if she hasn't been ritually cleansed.

In Christianity: The author of the book *The Status of Women in Islam*, gives an elaborate quotation from *Marriage East and West*, by David and Vera Mace:

> "Let no one suppose, either, that our Christian heritage is free of such slighting judgement. It would be hard to find anywhere a collection of more degrading reference to the female, sex than the early Christian Fathers provide: Lecky the famous historian, speaks of (these fierce incentives which form so conspicuous and so grotesque a portion of the writings of the Fathers-Woman was represented at the door of the hell, as the mother of all human ills She should live in continual penance on account of the curses she had brought upon the world. She should be ashamed of her dress, for it is memorial of her fall. She should be especially ashamed of her beauty, for 't is the most potent instrument of the devil). One of the most

> scathing of these attacks on women is that of Tetrulian: (Do you know that you are each an Eve? The sentence of God on this sex of yours lives in this age: the guilt must of necessity live too. You are the devil's gateway; you are the unsealer of that (forbidden) tree; you are first deserters of the divine law; you are she who persuaded him whom the devil was not valiant enough to attack, you destroyed so easily God's image! man. On account of your desert-that is death even the Son of God had to die). Not only did the Church affirm the inferior status of woman, it deprived her of legal rights she had previously enjoyed."

We quote the following from the Bible:

> "Now the snake was the most cunning animal that the Lord God had made. The snake asked the woman, 'Did God really tell you not to eat the fruit from any tree in the garden?' 'We may eat the fruit of any tree in the garden' the woman answered, 'except the tree in the middle of it if we do, we will die.' The snake replied, 'That's not true, you will not die when you eat it you will be like God and know what is good and what is bad. So she took some of the fruit and ate it. Then she gave some to her husband and he also ate it ... . God asked, 'Did you eat the fruit that I told you not to eat?' The man answered, 'The woman you put here with me gave me the fruit and I ate it'... . And He said to the woman, 'I will increase your trouble in pregnancy and your pain in giving birth. In spite of this, you will still have desire for your husband, yet you will be subject to him'."
>
> (Genesis, 3 - 1 to 7+12+16)

Encyclopedia Biblica provides an interesting reading about some of the Biblical Laws, or better still-Mosaic Law. "A woman, was betrothed." For a man to betroth a wife meant simply to acquire possession of her by payment of the purchase money which was a kind of dowry given to her father. It was not necessary to get the consent of the girl. And the marriage was valid. The woman being a man's property, he had every right over her. He had even the right of divorce, and it was the privilege of the husband only. The wife had no such rights, as it was regarded as a matter of course. This state of affairs was in vogue in Europe in varying degrees as late as the nineteenth century or after the French revolution.

Campaign for Women's Lib

In the 19th Century women could not tolerate such state of affairs any longer. They formed movements in Europe and America to emancipate women. This movement made efforts to make woman take part in the educational institutions. The engineers of the movement were Sophia Bryan, Frances Mary Buss and Dorothea Beale in Europe and Lucy Stone in America. They were fighting for the human rights of women. The place for a woman was in the home, her task was to produce children and to take care of them. She was to depend completely on her husband. She did not have an identity of her own as she was subordinate to man. There were many other things that made the movement for the emancipation of women gain momentum, especially when quotations from St. Paul were cited to show that it was not meant by God for women to be equal to men. Adam was created first, and from him Eve. These quotations were cited to attack the feminist movement. If you ever read European literature during the Cavalier period you feel as if they make you understand that it was the golden age of women in Europe. But, going very deep and reading the gaps between words you come to the conclusion that it was the epoch of chivalry. I would advise the reader to read Cervante's *Don Quixote* and see how women were treated. During that period people were thinking of horses more than of women.

3
Islam's Role

It is easier to appreciate what Islam has contributed to the well being of woman and how it liberated them from all those yokes. Islam has regarded the practice of burying a girl alive as a crime i.e., murder. In this respect the Holy Quran says :

> "And when the female infant buried alive is questioned: "for what crime she was killed?" (Quran, 81: 8, 9) (Even her father himself could not give her an answer).

Quran also criticizes parents on how they react when news is brought to them about the birth of a girl. On this the Holy Quran says:

> "When news is brought to one of them, of the birth of a female child, his face darkens and he is filled with inward grief. With shame does he hide himself from his people because of the bad news he has received. Shall he retain her on sufferance and contempt, or bury her in the dust? Ah! what evil choice they decide on." (Quran, 16 58, 59)

We shall appreciate the way man, used to deal with different situations and the way he regarded a woman in such an olden society (whether that society be in Arabia), fittest and, strongest. This was more so as man attacked man and man looted man. This was their common law.

Bahiy al-Khuury in his book: *al Marla bainal 'Bayti wal Mujtama-i* (Women between Home and Society) throws light on problem in a very good way:

> "...... Was a man, then, to blame, when he, in those days, arranged his life and other social activities in accordance with the conditions prevailing then, taking into account the invasions that could happen at any moment and the unexpected looting and ... "Was he to blame, 'then, when he went out looting or defending if he, exempted the pregnant, the one who nursed her baby and the like who were weak amongst women?
>
> "To which of the two births would he be happy; about the birth of a baby boy who would ride a horse, take up arms and fight the enemy or of that a baby girl that would not be able to do anything of the sort. Over and above, she would be a burden in the battle and she would have to be protected?
>
> "..... The Arabs did not welcome the birth of a baby girl, and this was so because of the nature of their society. Wars and invasions never ceased and taking revenge never stopped. All these things depended on the male, but a woman was unable to do any of these tasks, in addition to it, she was the desired loot for (the) service (of the enemy) in the eyes of the enemy, or she was for his entertainment....

We learn from Hadith (Sayings of the Holy Prophet peace and blessings of Allah be upon him) that a girl should not suffer injustice or inequality. He is quoted as saying what it meant :

> "He who has a daughter and does not bury her alive, or insult her, and does not prefer his son to her, Allah will enter him into Paradise."
>
> (There are many other sayings that encourage the bringing up of girls in, the same way as with equal treatment as the boys.)

According to the teachings of Islam woman is not blamed for Adam's first mistake. In some verses of the Holy Quran Adam is specifically blamed:

> "Then they twain ate thereof, so that their shame became apparent unto them, and they began to hide by keeping on themselves some of the leaves of the Garden. and Adam disobeyed his Lord, so Went astray.
>
> (Quran, 20 :121)

(Let us see what Abdullah al-Khayyat in his book, *The Muslim's Guide to Faith* has to say here. He quotes the Apostle (peace and blessings of Allah be upon him) as saying: "every child is born with an upright nature, but his father makes him a Christian or a Magian."

This means that every new born child carries within himself an innocent upright nature...... This is in complete contradiction with the Christian creed of the inborn sin. According to Islam no sin is inherited by a child Even Adam is not considered sinful in Islam. He forgot Allah's orders and had no intention to disobey his Lord's orders as said in the Quran.

Adam and Eve jointly disobeyed. Both repented and both of them were forgiven.

Fundamental Rights

Islam dealt with human rights of women at a time when in some parts of the world conferences were being held to discuss whether she had a soul or not and whether she was human or not, or whether she was to worship God as the man does or otherwise, or whether she will enter Paradise or not.

These conferences took place between the fifth and seventh centuries of the Christian era. It was at this very time that Islam came into being and gave the answer in such an amazing bravery:

> "O Mankind! Be careful of your duty to your Lord Who created you from a single soul and from it created its mate and from them twain hath spread (abroad) a multitude of men and women..." (Quran,4:1)
>
> "He, it, is Who did create you from a single soul and therefrom did create his mate that he might dwell with her in life...." (Quran, 7:199)
>
> "And Allah hath given you wives of your own kind, and hath given you from your wives sons and grandsons, and hath made provision of good things for you. Is it then in vanity that they believe and in the grace of Allah that they disbelieve?" (Quran, 16: 72)
>
> "The Creator of heavens and earth: He has made for you pairs from among your selves." (Quran, 42: 11)
>
> "And of His signs is this: He created, for you helpmates from yourselves, that ye might find, rest in them and He ordained between you love and mercy. Lo, herein indeed are portents for folks who reflect." (Quran, 30: 18)
>
> "O Mankind ! Lo! We have created you male and female, and have made you, nations and tribes, that ye may know each other ...." (Quran-49: 13)

Equality for All

Islam does not differentiate women from man in terms of religious obligations. It is interesting to find out that a woman has certain advantages (you may call them so if you like) over man in certain cases.

Let us quote some such cases :

She is exempted of the daily prayers and of fasting during her menstruation period (monthly course) and for forty days of her confinement after giving birth to a child. She does not have to make up for the missed prayers because of one of the aforementioned reasons. She may not fast during her pregnancy but she is not exempted from prayers and when she is nursing her baby if there is any threat to her health or her baby's she is allowed to miss fasts. She can make up for such missed fasting days whenever she can before the next Ramadan- (the ninth month of Islamic Era and the month in which fasting from food etc., is observed from dawn to sunset for the whole month).

Islam took into account the physical and psychological changes in the natural female function, e.g., a woman might be nursing her babe or looking after him; that it made the attendance of congregational prayers optional for her while it is compulsory for men. A man must attend all the congregational prayers, especially if he happens to live near a mosque or a place where Muslims meet to say prayers. It is not accepted that he says his prayers alone at home. While it is permissible for a woman to do so. Some of the theologians even say it is preferable that she say her prayers at home.

According to the Holy Qur'an, the conjugal life is a life of ease and comfort and mutual love and affection It has been called one of Allah's important symbols. The Holy Qur'an has mentioned:

> And of His Signs is this: He created for you helpmates from yourselves that ye might find rest in them, and He ordained between you love and mercy. (30:21)

In another verse of the Holy Qur'an, the mutual love and cooperation that exists between husband and wife and their solicitude for each other's comfort has been explained in the beautiful style as follows:

> He it is who did create you from a single soul and therefrom did make his mate that he might take rest in her. (7:189)

The above and other verses of the Holy Qur'an explains the conjugal relations of husband and wife in a charming style. They exhort a person to gratify his sexual desire in a lawful manner and derive spiritual comfort and elevation. Allah, the Exalted has created pairs of every living being so that they may provide solace and comfort to each other.

There is such inherent love and affection for wife and children in the heart of a person that sometimes he forgets the duties he owes to Allah, while engaged in his worldly pleasures. The wealth and affluence which Allah has bestowed upon him make him indifferent to his Creator. Allah, the Exalted has warned the believers:

> O' ye who believe! Lo! among your wives and your children there are enemies for you, therefore, beware of them. And if ye efface and overlook and forgive, then lo! Allah is Forgiving, Merciful. (64:14)

While interpreting the above verse, Maulana Shabbir Ahmad Uthmani has written: It often happens that a person being engrossed in the love and affairs of his family forgets the duties he owes to Allah. He does not even hesitate to commit sin. Thus he is deprived of many virtues and excellent qualities. He tries to fulfil the demands of his wife and children by hook or by crook, even if he has to take bribe. He becomes forgetful of the Hereafter. It is obvious that the attempt to please the family at the risk of loss in the Hereafter is not a good bargain and such family cannot be called his friend, rather it is his enemy, but he is not conscious of this fact. So Allah has warned against the attitude which is merely for the adornment of this worldly life at the risk and loss of piety and morality and the life in the Hereafter. But this does not mean that all wives and children are of this sort. There are many noble wives who protect the piety and morality of their husbands and help them in their pious deeds and there are many good children who lead a righteous and pious life.

Rules for Man

In order to fulfil the conjugal rights and gratify the sexual urge in a lawful manner, Islam has promulgated certain rules and regulations and has ordained its followers to observe them. It is obvious that the two strangers who are being united in wedlock possess different hearts and minds and trends and inclinations. Their social customs may also differ. Therefore, one cannot expect perfect mutual cooperation and harmony between them at the first stage. Then there is variation in the mental and intellectual levels of men and women. They have different habits and temperaments. In view of all this, Islam has given some important instructions and also assigned some rights and duties to both the husband and wife. We will first of all discuss in detail the rights and duties assigned to husbands.

It is not surprising that sometimes there is some clash and quarrel between a husband and wife which provides an opportunity for the devil to intervene. Chastity and piety are in danger especially when the woman is touchy, short-tempered or capricious. Islam has not ignored this important factor and has given useful instructions to avoid any clash. A man has been advised to show patience and tolerance if his wife annoys him by her utterance or action. It has been mentioned in the Holy Qur'an:

> But consort with them in kindness, for if ye hate them it may happen that ye hate a thing wherein Allah has placed much good. (4:19)

There is a Divine dictate in the above verse that if the attitude of a wife is against the nature and temperament of a person, he should not fly into a rage, but should show wisdom and tolerance. It is possible that he may be abhorring her due to her nature and temperament, but Allah has placed some good in her which may make him successful in this world and in the Hereafter. This fact has been explained in the following Hadith:

> No believing man should injure any believing woman merely because he hates any habit in her. Just possible her other thing may appeal him. (Muslim)

There may be good qualities in a woman along with her bad habits. So a man should like her for her virtues, overlooking her weaknesses.

Holy Prophet's Instructions

Pointing out the inherent weaknesses of women, the Holy Prophet (peace and blessings of Allah be upon him) has said: I advise you good treatment towards women as they are born of rib and the most curved thing in the rib is its upper part. If you want to straighten it, you would break it and if you leave it, the curvature would subsist forever. So accept this advice concerning women. (Bukhari)

In the above Ahadith, curvature has been said to be inherent in the nature of a woman. This is inseparable from her. However, it can be rectified to a reasonable extent by politeness and softness. So an attempt should not be made to straighten it and a man should never expect that the woman would cooperate with him in all matters. Their natures are poles apart. If any person commits this blunder under some misconception he would have to face bitter consequences. But one should also not remain indifferent and let the woman do as she likes.

The household affairs can be managed efficiently if both husband and wife show mutual love and cooperation. Woman is man's trusted companion and we cannot ignore her. If the outside matters are in the hands of man, the domestic affairs are controlled by a woman. Cooking, education of children and other household matters are managed by the woman. Then how could the household affairs be managed smoothly and quickly without the mutual cooperation of both parties? Someone has rightly said: Husband and wife are the two wheels of the cart of life. Unless they move together, the cart cannot go ahead. We should therefore treat women politely and gently which should inspire sentiments of love and affection in their hearts. Moreover, men have been advised to show patience and forbearance over the shortcomings of women. A slight lapse on a woman's part may prove disastrous and ruin the honour and prestige of husband and that of the whole family.

If a man begins to quarrel over trivial matters it would become impossible to pull on. Man is more tolerant and forbearing and so it is his duty not to lose patience in such critical hours.

4

Dignity of the Household

In our society, the importance of the large-scale ideological and economic factors in the everyday life situation of the individual, and the way in which this ideology has opened up the possibility of divergent adaptations and a new household economy. Moreover, the burden that economic changes place on adult males (who still are the main providers in most families), as well as career married women, has increased. This has complicated and intensified the tradition of child-rearing, cooking, washing, cleaning the house, taking care of the family and social networks, as well as the time spent on purchasing goods and supervising children after school. The large-scale economic reforms, and the new household economy, have affected the life of family members in different ways. The form and the rituals of household activities in everyday life are central themes in the following section.

The economic crises of the Islamic state and the new ideological demands have incurred cumulative and overlapping perspectives. This has left a narrow range of options for young and ambitious couples, forcing them to seek opportunities outside the home country, as exemplified by Mahry's extended family. Marriage and higher education has traditionally served as a passage for social and economic independence, although it has often been the case that newly-weds stay in the house of the wife's or husband's father for a while, before establishing an independent household. For ten years Halimeh, a 44-year-old female school teacher, shared a residence with her sister-in-law before she and her husband could save enough money to buy one of the two-room flats offered to school employees.

Marriage has always been an economic security for the wife, and the husband is traditionally responsible for the economic security of the family. The reality of the current socio-economic situation for the average lower and middle-class category, is such that extra economic support is necessary, either from the wife-particularly in the case of young married couples-or from parents.

A young family's economic independence and higher social status, such as in the case of Mahry and her siblings, depends upon occupation and further education. Mahry and her family had less chance of obtaining higher education because of the increased number of applicants, and also because of new Islamic ideological criteria for the selection of religiously active candidates. A new mode of adaptation, and a new economic niche, has emerged for family members who are able to take on additional roles.

As a result of constant price increases on household goods, the consequences of these economic niches have affected males and females differently. Managing the household economy is difficult in lower and middle-class families, even when the breadwinner (often the man), has previous work experience, or higher education. Families are dependent on a single income from employment in the public sector, such as teacher or office work jobs.

Grown-up children, despite their higher education, are economically dependent on their parents, who returned home from abroad during the Iranian revolution in 1978. This dependency may be permanent for some, thus placing a burden on the parents. In post-revolutionary Iran, large numbers of urban middle and higher-class Iranians left home.

Significance of Organisation

Two distinctive, significant and completely new household structures emerged in post-revolutionary Iran. These were: (a) the extended household composed of parents and married children who shared a residence, and (b) the households consisting of elderly couples who remained in Iran, while their children left home and took permanent residence abroad. The former household composition is common among families where a majority of the members stayed in Iran, and only a few moved abroad. The latter household composition consisted of elderly couples who voluntarily lived alone at home, visiting their children only once in a while abroad. These are often better-off couples, contrasting dramatically with the lower and middle-class extended household, where parents accommodate a married daughter or son and their families.

To maintain the economy of daily life many young educated men started a business of their own, or with other male relatives. The inevitable solution for lower and middle-class families was to have two members of the family in employment. Alternatively the breadwinner of the family would take two jobs, one in the official sector and another in the private sector. In the case of Mahry, close and distant male relatives were employed as civil servants, teachers, low-ranking army officers, social health personnel, etc. Due to the high cost of living they worked in their spare time as independent taxi drivers, as salesmen buying and selling land, as dealers in foreign currencies or rationed goods, or as shop assistants. In comparison, women were either housewives or, as is the case among a few middle-aged women, they were employed as nursery teachers, computer assistants, students, social health workers or, like Mahry, they worked with sewing and embroidery.

Most of the young families in the community, either rented rooms that cost them half of their salary as state employees, or they shared a residence with their parents or a close relative in order to save money. Many were also dependent on others for economic support, directly or indirectly, in the form of cash, household subsistence, and goods. Such socio-economic insecurity, along with the poor educational opportunities for themselves and the problems facing their children, as well as the general political harassment, has led many of these middle-class families to join the flow of migrants of the 1980s.

Household work is not only a distinctive personalised domain, but is also a part of the larger economic and post- revolutionary ideological development, as well as being a focus of change. Domestic work in post-revolutionary Iran involved a series of new tasks and more intensive work schedules for women.

Adaptability of household members to changing conditions depended on the availability of facilities and resources. A married woman explained that due to the intensive work schedule and, for example, the lack of communal facilities, she had to do the laundry at night when water was more easily available, and the shopping before sunrise so as to be able to prepare the mid-day meal for the family. This example illustrates how the mode of work among women mainly concerned with 'domestic' tasks has intensified due to broader political and economic conditions. One could hardly escape the daily observation of lower and middle-class women (often mothers), accompanied by small children, waiting impatiently for several hours in queues, in order to purchase hygienic supplies of milk, foods, and other 'domestic' items, at a more reasonable price than in the open market. Commonly they were worried about the daily household routines; for example, one waiting in such a queue told how worried she was at being delayed in preparing the noon meal for her husband and children coming home from work and school.

Foreign goods, such as electrical appliances, were very expensive and considered as luxury items by lower middle-class families. Moreover, these items provided a new form of enterprise for well-off families. Being able to sell foreign goods in the home market greatly boosted the income of such well-off families. The extended household has to some extent solved the problem of married children who are not able to establish an independent household without economic support from their parents.

High prices of household equipment and house rent made it impossible for young families with average economic means to establish an economically independent household. However, such an intensive relation and extended household dependency has increased family conflicts dramatically, particularly in already controversial relationships such as between daughter-in-law and mother-in-law.

Opportunities Available

Career options are limited for young members of lower-class families. Petty trading seems to be an acceptable strategy for boys. Wheeler-dealers, and street vendors, are two forms of economic activity adopted by recent school-leavers. Bazar-e azad activity has opened a series of channels through which household items rationed by the state flow into the black market. Such enterprises, and the extra income earned, are often considered insecure, illegal, not quite respectable and even immoral. Middlemen, such as wheeler-dealers, after spending long hours in queues, buying goods such as cigarettes and eggs from the co-operatives shops, and then selling them at black-market prices. This type of occupation may serve as a source of income for young and middle-aged male members of low-income families. For families with low incomes, daily petty trading is not a permanent enterprise.

Self-employment yields more income than a low-paid permanent job. Establishing a business requires both economic and social capital, without which it is difficult to obtain goods to sell, or to rent a shop. When renting a shop a deposit is paid. The price has increased with inflation from around 50 thousand tomans in 1979 to an average of one million tomans in 1990. This means that it is virtually impossible to establish a permanent business. It also means that large profits can be made from letting shops, houses, flats and rooms. Those who have parents with a large capital may set up a small business.

While the father is still alive, they will be allowed to enter the family business as part of their eventual inheritance. The street-corner traders sell items such as dollars, cigarettes, rationed foods, and stockings. Dast-forosh is an enterprise open to even those with little capital, and is often a second source of income for individuals such as a grown-up son, or a head of a household. Any form of self-employment to supplement the limited household income, is justified on the grounds that multiple sources of income are necessary. Since a single-income job in the public sector cannot meet all of the household's real expenditures, the idea of a second job has become widely accepted.

Resourceful entrepreneurs will be able to provide for family consumption, as well as accumulate considerable wealth. In contrast, permanent business activities are generally open only to better-off middle-class merchants and craftsmen, and other traditionally independent producers and distributors. These are often co-operative family businesses jointly owned by close male relatives, such as a father and his sons, brothers, cousins and in-laws. This contrasts with the petty trader who sets up his business independently. Recently, because of restrictions, male shopkeepers are forbidden to sell female lingerie, or to open female hair-dressing salons.

As a consequence, female shopkeepers and co-partnership with a female relative has increased. The open market makes non-rationed items available to the public, such as electrical appliances, clothing, and domestic goods, as well as scarce medicines. The scarcity and long queues have forced many people to purchase items in the black market.

The rise in prices of local commodities may be explained by: (a) the government extra export policy for earning foreign currencies; (b) the rise in the exchange rate for dollars; and (c) the two devaluations of the rial. Devaluation of Iranian currency has been of particular importance for the family household economy, since family incomes are in the form of rials. Subsequently they are the hardest hit by inflation, exchange rates, and the black market policy of the state.

Broad structural and economical changes, such as the rationing system for the distribution of goods, has encouraged the development of a new transactional pseudo-occupation niche. Some of these new enterprises are considered immoral, in terms of their transactional and insecure nature. Self-employment and free-enterprise activities are considered to offer greater opportunities for meeting the daily increases of expenditures. Government employees, who are particularly well educated, and with fixed low wages, have become very disappointed with the monthly income of their permanent jobs. It is not adequate to cover their household expenses, such as rent. The difference in the earnings of these well-qualified government employees, and those whose main source of income is selling dollars in the black market, has marginalised the former category both socially and economically.

Wages for average civil servants and employees in official sectors, such as education, have remained relatively the same as they were before the revolution. According to a study by Behdad, in 1980 there had been an increase in the official minimum wage and a change in the rate of income tax to 12 per cent.

Most workers were affected by the new law stipulating minimum wages, the exception being urban workers in large firms. It must be keep in mind that family economic viability in post-revolutionary Iran is a problem for most government employees, hence the interest in free business and double waged jobs.

The most profitable enterprises involve trading in foreign currencies and goods, such as dollars, pounds, gold, household items and land, and money lending. Thus, the families that had invested capital in such commodities as land, houses, cars, gold, shops, etc., prior to the outbreak of the war between Iran and Iraq in 1980 are now in position. Expansion of the black market has an advantage as it further benefited those who have access to foreign currencies, imported goods, and are able to travel abroad frequently.

Land ownership has always been an important source of local identity and power in Iran. After the revolution, long-term investment in land has more than ever become an important form of capital, as well as a strategy for rapidly accumulating wealth. The dramatic rise in land prices since 1980 has applied even to the purchase of the isolated land outside the city limit, which is not even supplied with electricity and water.

Social Movement

An example of rapid social mobility through land ownership is the case of an educated civil engineer. He qualified in England in the 1970s. He and his family returned to Iran shortly after the Iranian revolution in 1980. He started to work for his former employer, where he had previously been employed in a junior position. Due to his high foreign qualification he was soon offered jobs in different cities, including one in a province where he received high wages due to the difficult geographical conditions. Shortly after he returned home from England he bought a piece of land at a low price. The land was on the non-residential periphery of a town without electricity and water supplies. It cost him 60 tomans per square metre in 1980. However, inflation increased its value to 5,000/6,000 tomans per square metre in 1989.

In the long term ownership of land is highly beneficial, the rapid increase in value making it a secure investment. The demand for land has particularly increased as a result of demographic changes. These can be explained as follows: (a) rapid population growth; (b) the continuous migration from small towns and nearby villages to large towns. The rapid expansion of towns toward the city limits increased the value of cheap and isolated land from 20-60 tomans per square metre in 1979, to 6,000 tomans per square metre in 1989-90. Such land could not, however, be used for building a house until it had been included within the town's official boundaries.

The profit from land ownership was greater than from the ownership of fruit gardens, the latter providing only a small annual income for urban middle-class and business families. This was the common enterprise that led to the serious destruction of the famous orchard land in Shiraz. The grape and apple farms changed into building sites, thereby bringing a high profit to their owners. It would be interesting to evaluate the impact on agricultural production.

Land confiscated during the revolution has been sold cheap to religio-politically privileged community members, such as war veterans, employees of the Islamic institution for rehabilitation, and to families of martyrs or hostages. In recent years government supporters have been favoured for the redistribution of economic and social opportunities, such as obtaining employment, education, rationed goods and land. Special allocations have been given as the rewards for their support. Thus, economic advancement has been possible not only for those who have accumulated capital under the former regime, but also for those who have gained high status as first-class citizens in the Islamic regime, whatever their class background may have been.

Gifts of gold signify sets of kinship relations and are part of large chains of acts distinguishing close relatives, high-ranking guests and close friends. The value of gold is both an objective and a subjective cultural phenomenon, and concerns the relations between people on various levels. Gold has always been associated with prestige and high status and is often exchanged as valuable gifts among Iranians. There is a strong tendency for women to own some gold, receiving and giving in accordance with expectations. The saving and management roles women play within the family in this context is considered to be related to their orientation toward the future. Gold functions for women both as prestigious ornaments, and as a status symbol. Gifts of gold signify a 'proper' bride and provide capital for the family and her husband.

While purchasing land has remained the principal investment and economic transaction for men, gold has played a similar role for women. The constant rise in the value of gold, along with inflation, has meant that its importance not only as solid capital, but also as a status symbol, has grown.

The common strategy is to buy as many articles of gold as possible when the prices are low, and then sell or exchange these items when the prices have gone up. Accumulation of gold is considered a wise policy, both from the point of view of the individual and the family.

Gold is a significant gift requested by the bride. The amount to be received is often agreed upon at the time of engagement. Gold jewellery, or a number of gold coins, may be agreed upon as being a part of, or the entire *mahryeh*. The increasing tendency among middle-class brides to have mahryeh in gold coins than rials is because gold is more stable in price and more likely to rise in value than fall. The quantity of gold received as wedding presents depends on how wealthy the relatives are, and the number of guests. Such gifts may also be given on other significant occasions, such as at the birth of a child, during the first pregnancy, upon obtaining a higher degree, or on the Iranian New Year in March.

The young married women were considered inexperienced, and were constantly advised by their mothers and sisters about future relations with their husbands and their families. Planning a secure future, the mothers advise their daughters to buy gold instead of toys and decorative items, and to be concerned about the future. Such issues have become important lessons given by mothers to their married daughters. The importance of the gift of gold as capital is revealed at times of family crises. It is increasingly common for married women to give their savings to their desperate husbands to start a business or purchase property. Such a form of economic support brings extra recognition and respectability for the wife. The husband is often willing in return to register part, or whole, of the purchased property in her name.

On one occasion Farideh, a 30-year-old married housewife, proudly exclaimed how she sold all of her wedding jewellery and the children's gold to give tomans to her husband, so he could purchase a piece of land that was especially offered to him at his place of work. Her husband in return registered the land in her name. Another situation in which a woman's gold reserves may be vitally important to the whole family is exemplified by Mahtab, an elderly mother with a family of ten, who was forced to seek shelter in Shiraz during the Iraqi bombardment of Abadan in 1981. The only property they could bring with them was her gold (one kilogram). Soon she decided to sell it, despite the market rate being low, because she considered it important to provide the necessary clothing and accommodation for her daughters, and to protect the family. The only thing she had been reluctant to sell was a ring that had once belonged to her mother.

A third example is that of a 55-year-old woman, who sold all of her gold jewellery and borrowed money from her oldest daughter, in order to visit two of her children living in Norway. To her the value of the visit was worth more than her gold. She thought, what would be the use of saving when she might never again have the chance to see her children and grandchildren?

The distance, and the high cost of the journey, signified the importance of the visit and, and as she put it, 'it may be the only chance in my lifetime'. She had to insist on the importance of such a visit since her old husband thought that it was more important to take care of the house, and was thus reluctant to give her any financial support. Finally she alone provided the money for her journey to visit her children. She frequently talked about this as an event to gain respect.

A fourth example is that of a couple educated abroad, who had recently returned home and needed to pay for the transport of their household goods from Germany to Iran. The wife, Shahla, decided to sell her own gold, as well as her daughter's, to pay the required sum. She considered the household items to be of equal value to the gold since these were enormously expensive and scarce in Iran. Her mother, Mahtab, proudly returned to this case, telling others how her daughter managed her family life, thus presenting her daughter as a good wife to a good husband.

Dignity and Status

Contributions to the family economy in times of crises would allow the wife to emphasise her honourable identity and enable her to negotiate with her husband. The latter may, as noted, often agree to reward his supportive wife by registering some property in her name.

Some women insist on keeping some of the gifts of gold received through their own lineage by transferring it to their daughters or daughters-in-law, or to their mother's lineage (sister's daughter). Such a form of gold exchange signifies sets of kinship relations in which the wife competes with the husband's for support. Thus, women often adopt far-sighted perspectives on the value of gold, a view that their husbands may not necessarily share, but from which they often benefit.

Dowry consists of household goods that the bride will bring to her husband's house. Mahr is a sum of money or valuable items such as gold and land that the husband pledges to pay the bride upon marriage. This amount will be written as a legal document for the bride's security, and may become a legal debt upon the bride's request. These two forms of payment play important roles in the dynamics of the marital relation, giving a woman a high degree of security and also a deterrent for a divorce.

It is generally assumed that the larger the dowry (i.e. consisting of kitchen utensils, carpets, bedroom furniture, etc.), the greater is the respect shown to the daughter and, thus, the greater is the prestige gained in the eyes of the husband's female relatives. Due to the open market prices of dowry items people purchase presents through the newly established Islamic state marriage institution, which offers a few items for those newly wed. These might include items such as a stove, a machine-made carpet, and an oil heater. Two or three items were sold to each newly married couple in 1989.

The better the daughter's education, job and appearance, the less pressure is placed on the parents to provide an expensive dowry. This point of view was expressed by at least ten of the working women, aged between 30-45, including 4 teachers (1 nursery, 2 school, 1 university), 3 hairdressers, 1 social worker, 1 accountant, 1 office worker. Of these two had resigned, one of whom was Narges, a 40-year-old woman and former accountant, the other being a teacher who had several times taken leave to avoid the political stress associated with her working conditions.

Working women have often purchased household goods either through the co-operative institution where they worked, or when such goods were available at a special price. Six of them had been working before marriage. As part of their dowry they brought these goods to their husband's house without putting economic pressure on their parents. The average parent, with several marriageable children, may find themselves in serious economic difficulties, unable to provide a dowry for their daughters. However, some parents, in order to reduce these expectations, will give a little dowry to the daughter and in return agree for a simple wedding party and a smaller gift of gold.

In order to reduce the expenses of the groom, a one-day celebration for the two phases of the wedding is the most usual form of marriage. The first phase of the wedding party starts with the *aqad* ceremony, in which the Muslim marriage contract will be written. At that time the close relatives of the bride and the groom are invited, and a warm meal will be served at the expense of the bride's family. In the afternoon the second phase of the celebration, known as the wedding party, will be held. Then dinner will be served to a large number of guests, including distant relatives, friends and close neighbours. This part will be held at the expense of the groom. The wedding marks a recognition of the Muslim marriage contract. It is seldom the case that a bride moves to live with her husband before the second phase of the marriage celebration.

Devaluation of the rial brought a series of dramatic changes to families and the household economy. The reduced value of rials provided grounds for parents of brides to request higher *mahr*, to guarantee more security for women at the time of divorce. The average mahr requested by the bride's family increased from a few hundred thousands before the revolution, to 3 million for the average middle-class family in 1989, and to 10 million in 1994. Knowing the existence of such a threat causes the girl's family to request a higher amount of mahr.

In the past, the mahr was so low that initiating a divorce today has been easy for some husbands, being only a matter of paying an insignificant amount of cash to the wife. The predicament of a woman facing divorce due to low mahr, can be illustrated in the case of Narges. In 1970, when she married, her mahr was 100,000 tomans; (a high sum at that time). When she divorced in 1989 the average mahr was 3-5 million tomans; among the better educated and well-off families. Her husband thought it was an easy matter simply to give her the total amount of 100,000 tomans in cash, thus fulfilling the sole legal condition for a restricted third-degree divorce. For the husband this equalled the price of a pair of car tyres.

The high amount of mahr today makes it impossible for husbands to pay it to their wives in case of divorce. However, to women the sum is more a matter of status, providing them with more power and ability to negotiate with the husband in case of divorce. Family insecurity and the increasing number of divorces on one hand, and the continuous devaluation of rials on the other, induces parents to increase their demands of mahr, thus hoping to guarantee greater security for their daughters in marriage.

The legal, moral and social status of woman is not affected in any way if she engages herself in the maintenance and upliftment of the home. Islam, on the one hand, safeguards all her rights by law and on the other, instructs society to render her a kind and fair treatment. Islam creates such an environment that whatever position woman assumes, she holds it with all her dignity and honour. As long as such an encouragement prevails, no change can ever occur in her honour and dignity. There are three prominent positions of woman at home — a daughter, a wife and a mother. Islam bestows great rank and position on her in all her three roles. No one can pull her back from this high position while she remains in the fold of Islam.

In Mother's Capacity

Islam assigns the highest rank, after Almighty Allah and His Prophet, to mother. Islam instructs man to give just and fair treatment to both father and mother and commands him for their obedience because both of them confer benevolence on him. But, in the Qur'an and Hadith, reference to the great benevolence of mother occurs more evidently and prominently. The Qur'an says:

> And We have enjoined on man (to be good) to
> his parents: in travail upon travail.
>
> Did his mother bear him,
>
> And in years twain
>
> Was his weaning (hear the command)
>
> 'Show gratitude to Me and to your parents:
>
> To Me is (your final) goal. (31:14)

At another place Allah Almighty says:

> We have enjoined on man
>
> Kindness to his parents:
>
> In pain did his mother

Bear him, and in pain

Did she give him birth

The carrying of the (child)

To his weaning is

(a period of) thirty months. (46:15)

In all the works of child upbringing like feeding, nursing, education and training, the father participates with mother. But it is only the mother who bears all the pains and troubles of pregnancy and delivery individually. To bear the burden of pregnancy for nine long months, to give birth to a child after a great struggle of life and death and to feed her child out of her own blood and to lead a life of full care and strict precaution in all these stages is not at all an easy task. Father does not undertake all these hardships and does not bear all this pain. Therefore the benevolence and favours of mother on man are more than those of the father.

There are several Hadith which draw our attention towards rendering great service and obedience to mother and to behave politely with her. Some of its precepts are being discussed here.

Prophet Muhammad (peace be upon him) instructed man to give fair and just treatment to both father and mother. But the Prophet stressed the fair treatment more to mother. The Prophet said:

> 'I enjoin man about his mother, I enjoin man about his mother, I enjoin man about his mother, I enjoin man about his mother.

> Hazraṭ Aisha reported that she enquired: 'O Messenger of God, who has the greatest right on woman?' The Prophet Muhammad, upon whom be peace, replied, 'Her husband (has the greatest right on her)'. She then asked, 'Who has the greatest right on man?' The Prophet replied, 'His mother (has the greatest right on him).'

Some of the people are of the opinion that since mother is weaker than father, hence the Prophet (peace be upon him) instructed man to serve and obey the mother much more than the father. Probably it is also true. However, the fact is, mother confers more benevolence on man than father and therefore she deserves more attention and obedience.

In traditions, disobedience to parents is included in Kaba'ir, i.e. , great sins.

A separate instruction is also given forbidding disobedience to mother which is condemned as an unlawful act. Prophet Muhammad (peace be upon him) said:

Allah has forbidden you to be undutiful to your mothers, to withhold (what you should give) or demand (what you do not deserve), and to bury your daughters alive. Prophet Muhammad (peace be upon him) mentioned sins and said that when his Ummah perpetrates these sins, great difficulties and torment will fall upon them. One of such sins is:

> 'Man would accept the words of his wife and would disobey his mother; would adopt a pleasant behaviour with his friend and the behaviour with his father would be severe.'

In one of the Hadith, disobedience to parents is regarded as one of the signs of the approaching Dooms Day.

The just and fair treatment to mother is regarded as a means of atonement for one's sins and the attainment of Paradise.

Hazrat Aisha states that Hazrat Harsa bin Noman behaved with his mother in a most respectable, pleasant and polite manner. Once Prophet Muhammad (peace be upon him) said:

I saw heaven in my dream where I heard somebody reciting the Qur'an. I asked whose voice was that. I was told that it was the voice of Hazrat Harsa bin Noman. Then the Prophet said that it was the reward of fair treatment to mother.

Hazrat Abdullah bin Amr says that someone confessed to the Prophet that he had committed a great sin. Is there any way of repentance for it? The Prophet asked: Do you have your aunt (maternal)?' The man replied, 'Yes'. The Prophet said: 'Render her just and fair treatment.'

It evidently shows that it is not the service to mother alone but the service to her relatives too, can be one of the means of the expiation for sins.

Service to mother is superior to the service to father. It is next only to the mother that the position of any other person can be determined. Hazrat Abu Hurairah relates that a person questioned Prophet Muhammad (upon whom be peace): Who deserves my polite behaviour most? The Prophet replied: 'Your mother'. The man asked: Who (deserves) the next? The Prophet replied: 'Your mother'. The man enquired for the third time that who deserves the next? The Prophet made the same answer: 'Your mother'. When the man repeated the same question for the fourth time, Prophet Muhammad (peace be upon him) said, 'Your father.'

There is one more Hadith according to which a companion of the Prophet asked him who deserved the greatest right for his decent and just treatment. The Prophet replied: 'Your mother'. The man asked who stands next to her? The Prophet replied: 'Your mother'. The man asked the same question for the third time. The Prophet gave him the same answer again. When he put the same question for the fourth time, the Prophet replied: 'Your father', then whoever stands as much nearer to you in relations deserves as much decent treatment.

Qazi Ayaz states that some people say that both mother and father deserve just and fair treatment. But mother deserves more rights for service. Imam Nawawi says that this opinion is the correct one since most authentic Hadith support it. Haris Muhasbi says that consensus seems to be that in matters of service from children mother has more rights than father.

There are different Traditions on the question whether the polite behaviour with mother should be double or triple? Imam Tahawi says that in this connection those Traditions are more authentic in which it is said that a man should offer kind and mild treatment to mother three times more than what he should offer to his father.

Imam Ahmad says that father should be obeyed, but as far as the fair treatment is concerned, out of the four parts, three belong to mother.

Islam does not stress the legal rights of mother and father alone but also prescribes a kind and decent treatment to them. Islam holds that the legal rights of parents should be observed heartily and with love and devotion and should not be regarded as burden. It also unfolds the fact that apart from the legal rights, one should give as noble and humble treatment to parents as possible and in this treatment again, mother deserves more affectionate treatment. Mother should be offered better behaviour than what is offered to father.

In Wife's Capacity

In Islam woman possesses an independent entity of her own. Because of Nikah, neither her personality gets dissolved in the personality of her husband nor does she become his subject or servant. When she holds some new responsibilities after marriage, she becomes the owner of some new rights at the same time. As she cannot refuse these responsibilities, in the same manner her rights cannot be taken away from her.

Now let us see how Islam views the relationship between wife and husband and what legal and moral basis Islam provides for this relationship.

The relation of husband and wife is, in fact, the relation of love, affection and intimacy. The natural love and attraction which God has placed between husband and wife is described in the Holy Qur'an thus:

And among His Signs

Is this, that He created

For you mates from among

Yourselves, that ye may

Dwell in tranquility with them

And He has put love

And mercy between your (hearts),

Verily in that are Signs

For those who reflect (30:21)

What is suggested is that there should be a relation of love, sympathy and affection between husband and wife. It is all their natural urge indeed. If hostility and animosity take the place of love and affection, it is against nature on which Allah Almighty has created them.

There is always a head of any minor or major institution. The structure of the family and the relationship among its members and its problems are more complicated and varied than all the other institutions and their problems. Order and discipline cannot be there in a family in the absence of its head. If there is no head of a family or no one is responsible for a family, it would definitely get disorganised. In Islam, man obtains the position of a head of the family for several reasons. This does not mean that man has acquired unlimited and whole and sole authority on his wife and that she is merely his subject. It actually means that while it is the responsibility of woman to accept her husband as a leader and obey and follow all his 'lawful demands', she also enjoys her rights. It is compulsory and obligatory for a man to perform these rights rather to pay all her dues. Hence the Qur'an says:

Men are the protectors

And maintainers of women, because God

Has given the one more (strength)

Than the other, and because

They support them

From their means

Therefore the righteous women

Are devoutly obedient and guard

In (the husband's) absence

What God would have them guard (4:34)

Again in another place, says the Qur'an::

And women shall have rights

Similar to the rights against them, according

To what is equitable;

But men have a degree

(of advantage) over them

And God is Exalted in Power, Wise. (2:228)

Woman, while accepting the superiority of man in domestic life, gains and enjoys all rights of maintenance allowance, residence, alimony, and education and training and several other rights. If man falls short of performing all these rights of woman, she can secure them through law.

Islam exhorts man not only to discharge the legal rights of his wife but to behave with her decently and justly. Nice treatment with wife is required in every condition. Sometimes man dislikes the face, temperament and habits of his wife, which affects their relationship. In such cases man is instructed to consider the better aspects of his wife because if he dislikes one aspect of hers, there can be then praiseworthy qualities in her. Therefore it is the demand not only of morality and nobility but also of wisdom and sagacity that man should keep farreaching interests before him and should not spoil the cordial relationship with his wife. Sometimes a certain thing appears unpleasant to man, but in it are hidden unaccountable aspects of goodness. In this connection, Islam lays down such a noble and ideal rule that cannot be found anywhere else. Allah Almighty says in the Qur'an.

> On the contrary live with them.
>
> On a footing of kindness and equity
>
> If ye take a dislike to them.
>
> It may be that ye dislike
>
> A thing, and God brings about
>
> Through it a great deal of good (4:19)

A lucid elucidation of such a polite behaviour with wife can be found in the sayings of Prophet Muhammad (peace be upon him).

Hazrat Muawiya Qushairi once enquired about the rights of wife of the Prophet (peace be upon him). In reply the Prophet said:

That you should give her food when you eat, clothe her when you clothe yourself, not strike her on the face, and not revile her or turn her out of the house (if separation becomes necessary) but live separately within the house itself (temporarily).

The same Tradition is expressed again in some other words:

> Feed her what you feed yourself with, her clothing should be of the same standard as yours, do not beat or abuse and rebuke her.

First, husband should follow the same standard of eating and drinking, clothing and dressing for his wife which he keeps for himself. It is unjustified if he keeps a high standard of life and compels his wife to subsist on a lower standard. Secondly, in association and relationship with her, his performance should be honourable. He should not treat her harshly or cruelly.

If any action of woman looks unpleasant or disagreeable, Prophet Muhammad (peace be upon him) advised man to endure and to have patience because this unpleasantness may prove temporary. Where some act of hers is unpleasant, some other acts may be pleasing to heart. To express lament and to show hatred and to be enraged at the slightest provocation will spoil mutual affectionate relationships for ever. Hazrat Abu Hurairah relates that Prophet Muhammad (peace be upon him) said:

> A believer must not hate a believing woman; if he dislikes one of her traits, he will be pleased with another.

Sometimes man demonstrates high morals and displays good conduct with others but his behaviour with his wife is reproachable even though his wife who is his life-partner is most deserving of polite and decent behaviour. Hence the man whose behaviour with his wife is just and fair is regarded as the best man. In a Tradition Hazrat Abu Hurairah relates that the Prophet said:

> The believers with perfect faith are those who have the best disposition and the best of you are those who are best to their wives.

In a Tradition, showing courtesy and love to wife and children is regarded as an attribute which completed faith (Iman). Hazrat Aisha related that Prophet Muhammad (peace be upon him) said:

> Among the believers, the man whose moral is best, has the perfect faith and who behave with his wife and children with more love and affection.

In another Tradition Hazrat Aisha relates that Prophet Muhammad, upon whom be peace, said:

> The best of you is he who is the best to his family, and I am the best among you to my family.

Islam regards the standard of relationship between husband and wife free from contention and strife as commendable. Wife should try to keep her husband delighted and contended, to obey him in rightful works and to safeguard his honour and dignity and wealth and property. On the other hand, husband should consider such a chaste and virtuous wife to be an excellent asset of life and should offer more decent and polite behaviour to her.

Hazrat Abu Hurairah says that Prophet Muhammad (peace be upon him) was asked about the attributes of a virtuous and righteous woman. The Prophet said:

> 'The one who pleases (her husband) when he looks at her, obeys him when he gives a command, and does not go against his wishes regarding her person, or property by doing anything of which he disapproves.'

Hazrat Abu Amama relates that Prophet Muhammad (peace be upon him) said:

> 'After fear of God, a believer gains nothing better for him than a good wife who obeys him if he gives her a command, pleases him if he looks at her, is true to him if he adjures her to do something, and is sincere towards him regarding her person and his property if he is absent.'

Hazrat Abdullah b. Umar b. Aas says that the Prophet said:

> 'The whole world is to be enjoyed, but the best thing in the world is a good wife.'

Hazrat Omar asked Prophet Muhammad (peace be upon him) that Allah Almighty forbids to store gold and silver, what type of wealth, then, we should keep with us? Prophet Muhammad (peace be upon him) said:

> 'Each one of you must possess with you, a thankful heart, a God-remembering tongue, a (Muslim) believing wife who assists him in the works for Akhirah (eternal life).'

It is quite evident from the above Traditions what type of relationship Islam wants to promote between husband and wife. If such a type of relationship exists between them, both of them will be assistant and well-wisher of each other, their life will be pleasant and ideal and all the unpleasant problems of rights and demands which cause disturbance and destroy the domestic life would never occur in their life.

In Daughter's Capacity

Before the proclamation of the Prophethood of Prophet Muhammad (peace be upon him), parents were much proud of their sons and they were supposed to be their great asset, because they gave more strength to their tribe and they were assistant in their great exertion in the field of finance. But daughters were considered to be burden on them and they were supposed to be the cause of ignominy or disgrace and on their very mention their heads dropped in shame. The Qur'an portrays a very graphic picture of the feelings of a parent on the birth of his daughter at that time.

> When news is brought to one of them of the
>
> Birth of a female (child), his face
>
> Darkens, and he is filled
>
> With inward grief!
>
> With shame does he hide

Himself from his people, because of the bad news

He has had Shall he retain it

On (sufferance and) contempt, or bury it

In the dust. (16:58-59)

One of the results of these obnoxious feelings for daughter was that some tribes used to bury their daughters alive. The Qur'an vehemently criticised the murderıng of children and regarded it a capital offence and put an end to this abhorrent practice once and for all. The Qur'an says that on the Last Day, one would have to answer for the hard-heartedness to God. The Qur'an says:

When the female (infant)

Buried alive, is

Questioned

For what crime

She was killed (81:8-9)

Islam inculcated totally different feelings for girls in place of their barbarous and brutal feelings.

The first and foremost that Islam says is that it is the will and wish of God that favoured some with children and to some He debarred and to some He gave only sons and to some He favoured with daughters alone and to some He blessed with both sons and daughters. None of this case is a cause of honour or disgrace or cause of dishonour or ignominy. All this is a natural phenomenon representing as it does the boundless knowledge and wisdom of God. Those who consider it a standard of dignity or ignominy are cavilling at His wisdom. The Qur'an says:

To God belongs the dominion of the heavens

And the earth. He creates what He wills

(And plans). He bestows (children) male or

Female according to His will (and plan)

Or He bestows both males

And females and He leaves

Barren whom He will

For He is full of knowledge and power.

(42:49-50)

There is exhortation in Islam for the proper nourishment and sustenance of daughters. It is regarded as a good deed and a means for the attainment of Heaven. Hazrat Aisha relates that Prophet Muhammad (peace be upon him) said:

> 'Whoever is in charge of (put to test by)
>
> three daughters and treats them generously,
>
> then they will act as a shield for him
>
> from the (Hell) Fire.'

In Traditions, the upbringing and nourishment of two or three daughters or sisters or even one daughter or sister is referred to as a means for entering Heaven. From this the reward or requital to the person who brings up more than three daughters or sisters can be well realised. Hazrat Itba bin Aamir relates that Prophet Muhammad (peace be upon him) said:

> 'Whoever has three daughters, and bears with the miseries in their connection, feeds and clothes them with the earnings of his labour, they will become a curtain on the fire of hell, for him.'

Hazrat Abu Sayeed Khudri relates that Prophet Muhammad (peace be upon him) said:

> 'Whoever amongst you has three daughters, or three sisters, and he treats them gently, he will surely enter heaven.'

Hazrat Abu Sayeed relates one more Hadith that Prophet Muhammad, upon whom be peace, said:

> 'Whoever has three daughters or three sisters or two daughters or two sisters and he adopts a good company with them and fears Allah about them, He has (place for him in) Heaven.'

Hazrat Anas relates that Prophet Muhammad (peace be upon him) said:

> 'If anyone cares for two girls till they grow up, he and I will come on the day of resurrection thus', and he joined his fingers.'

Hazrat Abu Hurairah relates that Prophet Muhammad (peace be upon him) said:

> Whoever has three daughters and he bears with the difficulties and financial problems, in connection with them, Allah will make him enter Heaven, for courtesy towards them.' Abu Hurairah reports that a man enquired if he has two daughters (and bears with the difficulties in connection with them). The Prophet replied, 'Even if he has two daughters (Allah will bless him with Heaven)'. A man asked, if he has one? The Prophet said (He will) even if he has one.'

Hazrat Abdullah bin Abbas relates a similar Hadith that Prophet Muhammad (peace be upon him) said:

> 'If anyone takes care of three girls or the like number of sisters, training them and showing kindness to them till God enriches them, God will guarantee him paradise.'

Hearing such a great reward, a man humbly enquired Prophet Muhammad (peace be upon him) that if anyone renders the same service to two daughters or sisters in the same way does he get the same reward? The Prophet replied, 'Yes, he would get the same reward'. The one who relates the above Hadith says that if the man would have enquired for one daughter or sister, the Prophet would have given the same reply.

It shows that for providing nourishment and giving proper training to one daughter or sister a man deserves a seat in paradise. If he nourishes and brings up more than one daughter or sister, his rank may be raised accordingly.

It is stated in the Hadith that with the good nourishment of daughters, they should also be given good education and training and should also select a good match for the marriage and should continue fair and just treatment with them. Hazrat Abu Sayeed Khudri relates that Prophet Muhammad (peace be upon him) said:

> 'Whoever nourishes three daughters, educates and trains them, gets them married (and afterwards) offers a gentle behaviour to them, for him there is heaven.'

Generally more love and affection is showered on sons in feeding, clothing, education, training and in every respect more preference is accorded to them. This is total injustice and oppression. In Hadith such a treatment is forbidden and condemned.

Hazrat Abdullah bin Abbas relates that Prophet Muhammad (peace be upon him) said:

> 'Whoever has a girl, who has neither buried her alive nor gives a mean treatment to her and not

> even gives preference to his son over his daughter, God will make him enter Heaven.'

In all these Hadith on the proper nourishment, education training, arrangement of marriage and equal treatment to daughters or sisters, glad tidings is given for liberation from Hell and the attainment of Heaven. One who does not have faith in God and the eternal day and one who gives all importance to the present world alone does not realise the significance of these Traditions. But the very goal of the believer (Momin) is success on the Judgement Day. There is all what he wishes in this goodness for a believer.

With the inducement of the proper care for girls, this conception is also laid down that she is not worthless or valueless as the world considers her, but she is the most valuable boon of nature. The love and affection which she possesses in herself, a boy does not have it.

Hazrat Aqba bin Amir relates that Prophet Muhammad (peace be upon him) said:

> Do not hate girls. They are comforter and much precious.

Such a teaching for a fair and just treatment of girls is an example which is found nowhere. According to Islamic law, if the child does not own any position and does not have any proper means for living, his maintenance is obligatory on his father. In accordance with this rule, the maintenance or allowances for daughters is obligatory on his father till her marriage and in the absence of his father, it is necessary for her nearest relative to ensure her maintenance. After marriage, the responsibility of her maintenance shifts to her husband and on the death of her husband or in case of divorce and if the woman is not self-sufficient in financial matters, the responsibility goes to her children or in case she has no children, the responsibility for her maintenance falls on her nearest relative. This is a legal right and in the Tradition its importance is well emphasised.

Hazrat Suraqua bin Malik relates that Prophet Muhammad (peace be upon him) asked him:

> 'Shall I not show you what is the greatest charity. He said: Messenger of God, certainly show (it). The Prophet said, 'To be grateful to your daughters who (after becoming widow or being divorced) is sent back to you and there is no one save you, her earning man.'

The Companions of the Prophet were so thoughtful about their widows and daughters that it can be well understood from this example that Hazrat Zubair endowed some of his houses. In the details of this endowment the following statement was also included.

Whosoever of his daughters (being divorced or by becoming a widow) would come back to her house, she would stay in it.

Neither she would put it in loss nor would she be put in loss. If she is self-sufficient in respect of finance without depending on her husband, she would not have any right in it. In this way, in the family system of Islam, the legal right of woman are secured.

5

Better Citizens

Farid Wajadi Afandi in his famous book entitled *Al-Mir'at al-Muslima* has discussed the habits and temperaments of women. Maulana Azad has translated this book into Urdu and added footnotes to it. In this book the author writes quoting references from the Encyclopaedia: It is a fact that the construction of the female body resembles that of a child. Due to this reason the woman is sensitive like a child and is readily affected by external impressions. It is the habit of a child that he begins to cry over a painful sight and leaps up with joy over a cheerful thing. The same is the case with the women, who are easily carried away by all sorts of sentiments than men.

Experience shows that women are generally hardworking and self-contented. They love their husbands from the core of their hearts, bring up their children with the utmost care and are the best household managers. They are sincere and loyal. There are more virtues and less weaknesses in them.

The laborious and hardworking nature of a woman can be judged at the time of difficulty.

Modern research has proved this fact. The great scholar Lumbrose has written: Just imagine the hardships and tribulations a woman has to go through during pregnancy and at the time of delivery, otherwise the accomplishment of this delicate and difficult task of multiplication of the human race would not be possible.

No doubt woman is a delicate creature. She has a weak and delicate heart. Coquettishness is in her nature. She is of buoyant and jovial nature. She is also easily annoyed and flares up at trifling matters. A man should adopt some reasonable attitude taking into consideration all these things. In the verses pertaining to divorce, men have been admonished not to commit tyranny and aggression.

Divine Rulings

It has been said in the Holy Quran:

> Retain them not to their hurt so that ye transgress (the limits). He who doeth that hath wronged his spul. Make not the revelations of Allah a laughing stock. (2:231)

In the above verse men have been forbidden from tyranny and oppression; but the miraculous style of the verse is very comprehensive. Allah, the Exalted, forbids men from persecuting women. The Holy Prophet (peace and blessings of Allah be upon him) has observed: No one of you should beat a woman like a servant and then next day go to her for sexual gratification.
(Bukhari)

The Holy Prophet (peace and blessings of Allah be upon him) has prohibited the beating of woman. The Holy Prophet (peace and blessings of Allah be upon him) said: Do not beat your wife like a maid servant. (Mishkat)

Once the Holy Prophet (peace and blessings of Allah be upon him) was questioned about the rights of women over men. He answered: When you dine, dine with them and when you dress, dress with them. Do not beat them on their face, nor rebuke them nor separate them. If you do so, do in the house. (Mishkat)

The Holy Prophet (peace and blessings of Allah be upon him) has issued the above commandment as men have the right to admonish women under special circumstances but it is not permissible to admonish them publicly.

The kind and benevolent treatment of the Holy Prophet (peace and blessings of Allah be upon him) towards his wives is a practical example for all the believers. He never even thought of giving physical punishment to his wives.

However, the Holy Quran has allowed the infliction of physical punishment on women in special situations:

> As for those from whom ye fear rebellion, admonish them and banish them to beds apart; and beat them. Then if they obey you, seek not a way from them. (4:34)

But this prerogative should be applied very rarely when it is absolutely necessary. According to the Holy Quran, if the woman is stubborn and persistent in her behaviour, man should try to convince her by argument. If he does not succeed to bring her round, he should separate his bed. Even then if he does not succeed, he is allowed to beat her. But what could be the nature of beating? In this connection, the Holy Prophet (peace and blessings of Allah be upon him) has said: Give them a light beating. This implies light punishment or rebuke.

Holy Prophet's Golden Advice

The Messenger of Allah (peace and blessings of Allah be upon him) in his famous historical address observed, besides speaking on other important points:

> Instruct each other to do good to your womenfolk for they are assigned to you and have no control over anything by themselves and if they are guilty of immodesty, you are allowed to beat them without leaving (serious) injury. But if they repent you must treat them

> better. Lo! you have your rights against your wives and they have theirs against you. It is their duty to observe chastity and to avoid immorality and their right against you is that you must feed and clothe them with fairness.
>
> (Tirmidhi)

It is evident from the above Hadith that the permission for the beating of women granted by the Holy Quran may be utilized very sparingly, only in the case of manifest immodesty. Every word of the above extract of the speech of the Messenger of Allah (peace and blessings of Allah be upon him) is full of profound insight and wisdom regarding the mutual relations of husband and wife.

In order to ensure discipline and stability in domestic life men have been given power over women. If both were vested with equal power, it would have ruined the peace and harmony of the domes tic life as two kings cannot rule over one state. Secondly, men have been given permission to rebuke or to avoid sexual intercourse or to beat, not causing any serious injury, if the woman is found guilty of manifest immodesty. Then the rights of husbands against their wives and those of wives against their husbands have been explained. The husband has been instructed to feed and clothe his wife with fairness. He must not take undue advantage of the power vested in him and do what he wishes; but it is his duty to fulfil the needs tastes and interests of his wife as she is dependent on him. Experience shows that if any person is dependent on the other in a certain sphere of life and the latter does not care for his sentiments and tastes, the former's feelings are injured and he feels disgusted.

Before the advent of Islam there was no restriction on the Arab men and women meeting and talking with each other just like the modern western people of today.

Islam put an end to these practices of the Days of Ignorance. The second duty of women is that they should ask the permission of their husbands before they allow any man (Mahram or Ghair Mahram) to enter their houses and should not let such men enter their houses whom their husbands do not like.

Holy Prophet's Domestic Life

> The Holy Prophet (peace and blessings of Allah be upon him) has taught that a Mumin should be an embodiment of virtues and of excellent moral conduct and behaviour and that the best of you in this respect are the kindest of you to their wives. The Messenger of Allah (peace and blessings of Allah be upon him) has observed: The most perfect of the believers in faith is the best of them in moral excellence, and the best of you are the kindest of you to their wives.
>
> (Tirmidhi)

According to the above Hadith, the sign of the most perfect and best believer in faith is that he is the kindest to his wife. The husbands should, therefore, be kind and benevolent to their wives and should always try to fulfil their lawful needs and desires to please them. He whose treatment with his wife is the best possesses the most excellent virtues among us. During a short meeting, a person may pose excellent behaviour and manners; but the permanent and lasting company of his wife exposes his real character and temperament. The wife is the real test of his natural and inherent qualities.

Once the Messenger of Allah (peace and blessing of Allah be upon him) said: Avoid beating the living creatures of Allah. In Arabia the women were treated no better than animals. They were entirely at the mercy of men. Men had the right to take the life of a woman or to beat her as an ordinary thing. But with the advent of Islam, the persecution of women ended and they heaved a sigh of relief.

> The result of the emancipation of this downtrodden humanity began to be felt in society as is evident from this Hadith. One day Hadrat Umar (Allah be pleased with him) came

to the Messenger of Allah (peace and blessings of Allah be upon him) and said: Women have become daring to their husbands. Hearing this the Messenger of Allah (peace and blessings of Allah be upon him) said that the above instructions may not be observed strictly; but the husbands took an undue advantage of the 'relaxation' and complaints began to pour in. Thereupon the Messenger of Allah (peace and blessings of Allah be upon him) said: Many a woman surrounded the family of Muhammad and complained that their husbands were not good people. (Riyad Al-Salihin)

Who could bear to listen to the complaint from the tongue of the Messenger of Allah (peace and blessings of Allah be upon him)? The result was that there came a moderation in the men's behaviour.

One main aim and object of the Messenger of Allah (peace and blessings of Allah be upon him) in calling for the meeting of the Ummahat-ul-Muminin (mothers of the believers) in Madinah, eight or nine years before his death was, besides other things, to give a practical lesson that mutual love and harmony should exist between husband and wife. He used to say: The best of you is the kindest of you to his family and I am the kindest of you all to my family. And when your wife dies pray for her. (Mishkat)

It is evident that pious and good behaviour does not mean temporary posing; but your treatment of your wife and children should fully reflect these virtues. The Messenger of Allah (peace and blessings of Allah be upon him) not only instructed the people to be good and kind to their wives, but also acted upon this principle

> in his practical life. He used to say: The most perfect of the believers in faith is the best of them in moral excellence and the kindest of them to his wife and children. (Mishkat)
>
> The Messenger of Allah (peace and blessings of Allah be upon him) used to do what he said. There are a number of Ahadith that the Messenger of Allah (peace and blessings of Allah be upon him) did not forget Hadrat Khadija (Allah be pleased with her) after her death and remembered her frequently. Not only did he talk of her often, but he used to treat her female friends kindly. It has been said by Hadrat 'A'isha (Allah be pleased with her): Never was I jealous of the Prophet's wives. Although I never saw her, but he remembered her so often (that she was not a stranger to me). His love and devotion for his first wife can be judged from the fact that whenever a goat was slaughtered in the house, he remembered her and distributed a portion of the meat among her female friends. (Mishkat)

Hadrat 'A'isha (Allah be pleased with her) once asked him (Allah's Messenger) if she had been the only woman worthy of his love? He used to say: Khadija bore me children and she was such a pious and faithful lady.

Exemplary Husbands

Due to the above practical teachings of Islam, the Prophet's Companions also moulded their lives accordingly. They had sincere love and devotion for their wives. An illustrious Companion of the Holy Prophet (peace and blessings of Allah be upon him) Hadrat 'Abdullah bin 'Umar (Allah be pleased with him) was returning from Jihad. On the way someone told him that his wife was ill. He was perturbed to hear this news. He hastened to reach home and see his wife. On this occasion he offered his Maghrib (evening) and 'Isha (night) prayers consecutively.

It has been reported about Hadrat 'Abdullah bin 'Umar (Allah be pleased with him) that his father asked him to divorce his wife for certain reasons. He was in a strange fix. On the one hand, he could not disobey his father's command and on the other hand, love for his wife stood in his way. He was on the horn of a dilemma and almost refused to divorce her. His father (Hadrat 'Umar) presented this matter to the Messenger of Allah (peace and blessings of Allah be upon him) who decided that he ('Abdullah bin 'Umar) should obey his father. Then he divorced his wife (Uswa Sahaba). Hadrat Imam Hasan (Allah be pleased with him) the son of Hadrat Fatimah (Allah be pleased with her) divorced his wife for certain reasons and paid her dowry. When the news of the divorce reached her she was dumbfounded and began to weep. When the Messenger came back and told him about the pathetic condition of his wife, he also burst into tears and said: Had I not pronounced irrevocable talaq (divorce), I would have affected a reconciliation.

A similar incident of Hadrat Abu Bakr's son has been reported. He loved his wife so dearly that he did not proceed on Jihad on several occasions and stayed in the house, thus depriving himself of Allah's blessings and rewards. When Hadrat Abu Bakr (Allah be pleased with him) heard this he asked his son to divorce his wife. The son tried his best to put off this matter, but when his father insisted he was compelled to divorce his wife. But the flame of love continued to burn in his heart and he began to recite painful couplets. When Hadrat Abu Bakr (Allah be pleased with him) came to know about this, he called his son and asked him to re-establish marital relations as the divorce had not yet become irrevocable.

The love story of Hadrat Buraira and Mughith has been narrated in Ahadith. Hadrat Buraira who was a maid-servant was married to Mughith. When she became free, she had the right to live with her first husband or not. Hadrat Buraira decided not to live with Mughith. When he came to know of her decision, he could not bear the pangs of separation and loitered about in the streets of Madinah weeping and crying.

The excellence of the rules and regulations promulgated by Islam in the past have raised the prestige and honour of downtrodden humanity. It has given women their due rights and ample opportunities to show their worth and capabilities.

Rights for the Life Partner

> Worship and prayer etc., are very significant things; but Islam does not allow that a person should remain always busy in 'Ibadah (acts of devotion), and deprive his wives of their legal rights. It discourages the monastic way of life. The Messenger of Allah (peace and blessings of Allah be upon him), showed his displeasure over the action of some of his Companions who spent the whole night in 'Ibadah (worship, prayers etc.) and were heedless of their conjugal duties. The Messenger of Allah (peace and blessings of Allah be upon him) called them and instructed them: Verily, your wife has right against you. (Bukhari)

In order to prove himself to be a good husband a man should not only try his utmost to fulfil his wife's needs and please her; but also act upon the following instructions of the Messenger of Allah (peace and blessings of Allah be upon him).

> The husband should be dressed neat and clean so that his wife should be pleased to see him and admire in her heart his aesthetic sense, polished manners and the excellent style of his dress. He should not be dirty, ugly looking or rough or shabbily dressed. If the husband wants that his wife should be neat and good looking, it is also the desire of the wife that her husband should be handsome looking and of cheerful disposition. Islam does not allow a person to wear ugly looks. The Messenger of Allah (peace

and blessings of Allah be upon him) led a scrupulously neat and clean life. He had a smiling, cheerful countenance. He always was careful of his personal cleanliness. While he was in the house or on a journey, he did not forget to keep a mirror, a comb and a box for holding collyrium and other toiletries. The Messenger of Allah (peace and blessings of Allah be upon him) did not like people to remain dirty. Hadrat 'Ata bin Yassar (Allah be pleased with him) reported that the Messenger of Allah (peace and blessings of Allah be upon him) was sitting in the mosque when a person, the hair of whose beard and head was shabby and dishevelled entered. The Messenger of Allah (peace and blessings of Allah be upon him) asked him to arrange his hair. He got his hair arranged. When he turned his face and the Messenger of Allah (peace and blessings of Allah be upon him) saw him in a good condition he observed: Is this condition not better than the former which was like a devil? There is another Hadith: Verily, Allah is good and likes goodness. He is clean and likes cleanliness. (Mishkat)

It is evident from the above Ahadith that both the husband and wife should pay special attention to their personal cleanliness. It is the duty of the husband to provide such articles as will enable his wife to keep herself neat and clean. It is the duty of the husband to provide such things as a comb, oil, soap, etc., according to the practice in vogue, and perfume whereby she can make herself sweet smelling. It is also his duty to provide water for washing the clothes and body.

(Alamgiri)

> It has been stated in the Hadith that at the time of return from a journey the husband should try to inform his wife before hand. It is necessary because women often do not take much care for their personal appearance in the absence of their husbands. So that the woman may remove her dirt and remove the hidden (superfluous) hair. (Bukhari)

Favouring the Better Half

It is the moral responsibility of the husband to be good and kind to his wife. If any misfortune befalls her, he should not withdraw his love and favour; but in the difficult time his treatment should be more kind and sympathetic. If she happens to fall ill, he should take her to the doctor. If she is in difficulty, an attempt should be made to solve her problem. If her face becomes uglier due to illness, indifferent and harsh treatment should not be adopted with her; but every effort should be made to console her. If he would not sympathise with her, her feelings would be injured and her jovial and buoyant face would become dejected. The indifferent attitude of her husband would rend her heart with frustration.

> Just imagine, you bring a beautiful, fascinating lady and are ready to sacrifice everything for her. You have purchased the best wedding dress and ornaments just to please her. But by chance she falls ill, and smallpox makes her face ugly or snatches away the light of her eyes. When she looks into the mirror, her eyes become wet with tears or if she becomes blind, the whole world plunges into darkness for her. She weeps bitterly day and night. To add to her calamities, you threaten to turn her out. She is tortured for no fault of her own. Where has her husband's love gone? How has spring turned into winter? All these are the vicissitudes of fortune. Just think, is it proper or human? Is this not a disgrace to

> love and sheer injustice? It must also be kept in mind that the painful sighs and tears of a helpless and downtrodden woman do not go waste. Islam does not permit this terrible attitude and hard-heartedness. The Prophet (peace and blessings of Allah be upon him) said: He who does not make mercy, Allah will not make mercy on him. (Riyad Al-Salihin)
>
> What has been said above is only to give an understanding of the problem. It is the duty of the husband to try his utmost to win the heart of his wife. He must have full regard for her feelings and sentiments. There is a well known story that one night while Hadrat 'Umar (Allah be pleased with him) was on patrol, he heard the voice of painful songs from a house. Hadrat 'Umar (Allah be pleased with him) asked the reason for this. He was told that the husband of this woman had proceeded on Jihad. He was deeply moved at her sincere love for her husband and asked Hadrat Hafsa (Allah be pleased with her) how long a woman can bear her husband's separation. Her answer was: For four months. Thereupon he issued the following order to his Commanders: A married person should not remain away from his wife for more than four months. (Dur Mukhtar)

It is evident from the above historical incident that it is also among the duties of the husband that he should not be indifferent to the feelings, sentiments and the natural sexual urge of the wife. If he was to stay in a foreign country for long, he should keep his wife and children with him. This fact has also been explained by the Holy Qur'an in a verse regarding Ila. If a person resorts to *Ila* (a vow of temporary cessation of marital relations) without naming a period, he is bound either to re-establish the normal relations after four months or to divorce his wife. After the lapse of this period, the husband has no right to keep his wife and she is free to marry any man. The Holy Quran says:

> Those who forswear their wives must wait four months; then, if they change their minds, Lo! Allah is Forgiving, Merciful. And if they decide upon divorce (let them remember that), Allah is Hearer, Knower. (2:226-227)

> The husband must have confidence in his wife. He should entrust all the household affairs to her so as to give confidence to her and enhance her prestige and honour. The Messenger of Allah (peace and blessings of Allah be upon him) said: A woman is the custodian of the house of her husband. (Bukhari)

The other Ahadith also testify to this fact. It has been said therein that women are custodians of their husband's property. Moreover, confidence in a woman adds to her prestige and honour and she considers herself as in charge of the household affairs. The husband's responsibilities and worries are then decreased with the result that he would lead a peaceful and comfortable life.

> One right of a wife on her husband is that the husband should not divulge her secrets to others but must keep it a secret. The Messenger of Allah (peace and blessings of Allah be upon him) has strictly forbidden husbands to divulge the secrets of their wives: The most wicked among the people in the sight of Allah is the man who goes to his wife and she comes to him, and then he divulges her secret.
>
> (Muslim)

> The secrets of conjugal life must not be divulged or discussed publicly. While commenting upon this Hadith, Imam Nawawi has written that it is strictly forbidden to discuss

> the sexual relations of husband and wife. To explain the detail of the sexual intercourse is an abominable act. According to the above Hadith it is forbidden to expose the secrets of husband and wife, such as sexual intercourse and details thereof and what happened with the woman and (divulgence of), anything said or any act committed by her. (Sharah Muslim)

Monetary Support

Among the great responsibilities which Islam has put on the husband, his duty is also to provide necessary expenses for the maintenance of the house such as food, clothing, lodging, etc. So that his wife can rear her children without much worry.

It has been mentioned in the Holy Quran:

> Let him who hath abundance spend of his abundance, and he whose provision is measured, let him spend of that what Allah hath given him. Allah asketh not of any soul save that which He hath given it. (65:7)

None has to bear more burden than he can bear, but the responsibilities placed on him are proportionate to his power and ability. It has been mentioned in another verse of the Holy Quran:

> The duty of providing food and clothes to nursing mothers in a seemly manner is upon the father of the child. No one should be charged beyond his capacity. (2:233)

> The responsibility for providing the means of sustenance has been put on the husband so that the woman can bear and rear her children with full concentration of mind. This helps in the proper development of the personality of the child. We have already quoted a Hadith that

among the duties which a husband owes to his wife, one duty is: You should be fair to them in feeding and clothing them. (Tirmidhi)

The incident of Hind bint 'Utba, the wife of Abu Sufyan, is known to everyone. She went to the Messenger of Allah (peace and blessings of Allah be upon him) and complained: My husband is miserly. He does not give sufficient provision to my children of his own accord. After relating her story she asked: If I feed his children out of that held by him, is there any harm to me. The Messenger of Allah (peace and blessings of Allah be upon him) said: Take honestly what is enough for you and your child. (Bukhari)

The Messenger of Allah (peace and blessings of Allah be upon him) also made arrangements for household expenses. He had set apart a garden for this purpose. He deposited the income of that garden for defraying his household expenses for the year. The Messenger of Allah (peace and blessings of Allah be upon him) used to sell the trees of Bani Nudair and deposited the amount to provide means of sustenance for the whole year. (Bukhari)

The Jurists call Nafqa (household expenses), Wajib (incumbent), on the husband irrespective of whether the wife may be poor or rich. Household expenses mean food, clothing, lodging etc. In the dictionary the word Nafqa means expenses for wife and children and according to the Shari'ah it implies food, clothing and lodging.

(Dur Mukhtar)

Proper Freedom

Another right of a wife over her husband is that the latter should allow her to see her parents and her near relatives i.e. Mahrams. The Messenger of Allah (peace and blessings of Allah be upon him) used to see his affectionate daughter and Hadrat Abu Bakr and Hadrat 'Umar (Allah be pleased with them) also used to go to the Prophet's house to see their daughters. A large number of such instances have been mentioned in the Ahadith. The Jurists are of the view that if the wife goes to see her parents once in a week, the husband should not object to it. But this is permissible if the parents are unable to see her for some genuine reason, otherwise, they should themselves go to see her.

If there is a dispute between husband and wife and there is a danger that it would take a serious turn, the husband has been instructed not to take a hasty step. If the situation is not improved even by beating, a judge should be appointed from each side to resolve the dispute. The Holy Qur'an says:

> And if ye fear a breach between them twain (the man and wife), appoint an arbiter from his folk and an arbiter from her folk. (4:35)

But it must be kept in mind that the judges should be honest and sincere. It is then that they would be able to resolve the dispute, otherwise they would further aggravate the situation. The Holy Quran testifies to this fact:

> If they desire amendment Allah will make them of one mind. Allah is ever Knower, Aware.
> (4:35)

Hadrat Maulana Ashraf Ali Thanvi gives the following comments on this verse:

> "And the women who are arrogant in their behaviour should be first admonished. If they do not change their behaviour, do not share their bed. If they still disobey you beat them

> not causing any injury. If they obey you, do not commit aggression on them on one or another pretext. If the circumstances are such that there is risk of the situation being worsened, a judge who is competent to resolve the dispute may be appointed from either side who should investigate the matter and admonish those at fault, the husband or wife, or both. If the judges are sincere in their mission, they would by Allah's favour succeed in effecting a reconciliation between them. Allah is All Knowing, All Aware. Allah knows how mutual love can be restored between them and when He sees the good intention of the judges, He will guide them on the right lines. The judges must sincerely try to remove the doubts and suspicions existing in the minds of husband and wife and patch up the differences between them. The husband and wife should also cooperate with the judges and act upon the decision arrived at by them."

Housewife's Role

We have so far discussed in detail the rights of the wife against her husband. Now let us see what instructions have been given to the wife concerning her husband. We can judge from the rights and duties of both what strenuous efforts have been made by Islam to guard modesty and chastity and to ensure stability, love and harmony in conjugal relations.

Any rule or law which holds one party responsible, leaving the other free to do as it likes may be apparently nice but it cannot be called perfect or good. Only such rules and laws are complete as are applicable to all and guard the rights of one against the other. There is no denying the fact that woman is a weak and sentimental creature and because of this very reason she deserves our favour, love and regard and it is our duty to overlook her shortcomings. But this does not mean that she is absolved of her duties. Had it been so, the life of both husband and wife would be devoid of any purpose and charm.

Husband Supreme

Islam has kept in view the inherent weaknesses of woman. Due to this reason man has priority over woman. He has been appointed as the leader or president insofar as the family life is concerned, as he has the ability to solve the difficult matters. Allah the Exalted has said in the Holy Quran:

> Men are in charge of women, because Allah hath made the one of them to excel the other, and because they spend of their property.
>
> (4:34)

It means men have been given priority and eminence over women in the matter of knowledge and action. They are responsible for supporting them and providing food, clothing and lodging to his family. Hence he is the leader or president of the house.

There is no denying the fact that man is superior to woman due to his God sent virtues and capabilities. A woman has to go through certain periods in which she is rendered almost unable to do anything and she has to depend upon others, for instance, during pregnancy, suckling, rearing of children, menstruation and during the period of discharge of blood after childbirth. Hadrat Shah Wali Ullah has written:

> It is necessary and akin to nature that man should have authority over woman as man possesses perfect intellect, he is an expert politician. He defends vehemently and guards respect and honour. He has priority over woman as he provides food, clothing and lodging.

The modern research has proved that the brain of man is stronger than that of woman. He is more intelligent and wise. His mind is more mature. He possesses a strong body and muscles. We have already quoted the views of some writers. We give below some excerpts from modern research scholars:

The famous rationalist scholar and philosopher, Dr. Proudon writes in his book:

> "The perception and intuition of woman is as weak as is her intellect in comparison to man. Her character is also different. Her nature is also different. That is why her criteria of judgement of merits and demerits of a thing also vary. This difference between man and woman is lasting and abiding. It is her inherent nature."

Allama Farid Wajadi gives the following comments:

> "The five senses, on which depends the growth of mind and intellect also vary. The scholars Nicholas and Baily have proved that the five senses of women are weaker as compared to men."

He further writes:

> "Physiology has proved that there is variation in the weight and dimension of the female and male brain. The average weight of a male brain is 100 grams more in weight than a female."

Allama Wajadi has written:

> "Due to the intellectual faculty man has priority over woman. The average weight of a male brain is 49½ ounces and a female brain weighs about 44 ounces. 278 male brains were weighed. The biggest one weighed 65 ounces and the smallest one 34 ounces. But out of 291 female brains, the biggest weighed 54 ounces and the smallest

> 21 ounces. Is this not sufficient to prove that the intellectual faculties of women are weaker as compared to men?"

The above difference exists everywhere, in the civilized countries as well as in the backward countries. The author of Encyclopaedia writes:

> "Just as the difference in the physical strength and intellectual faculty exists in the most civilized city of Paris, in the same way it exists in the savage people of America."

That is to say, modern research has proved beyond doubt that men have more capabilities than women in every respect.

Equality in All Spheres

From the authority given to man it should not be construed that in Islam, a wife is the maidservant of the husband. This view is incorrect. Only a person who is ignorant of Islamic knowledge can hold this view. Sometimes it happens that a husband and wife have different opinions on certain matters. If there is any such dispute between them, the opinion of the husband should be given precedence over the opinion of the wife as he is the head of the family because of his special knowledge and capabilities.

Islam desires that all matters may be settled amiably with mutual consent of both husband and wife. There is equality between the two and both husband and wife have rights against each other and they also owe duties to each other. The Holy Quran has mentioned:

> And they have rights similar to those (of men) over them in kindness, and men are a degree over them. (2:228)

This brief verse contains a fundamental principle that men and women are equal in all respects and their rights and duties are also equal except that, as explained above, men have power over women. In all other matters concerning conduct and behaviour and 'Ibadah and social dealings they are equal and there is no reason for holding them in contempt. Islam has for the first time given such prestige and honour to womenfolk.

A philosopher has rightly observed:

> "If Allah wanted to make a woman the head of the family, she would have been born from the portion of the body where the head is set and if He wanted to make the woman a maid-servant, He would have created her from the lowest portion of the body having feet. As it was not Allah's will and He wanted equality, mutual love, harmony and respect and honour for each other, He created her from the side of man."

Despite the fact that man is the head of the family, he has been asked to consult his wife and settle all matters by mutual consent of each other. Where the Holy Quran has ordained that the mother should suckle her baby for a full two years and the duty of providing food and clothing, etc., to the woman who suckles rests with the father, it has also been ordained that if the woman desires to wean the child, it should be done by mutual consent of the husband and wife. It has been mentioned in the Holy Quran:

> If they desire to wean the child by mutual consent and consultation, it is no sin for them. (2:233)

It is obvious that mutual consultation is necessary in all matters. The gist of what we have said above is that Islam has framed rules and regulations for the married couple which if acted upon, would bring mutual love and harmony between them and protect their modesty and chastity.

In these hard times, we came across instances of rifts between husbands and wives of rich families over triflings. Their relations are strained. Both begin to live separately. Years pass on and both persist in their behaviour just to keep their false prestige. This period of separation is full of great hazards for both as no one is without sexual desire. Islam condemns such a way of life, there is no room for it in Islam. We shall discuss this point in detail in the next pages.

Meritorious Women

If the husband and wife had acted upon the excellent principles of Islam, the matter would not have gone from bad to worse. On such a critical occasion, if the husband's view-point, his being the head, were to be accepted, the dispute would surely have come to an end. The Holy Quran says:

> "So good women are the obedient, guarding in secret that which Allah has made them guard."
> (4:34)

In the above verse the virtue of a pious woman has been explained and she has been instructed to be loyal to her husband so that if there is any difference of opinion between them, it should not cause separation between them. The Messenger of Allah (peace and blessings of Allah be upon him) has further instructed the women to live amiably with their husbands:

> 'A woman who asks for divorce from her husband on triflings, is forbidden the smell of paradise.'

In the above Hadith women have been admonished that if any unagreeable thing occurs between the husband and wife, she should not demand divorce from her husband, as such, things do happen in married life due to difference in temperaments.

It is, however, the duty of a pious lady that in the event of a clash with her husband, she should overcome her anger considering her husband to be the head of the family. She should keep in mind that it is her duty to obey him. If she is sure that her husband has given her unjust treatment, she should try to convince him that he is wrong. She should however, be careful and cautious and present her viewpoint in a civilized manner.

God forbid, when any woman takes the law in her hand, the married life is bound to be disturbed and this small kingdom of the husband and wife will be ruined. The one inevitable result of this quarrel would be that both husband and wife would lose their honour and prestige when the people would come to know that they are unable to manage their household affairs.

Due to the husband's love for his wife, the latter must also please him, be solicitous for his ease and comfort and have respect for and honour him. She should always keep in mind that he is the head of the family and it is her duty to pay due respect to him. The Messenger of Allah (peace and blessings of Allah be upon him) has observed:

> "If I had ordained any individual to prostrate before the other individual I would have ordained the wife to prostrate before her husband." (Mishkat)

A husband who showers all his love and affection on his wife and spends his hard earned money to provide her comforts and amenities, taking her to be the centre of his devotions must be respected and honoured by his wife. A mere show of respect and honour is not sufficient; but there must be sincerity in these sentiments so that she may win his heart. For the wife the necessity for seeking her husband's pleasure exists in this world and also in the Hereafter.

> "When a woman whose husband is pleased with her dies, she would enter Paradise."(Mishkat)

A wife can win the heart of her husband through love and sacrifice. If the wife obeys him and fulfils his genuine demands, he will sacrifice all for her sake and do all that is in his power to please her. Loyalty and obedience in lawful matters are among the excellent virtues of a wife. The Messenger of Allah (peace and blessings of Allah be upon him) has observed:

> "A woman who had offered five times prayers and kept the fasts for the month (of Ramadan), and guarded her modesty and was obedient to

> her husband would be allowed to enter any of the gates of Paradise."
>
> (Mishkat)

Along with the duties like prayer, fasting and the guarding of modesty, it is also the duty of a woman to obey her husband. It is evident from the above Hadith that whereas it is necessary to fulfil the rights of Allah it is also the bounden duty of a wife to obey her husband. A woman who fails to fulfil the duties she owes to her husband cannot succeed. Once the Messenger of Allah (peace and blessings of Allah be upon him) was questioned as to who is the best woman, he answered:

> "The woman who pleases her husband when he sees her, obeys him when he orders and does not have any bad intention in her heart against his person nor against her husband's wealth."
>
> (Mishkat)

What more stress can be laid on woman obeying their husband? A woman who is not obedient to her husband is surely not a good woman in the sight of the Messenger of Allah (peace and blessings of Allah be upon him). She may be possessing an exalted worldly position and wealth and riches, but she is unfortunate and wretched, if she is not a good woman in the sight of the Messenger of Allah (peace and blessings of Allah be upon him).

The wife should fulfil her husband's lawful demands only. If he transgresses the limits prescribed by Allah and asks her to commit acts against the Shariah, she is allowed to refuse her husband. An incident has been narrated in the Hadith: Once a woman of Ansar came to the Messenger of Allah (peace and blessings of Allah be upon him) and said: I have got my daughter married. Perchance, the hair of my daughter have fallen down. Now my son-in-law demands that the hair of some other woman should be added to her hair so that she may look beautiful. Thereupon the Messenger of Allah (peace and blessings of Allah be upon him) observed: Curse be upon the woman who adds other's hair to her hair.

The wife must, however, obey her husband in permissible things. An obedient wife has been called the greatest of Allah's favours in Ahadith. The status given by Islam to the obedient wife can be judged from the following Hadith:

> The best of the things from which a believer can benefit next to the fear of Allah is a pious wife. If he orders her, she obeys and if he sees her, she pleases him. If she takes a vow before him, she fulfils and if her husband is away she has good intention against her person and property. (Ibn Majah)

It is evident from the above Hadith that the best of Allah's favours, next to fear of Him, is a pious and obedient wife who loves her husband dearly, has a smiling and cheerful fascinating face and amiable disposition. She guards her modesty and chastity. The Messenger of Allah (peace and blessings of Allah be upon him) has said: If the husband asks his wife to go from one mountain to the other and from there to the third, the true wife is one who obeys this command.

Islam wants that the relations between husband and wife should be stable and abiding. It has framed rules and regulations keeping in view the nature and temperaments of both. The duties which the wife owes to her husband must be fulfilled by her wholeheartedly. Once the Messenger of Allah (peace and blessings of Allah be upon him) said: A woman must fulfil the lawful demands of her husband and a woman cannot relish the sweetness of faith unless she fulfils the lawful rights of her husband.

We have already mentioned a Hadith that the husband is the head of the whole family including the wife, then how far is it correct on her part to disobey her husband? As she is the better half of her husband and his friend and life companion, it is the duty of a friend to give sacrifice for a friend. She should do everything cheerfully and of her own accord. She should never consider that she is a maid servant or a captive.

Sexual gratification is apparently a worldly act; but in this matter, too, if the husband calls his wife for sexual intercourse, she should obey him out of love for him. The Messenger of Allah (peace and blessings of Allah be upon him) has observed: "If a person calls his wife for his need, she must go to him at once, although she may be standing near the oven (for baking breads)."

There is an explicit hint in the Hadith that if she fails to comply with the husband's above order, she is guilty of sin. The Messenger of Allah (peace and blessings of Allah be upon him) has further observed:

> "If a husband calls his wife to his bed and she refuses to come, the angels hurl curses on her till morning." (Bukhari)

Once the Messenger of Allah (peace and blessings of Allah be upon him) said: "By Allah! If a husband calls his wife to bed and she refuses, Allah and his angels are displeased with her as long as her husband is not pleased with her."

> Basing his argument on the above Ahadith. Imam Nawawi has said that without any reasonable excuse of the Shari'ah, a woman is not allowed to reject her husband's demand for sexual intercourse. The husband should however, take care of the health of his wife. He should not overlook her health merely for the sake of the gratification of sexual instinct. Jurists are of the opinion that if the health of a woman is so weak that sexual intercourse is injurious, sexual intercourse with her should be avoided. If frequent sexual indulgence is harmful for her, the husband should not have sexual intercourse more than her strength permits.(Dur Mukhtar)
>
> The woman is, however, bound to obey her husband. The Messenger of Allah (peace and blessings of Allah be upon him) observed: "If

> the husband is present, the wife should not keep supererogatory fasts without his permission." (Bukhari)

The women of the Prophet's and Caliphs' times tried their utmost to please their husbands. An expression of slight anger by their husbands disturbed their peace of mind. They obeyed their husbands even when they held indifferent and discourteous attitude.

> Hadrat'A'isha (Allah be pleased with her) was once wearing silver rings in her hands. The Messenger of Allah (peace and blessings of Allah be upon him) seeing these rings in her hands asked: What are these, O' 'A'isha! She said: I have worn these to please you.
>
> (Uswa Sahaba)

Due to these excellent rules of social conduct and behaviour, both husband and wife had great love and affection for each other. How much love and devotion had Hadrat Khadija (Allah be pleased with her) for the Messenger of Allah (peace and blessings of Allah be upon him). As you know, Hadrat Khadija (Allah be pleased with her) was a rich lady. When she was married to the Messenger of Allah (peace and blessings of Allah be upon him) she sacrificed all her wealth for her husband's sake. Whenever he was in difficulty, Hadrat Khadija (Allah be pleased with her) helped him and consoled him.

> Hadrat 'A'isha (Allah be pleased with her) is also well known for her love and devotion for the Messenger of Allah (peace and blessings of Allah be upon him). She washed his clothes with her hands, applied perfume, crushed *miswak* (tooth stick) for him and kept it with care. She wove the rope for the sacrificial animal with her hand. Once the Messenger of Allah (peace and blessings of Allah be upon him) covered himself with a blanket and went to the

> mosque. The Companions pointed out that there was a spot on the blanket. He took off the blanket and sent it into the house. Hadrat 'A'isha (Allah be pleased with her) took a pot of water and washed the blanket with her own hands. She got it dried and sent it to the Holy Prophet (peace and blessings of Allah be upon him). (Uswa Sahaba)

The wives of the Companions also possessed the same sentiments of love and devotion for their husbands. They did their utmost to please their husbands. Hadrat Zainab, the loving daughter of the Holy Prophet (peace and blessings of Allah be upon him) was married to Abul 'As. The latter had not yet embraced Islam when the battle of Badr began. In this battle between the infidels and the Muslims, Abul 'As fought from the side of the infidels. The Muslims won the battle by Allah's infinite mercy and grace and a large number of Quraish were made captive by them. Abul 'As was also one among them. When the Holy Prophet (peace and blessings of Allah be upon him) declared that the captives should be set free on payment of ransom, Hadrat Zainab, the Holy Prophet's daughter and the wife of Abul 'As, sent her precious necklace as ransom for Abdul 'As. This necklace belonged to Hadrat Khadija (Allah be pleased with her) her mother and she had kept it with her in her memory.

Hadrat Hamna bint Jahsh's husband proceeded on Jihad and died as a martyr in the cause of Allah. When this news reached Hadrat Hamna, she was overwhelmed with grief and began to weep loudly.

Hadrat 'Umar's wife used to kiss the head of his loving husband during fasting out of intense love for him.

When Hadrat Hasan's wife received the dower money, after getting divorce from her husband, she wept saying: This sum is paltry as compared to the separated beloved.

It is the duty of a woman to greet her husband cheerfully when he enters the house. The smile of a woman has such a fascination for the husband that for a moment he forgets all his worries and anxieties. Even if he is totally exhausted and tired, he regains fresh vigour on seeing the smiling face and hearing the sweet words.

> The woman who cuts a sorry figure before her husband, turns her house into a veritable hell and adds bitterness to the life of her husband. The Holy Prophet (peace and blessings of Allah be upon him) has explained the virtue of the best woman: "When the husband cast a glance at her, it should please him." (Mishkat)

Whenever the wife should come to her husband she should be good looking and in neat and clean dress. All the household goods should be well-dusted and neat and clean.

The wife should not hesitate to serve her husband. The Prophet's wives served him. Hadrat Fatima, the Holy Prophet's daughter used to look to the needs of her husband and did all the household work. In Bukhari there is a separate chapter under the heading: 'The work of a woman in her husband's house' wherein it has been mentioned that blisters were caused on Hadrat Fatima's hands by working the hand-mill.

The Muhaddithin have drawn the conclusion from the above incident that women should themselves do ordinary household work. If Hadrat Fatima (Allah be pleased with her) could work the hand-mill she must also be kneading the flour and baking the bread herself. According to Imam Malik, it is the duty of the wife to do the household work herself if her husband cannot afford a servant, even if she belongs to a rich and wealthy family.

Among the three persons who did not participate in the battle of Tabuk and were boycotted by the people at the Holy Prophet's command, was Hilal bin Umayya (Allah be pleased with him). After a few days the Holy Prophet (peace and blessings of Allah be upon him) commanded their wives to boycott them till the decision about them was revealed. Thereupon Hilal bin Umayya's wife went to the Holy Prophet (peace and blessings of Allah be upon him) and reported: My husband is an old man. There is no servant to serve him. Therefore, I may be permitted to serve him. The Holy Prophet (peace and blessings of Allah be upon him) granted permission to Hilal's wife to serve her husband.

Hafiz Ibn Qayyim has narrated the incident of Hadrat Asma', the wife of Hadrat Zubair. How solicitous was she for the needs of her husband and how hard did she work for him.

A great shortcoming of woman is that they are stubborn and persistent. They must shun from this habit. It is a common experience that whenever anything goes against their whim and desire, they fly into rage and begin to exchange hot words. Thus the relations of husband and wife are strained and the husband is fed up with his wife.

If there is something reasonable, the wife should try to convince her husband. It is not proper to quarrel and wear an angry look. If the husband is in angry mood, she should become polite. If it is quite necessary to express her displeasure, she should do so; but care should be taken that their relations do not become bitter.

If the husband is aggressive and rude, she should show wisdom and not do anything in a hurry. It is better that she should reconcile with him even if it is against her wishes. It has been mentioned in the Holy Quran:

> If a woman feareth ill treatment from her husband,
> or desertion, it is no sin for them twain if they
> make terms of peace between themselves.
>
> (4:128)

A careful study of what we have said above makes it amply clear that the rules and regulations promulgated by Islam foster the sentiments of love and harmony among husband and wife so that the real aims and objects of marriage are fulfilled to their fullest possible extent and the people lead a peaceful and comfortable life. By living amicably they can protect their modesty and chastity in the most excellent manner.

Due to this reason, the rights and duties of both against each other have been explicitly determined. If both of them fulfil their rights and duties they owe to each other, there remains no cause of complaint or rancour against anyone.

The Differences

Allah, the Exalted has strictly prohibited all such acts as create hatred and discord between husband and wife. One of the greatest evils of sorcery, according to the Holy Quran, is that it causes separation between husband and wife:

> And from these two people learn that by which they cause division between man and wife.
> (2:102)

The Holy Quran has mentioned the doom of such a person in the following words:

> And surely they do know that he who trafficketh therein will have no portion in the Hereafter.
> (2:102)

It is a great sin to cause rift between husband and wife. A person who is guilty of this act would be deprived of the bounties and rewards of the Paradise. The Allah's Messenger (peace and blessings of Allah be upon him) mentioning the evil tactics of the devil and his team said: The devil sits on his royal throne and sends his disciples among the people for mischief making. He who commits the greatest evil receives the greatest reward. When these mischief mongers come back, they submit their reports to their leader regarding their evil exploits and wrong doings. In the meanwhile, a devil steps forward and standing before the leader submits the following report:

> 'I have performed my duty, I did not take rest until I caused rift between husband and wife.'

> Allah's Messenger (peace and blessings of Allah be upon him) said: The devil is overjoyed to hear this news and embraces him and extols him saying: Bravo! you have done well. You have excelled all. (Mishkat)

Mulla Ali Qari writes that the cause of the devil's joy is that he likes large-scale fornication, illegal child-births and spreading of evils and vices on earth.

> Every one having a grain of sense knows the evil consequences of rift or clash between husband and wife, hence the person who creates hatred and discord between husband and wife deserves to be condemned whole-heartedly. He is the sworn enemy of humanity. Allah's Messenger (peace and blessings of Allah be upon him) said: "He who instigates a woman against her husband is not among us."
>
> (Mishkat)

Islam is a religion of peace and harmony. It puts an end to hatred and enemity among the people and exhorts its followers to live amicably. A person who tries to create hatred and discord among the people by instigating one against the other cannot be called the real follower of Islam. It is a heinous sin to cause hatred between husband and wife due to which the house is turned into a veritable hell. The clash between husband and wife might lead them to evil way of life and moral delinquency which do not behove a true follower of Islam.

6

The Positive Side

Islam has promulgated rules and regulations for all actions and deeds, so, it has also set some principles for entering the houses in order to maintain the sanctity of home-life. It is not permissible to enter a house without seeking permission of the head of the family.

In the places not used as residences such as schools, guesthouses, monasteries where there is no restriction to go or in the houses where no one resides, one may enter without seeking permission. If, however, restrictions are imposed on the entry of some persons, they should not go therein. It has been mentioned in the Holy Quran:

> It is no sin for you to enter uninhabited houses
> wherein is comfort for you. Allah knoweth what
> ye proclaim and what ye hide. (24:29)

Except the above, it is not permissible to enter the houses without prior permission. It has been said in the Holy Quran:

> O ye who believe! Enter not house other than
> your own without first announcing your
> presence and saluting (saying Assalamo

> Alaikum) to the folk thereof That is better for you that you may be heedful.
>
> (24:27)

If you want to go in the house of another person, you should first ask permission from the head of the house according to the Islamic principles. He may be the owner of the house or residing in it on rent or without rent and the inmates of house may be mahram or ghair mahram or males or females. He must ask permission under all circumstances from the head of the house or from the member of the family whom he has authorised to do so. If he refuses permission to enter, he should go back at once and should not insist or compel. If no one responds to his call he should call out thrice and if no one responds even at the third call, he should return. It is not permissible to enter a house about which it is not certain whether anyone is living there are not. It has been mentioned in the Holy Quran:

> If you find no one therein, still enter not until permission hath been given. And if it be said unto you: Go away again, then go away, for it is purer for you. Allah knoweth what ye do.
>
> (24:28)

Supposing there is none in the house, even then you have no right to enter a house which is not meant for general public use. Moreover, if the permission to enter is not granted, it is futile to insist and to enter forcibly in the house. It is a great sin and offence. It is also against moral and ethical principles. So the 'Ulama are of the view:

If the entry is refused one should neither insist for permission to enter nor ask that purdah should be observed. He should also not wait as all these acts are against good etiquettes. He should not knock at the door. The author of *Kashaf* has explained his view while commenting upon the above verse.

Numerous Benefits

There are many advantages of seeking permission to enter a house. In the terminology of Hadith it is called Istidhan. It is an obligatory duty in Islam and one must act upon it. No one knows how much harmful it is to himself or to the family if anyone enters the house suddenly. It is just possible that someone may be naked, his glance may suddenly fall on him/her. It is, therefore, proper that no one should enter the house without seeking permission. If a number of married sons and daughters of the same father are residing in a house, it is necessary to seek permission before entering so that the inmates of the house may become alert and recompose themselves. The principle should be observed in entering the female apartment.

The Holy Prophet (peace and blessings of Allah be upon him) instructed his Companions to seek permission before entering a house. Many such events have been mentioned in the Ahadith where the Holy Prophet instructed his Companions to act upon this principle. Hadrat Abu Musa reported that the Holy Prophet (peace and blessings of Allah be upon him) observed:

> Asking of permission is for three times. If you are permitted, well and good, otherwise, you should return. (Riyad as-Salihin)

A person who belonged to Bani 'Amir once went to the Holy Prophet (peace and blessings of Allah be upon him) who was in the house. When he arrived at the door of the house, he said, May I come in? When the Holy Prophet (peace and blessings of Allah be upon him) heard his voice, he said to his servant: Go to the person who is outside and teach him the way to ask permission in accordance with the Shariah. Ask him to say: Assalamo Alaikum! May I come in? That person heard the instructions which the Holy Prophet (peace and blessings of Allah be upon him) was giving to his servant and said: Assalamo Alaikum! May I come in? Thereupon the Holy Prophet (peace and blessings of Allah be upon him) gave him permission and he came in.

Hadrat Kuldah bin Al Hanbul (Allah be pleased with him) said: I went to the Holy Prophet (peace and blessings of Allah be upon him) and entered without saying Assalamo Alaikum. Thereupon he said: Go back and say: Assalamo Alaikum! May I come in?

It is clear from the above Ahadith that the correct way to ask permission is that one should first say Assalamo Alaikum and then ask permission to enter. To seek permission without saying Assalamo Alaikum is not correct. It is also evident from the above Ahadith that one should ask permission thrice and if there is no response even at the third call one should not insist and return.

> In a Hadith the incident of Hadrat Abu Musa has been narrated. He went to Hadrat 'Umar and asked permission thrice. No response came and he came back. Hadrat 'Umar was busy in some work. When he was free he said: Call Hadrat Abu Musa in. When the person went out to call Abu Musa in, the latter had gone. He informed Hadrat 'Umar accordingly. When Hadrat Abu Musa again came to see him on some other occasion he enquired from him: Why did you return on that day. He said: I asked permission thrice and having no response I returned as I heard the Holy Prophet (peace and blessings of Allah be upon him) saying: Should anyone of you seek permission thrice and has no response he should return.
>
> (Ibn Kathir)

There is another incident relating to the Holy Prophet (peace and blessings of Allah be upon him). He went to Sa'id bin Ubada and asked permission thrice after saying Assalamo Alaikum. When he had no response he returned. Meanwhile, Hadrat Sa'id came to him running and took him to the house.

The Dacorum

It is necessary for the visitor to ask permission first so that he could not see any one of the inmates of the house all of a sudden. It has been narrated that once the Holy Prophet (peace and blessings of Allah be upon him) was sitting in the house and scratching his head. Someone came and began to peep in. When the Holy Prophet (peace and blessings of Allah be upon him) knew it, he became very angry and said: Had I known it, I would have had his eyes torn out. Is he not aware: The visitor, must therefore not stand in front of the door; he should remain at one side.

Hadrat 'Abdullah has reported that whenever the Holy Prophet (peace and blessings of Allah be upon him) went to anyone he stood at one side of the door and said: Assalamo Alaikum! In those days curtains were not hung at the doors of the houses. If it is hung, there is no harm in standing in front of the door; but etiquettes demand that one should not ask permission to enter standing just in front as thus there is every possibility of seeing the inmates of the house.

It has been mentioned in a Hadith that a person came at the door of the Holy Prophet (peace and blessings of Allah be upon him) and asked permission standing in front of the door. The Holy Prophet (peace and blessings of Allah be upon him) beckoned him to stand at one side of the door as the law of seeking permission has been made due to gazing in.

It is forbidden to peep in from fissures of the doors or that of the windows as the very purpose of seeking permission is thus violated. According to a Hadith in Sahihain the Holy Prophet (peace and blessings of Allah be upon him) said:

> If a person peeps in your house without permission, you throw a stone at him so that it hurts out his eye; there is no sin upon you.
>
> (Ibn Kathir)

If he seeks permission to enter after saying Assalamo Alaikum and the inmate of the house asks who is he, he should tell his familiar name. It should not be said: 'It is I', as the person cannot be recognized in this way. The Holy Prophet (peace and blessings of Allah be upon him) does not like that an ambiguous reply should be given.

Once Hadrat Jabir went to the Holy Prophet (peace and blessings of Allah be upon him). He (the Holy Prophet) asked: Who are you? He said: It is I. The Holy Prophet (peace and blessings of Allah be upon him) disliked the reply and said: What do you mean by this I, I. The Companions of the Holy Prophet (peace and blessings of Allah be upon him) also taught their followers the way to seek permission and exhorted them to act upon it.

The permission to enter the house should also be asked from the *mahram* such as mother and sister, etc. It has been stated in the verse regarding 'Istidhan' that a woman from Ansar came to the Holy Prophet (peace and blessings of Allah be upon him) and said: I am in such a condition that I do not like any one, even my father to see me; but these persons come and go in this state. Thereupon the verse a particular was revealed. Various instances have been narrated in Ahadith from which it is evident that *mahrams* are also required to ask permission as no body knows about the condition in which the women would be sitting. In my opinion one should not enter without permission even if there is only wife in the house as she might be naked and no body likes to be seen in a state of nudeness.

A person asked the Holy Prophet (peace and blessings of Allah be upon him): Is it necessary to seek permission from mother? He said: Yes, permission needs to be sought from mother. He said: I live with her. In other words, she is not required to observe purdah from me then why is it necessary to ask permission? The Holy Prophet (peace and blessings of Allah be upon him) said: Ask permission from her also. He said: Even if you go to your mother you ask permission. Would you like to see your mother naked? He said: No. He (the Holy Prophet) said: That is why I say that you should seek permission before seeing her.

Hadrat Zainab (Allah be pleased with her) says: Whenever Hadrat 'Abdullah bin Masud (Allah be pleased with him) came in for some need, he first stopped at the door and coughed and then came in. He did not like to come in suddenly. Zainab was the wife of Hadrat 'Abdullah bin Masud.

Hadrat Abu 'Ubaida says: When Hadrat 'Abdullah arrived he asked permission loudly at the door. Hadrat Imam Ahmad bin Hanbul says: When a person enters the house he should cough loudly or strike his shoe with force so that the inmate of the house may know that some one is coming.

The purpose of Assalamo Alaikum for three times is that the inmates of the house may know about the arrival of the visitor. They may become alert at the second and may grant or refuse permission at the third.

Ibn Al-'Arabi is of the view that it is an incumbent act to ask permission before entering the house of others. As regards one's own house, it is not an incumbent duty. If, however, mother and sisters are living there, he should cough and then enter. At the door he should strike his feet so that the women may become aware of his arrival. Sometimes even mother and sister are in a condition that it is not proper to see them.

According to Imam Malik, it is necessary to ask permission before seeing the mother or sister. It was again and again enquired from Hadrat Ibn Mas'ud and Ibn 'Abbas whether it is necessary for the persons to ask permission from the mother and sister residing with him. He said: No one likes to see his mother naked, then why do you insist on this question.

If you ponder over the Islamic rules and regulations you would come to the conclusion that they are not only rules of wisdom and freedom but excellently safeguard modesty.

We are constrained to say that these rules and regulations of entering the houses which have been explained by the Holy Quran and the Ahadith ~ and practically followed by the noble Companions of the Holy Prophet throughout their lives are being overlooked by the Muslims of today. These rules and regulations need to be revived and enforced in our home-life.

Safety and Security

It is an admitted fact that the Divine Law is the most effective safeguard against immorality and debauchery. After the commandments relating to grown up and adolescent boys in the Holy Quran the Ahadith have also explained that the children too have the capability to think. So far as *ghair-mahrams* are concerned, it has already been explained that it is necessary to observe strict purdah from them. It is, however, allowed to expose the face and palms of hands in need; but if there is any fear of evil or mischief, these parts should also not be exposed. From mahrams purdah is for the whole body except face, palms of hands, arms, head and shanks, etc., which remain ordinarily exposed but it is not allowed to expose these parts unnecessarily. The servant is also a ghair-mahram and it is necessary to observe purdah from him. An infidel maid-servant also comes under the definition of a mahram.

What we want to tell you is that the young boys and maid servants who fall under the category of mahrams should also ask permission to enter at special times as during these times men and women do not generally exercise proper care and vigilance in observing purdah. Allah the Exalted has said:

> O ye who believe! let your slaves and those of you who have not come to puberty ask leave of you at three times (before they come into your presence): Before the prayer of dawn and when ye lay aside your raiment for the heat of noon; and after the prayer of night. Three times are of privacy for you. It is no sin for them or for you at other times, when some of you go round attendant upon others (if they come into your presence without leave). Thus Allah maketh clear the revelation for you. Allah is Knower, Wise. (24:58)

In the above verse, three special times have been mentioned. The one is that of the morning prayer. That time is fresh and pleasant and the time to wake after enjoying a sound sleep during which one cannot take proper care of purdah. The second time is that of noon when almost every one has a nap and res: after lunch. On hot days the people generally take rest at noon and during sleep it is not possible to observe purdah. The third is the time after 'Isha'. This is also the time for rest. After the daily hard labour one feels tired and goes to sleep. As all are asleep, one does not care to observe purdah. Moreover, the husband and wife generally make love during these times. It has, therefore, been ordained that even maid-servants and children should ask permission before entering their apartment. If they are busy in kissing and embracing or sexual intercourse, this scene would have a very adverse effect on their minds. They would have nothing but shame and remorse. There is, however, no restriction to enter during the other times. Moreover, it is difficult to forbid the children from coming in as they are used to come and go. The same is the case of a maid-servant. She has to enter so frequently for household work that you cannot put restriction on her.

Some commentators have written that the instructions of Istidhan in the first verses are applicable to the other people and strangers and those contained in this verse pertain to the relatives, that is to say, to the mahrams. According to some scholars the instructions contained in the verse are for the common men and for all times and those contained in the above verse are for specific persons and for specific times and this view is correct.

The word *malik* used in the above verse means a maidservant as Abd which stands for servant is according to the Shari'ah a *ghair-mahram*. A servant is permitted to come among men; but he is not allowed to go among women. The mahram on whom there is ordinarily no restriction to come are also not permitted to come during the special times, the detail of which has been given above. These preventive measures are based on prudence and wisdom. Maulana. Ashraf Ali Thanvi has given the following comments:

> O believers! your maid-servants and those who have not attained the age of puberty should seek permission to come to you at three times. Firstly, before the morning prayer and secondly at noon when you take off some of your clothes in order to take rest or sleep and thirdly, after

the 'Isha prayer. During these three times you should not come in. In other words, these three times are for rest and sleep and privacy and one is not very serious in observing purdah therein in the strict sense. So instruct your maid-servants and immature children not to come to you at these times without asking permission. At other times, however, there is no restriction on coming and going as they come to you so frequently. The servants fall under the definition of ghair mahrams and are not allowed to go in the company of women. Maid-servants and immature children are, however, free to come in and go without asking permission except at the three specific times. The other times are not for taking rest and sleeping and it is not difficult to observe *satr*. Man should cover his body from navel to the knee before his servants and a woman should observe purdah from an infidel maid-servant except her decoration. A man is not required to conceal any part of his body from the maid-servant who is lawful for him and if she is not lawful for him he should cover his body from navel to the knee. A woman is required to cover her body from navel to the knee from a Muslim maid-servant; so the latter is allowed to come in without asking permission. A man should cover his body from navel to the knee from a child and woman should observe purdah from him, except that of her decoration so he is also allowed to come in without asking permission except at the specific three times or because of some special reason. Allah, the Exalted has revealed, clear verses for you and He is all-knowing, All Aware.(Bayanul Quran)

The immature children are also required to ask permission to come on reaching puberty. Previously they were required to seek permission if they wanted to come in at specific times. The practice which is in vogue in India and Pakistan that those children who come in without restriction during childhood and before puberty come without asking permission even after attaining puberty and the women do not observe purdah from them is absolutely wrong and against the Shariah and should be put to an end. There is no ambiguity about this rule that the children when they come to puberty must also ask permission as the concession enjoyed by them in childhood now no longer exists. It is mentioned in the Holy Quran:

> And when the children among you come to puberty then let them ask leave even as those before them used to ask it. Thus Allah maketh clear this revelation for you. Allah is Knower, Wise. (24:59)

Uptil now the children were required to ask permission at three specific hours; but on attaining the age of puberty they are also required to ask permission at all times like the other people as in childhood and in the adolescence period they were neither aware of the implications of purdah nor women had any attraction for them and vice versa; but now there has occurred a change in them; their feelings and sentiments have awakened raging a tumult in them. Women might also feel attracted towards them. Now the rule which is applicable to the grown-up persons is to be applied to them. Maulana Ashraf Ali Thanvi has added the following comments:

> And when the children among you reach the age of competency or be nearing this age, they should also ask permission like the grown-up persons. Allah, the Exalted has revealed clear verses. He is all-knowing, All-Aware. The above commandment has been repeated to emphasize the advantages of the rules of seeking permission.

Institution of Veil

It has been explained above that for women it is necessary to observe purdah of the whole body except her face and the palms of her hands as is evident from the above verse so that no one should have any misconception about the implication of these words. It may be pointed out that although there is no *satr* of face and hands, yet they should not be exposed to a stranger if there is fear of evil and mischief. The aged women may, however, not cover their faces and hands although it is better for them to do so.

> As for women past child-bearing, who have no hope of marriage, it is no sin for them if they discard their (outer) clothing in such a way as not to show adornment. But to refrain is better for them and Allah is Hearer, Knower.
>
> (24:60)

It has been ordained even for the aged women not to display their decoration. It is evident that Islam does not allow the parts of the body which come under the given definition be remained uncovered without any reason. Maulana Ashraf Ali Thanvi has written:

> One thing we must understand. Although there is no satr of face and hands in the strict sense of the word, but it is not permissible that women should freely display their faces and hands to strangers as there is fear of evil and mischief. The satr of these parts of the body also becomes incumbent except upon the aged women who have lost attraction for men and have no hope for marriage, only such women are permitted to expose their face and hands and according to some their feet but they are not permitted to display their decoration. So far as a young lady is concerned, it is necessary for her to observe satr of these parts if there is fear of evil and

> mischief, but it is permitted to expose these parts in case of necessity or genuine excuse. It is, however, better that purdah should be observed.

Ibn Al-'Arabi says:

> The aged women are specifically exempted from it and the rest have been disallowed (this concession) as the heart has no attraction towards the aged women. But if they observe full satr it is better than discarding the veil.
>
> (Ahkamul Quran)

According to the Fuqaha (Jurists) although face does not come under the definition of satr, it is better that the women should be asked not to expose their face so that there should occur no mischief. Nature has created such an irresistible attraction and fascination in the face of a woman that man is automatically drawn towards it and his natural sexual instinct is excited. Allama Ibn 'Abidin writes:

> A woman should be forbidden to expose her face lest man should see her face as sometimes when the face is exposed the eyes look towards it with lewdness. (Dur Mukhtar)

In the above verse, particular words have been used which means that the women should not put on such thin clothes as do not help to maintain their satr; but reflect the outlines of their bodies and display their beauty. Ibn Al-'Arabi writes:

> It is also displaying one's decoration and charms that a woman should wear such a thin dress as reflects her body. (Ahkamul Quran)

He has mentioned the following Hadith in support of the above view. The Holy Prophet (peace and blessings of Allah be upon him) observed:

> Most of the dressed women are practically naked. They attract others or are drawn towards them. Such women should neither enter Paradise nor have its smell.

We have already mentioned the following verse of the Holy Quran:

> And stay in your houses. Bedizen not yourself with the bedizenment of the time of ignorance.
> (33:33)

Umm 'Alqama has reported that Hadrat Hafsa bint 'Abdur Rahman came to Hadrat 'A'isha (Allah be pleased with her) Hadrat Hafsa was wearing a thin dopatta. When Hadrat 'A'isha saw this, she tore it and threw it out and gave her a thick one. Hadrat Hafsa was the niece of Hadrat 'A'isha.

Hadrat 'A'isha has narrated another incident: Asma bint Abu Bakr (her sister) went to the Holy Prophet (peace and blessings of Allah be upon him). She was wearing thin clothes. The Holy Prophet (peace and blessings of Allah be upon him) turned away his face and said:

> O Asma! It is not permissible to look at a grown up woman except her face and the palms of her hand. (Mishkat)

There is a Hadith in Sahih Muslim. The Holy Prophet (peace and blessings of Allah be upon him) observed:

> Don thy garment and you should not walk naked. (Mishkat)

The above and many other Ahadith on this subject reveal that both man and woman should wear such garments as do not reflect their bodies. Thus their grace and beauty would remain immune from the wicked eyes and there would be no danger to their modesty and chastity.

If you ponder over what we have said about purdah, you would find that there are many advantages of this institution. The wisdom behind this institution becomes all the more manifest when we see the moral turpitude of the West.

Islam attaches utmost importance to chastity and morality and righteous conduct and behaviour. If the rules and regulations governing the moral conduct and behaviour of society are not perfect and right and do not impose any restrictions on adultery and prostitution and on the action and behaviour leading to these vices, the morality is bound to be cast to the forewinds.

Study the chapter on "Ethics" of the History of the World and see what is the basic cause of spoiling the morals and what are the reasons of the downfall of a country and a nation? In our view the root-cause of all the evils was that there existed no balanced rules and regulations for guarding the chastity and morality of the people.

Islam has given no concession in the rules and regulations pertaining to chastity and morality. You have already read the attitude of Islam about unlawful sex. Now we would tell you about the punishment prescribed by Islam for those who level false accusation against pious and chaste men and women in order to disgrace them.

Islam condemns that person who is guilty of spreading false rumours against a pious man or woman. It has been mentioned in the Holy Quran:

> Lo! as for those who traduce virtuous believing woman (who) know not. Cursed are they in the world and the Hereafter. Theirs will be aweful doom. On the day Allah will pay them their just due and they will know that Allah, He is the Manifest Truth. (24:23-25)

Study the above verse deeply. A very stern warning has been administered for this offence. A person guilty of this sin is doomed in this world and in the Hereafter.

If any person brings a false accusation of adultery/fornication against a chaste and pious lady and fails to produce four eyewitnesses, he would be liable to beating with eighty stripes. He would be deprived of giving evidence against any person in future it has been mentioned in the Holy Quran:

> And those who accuse honourable woman but bring not four witnesses, scourge (with) eighty stripes and never (afterward) accept their testimony - they indeed are evil doers.
>
> (24:4)

The above verse throws a light on the significance of morality and chastity in Islam. A person who is guilty of levelling a false charge of immorality against a pious man or woman and fails to bring four witnesses in support thereof will be liable to the following punishments: 1. He should be beaten with eighty stripes. 2. In future his witnesses should not be accepted, being the biggest liar. 3. There is no doubt in his wickedness.

7

Equal Status

Equality is a term which is hard to define. There is a sense in which all human beings are equal, but in actual life, we find that no two human beings are really equal in all respects. There are differences of tastes, temperaments, faculties, powers and outlook, all of which cannot be traced to differences of environment or upbringing. It is apparent that the rights and duties of men and their social position flow from these inborn differences. In spite of the fundamental and essential unity of all human beings, it is impossible in practice to level down all differences and inequalities, because some of them are the outcome of native differences. Inequality leads to injustice and oppression only where artificial impediments, whether in the shape of laws and customs or traditions, are super-added to natural inequalities so as to prevent men and women from developing their native capacities to the full. It is the task of religion, state and law to remove all hindrances to human development and create an environment where only natural inborn differences and inequalities may fix a man's station in life.

Gender Equality

The ideal of sex equality should also be studied from, the same angle. If by sex equality is meant that artificial customs, traditions and laws which prevent the female sex from playing its full part in collective life and developing its inherent capacities to the maximum extent should be removed out of the way, there is hardly any individual of sound understanding who would disagree. But if sex equality means that the type of mental and bodily faculties, psychological make-up and temperamental equipment possessed by the two sexes is identically the same and that men and women exist and have their, being not as complements to each other but as competitors and rivals in a common sphere of action, then it is an ideal about which most people would disagree. As we shall discuss later, even modern writers and specialists on sex are not agreed on this point.

As far as the Holy Qur'an is concerned, it promulgated the doctrine of human equality, including sex equality, in a comprehensive verse which negates all inequalities due to sex, race, colour, nationality, caste or tribe. Says the Qur'an:

> O people! be careful of (your duty to) your Lord, Who created you from a single being and created its mate of the same (kind) and spread from these two many men and women. (iv. .1)

This is a declaration in plain terms that, in essential human dignity and fundamental rights, all human beings of whatever sex or race or nationality stand on a footing of equality, because they all ultimately spring from a single source.

When Islam appeared in Arabia, women held a very low position in society. They were treated not only as social inferiors but like slaves and chattel. When a man having many wives died, the latter were inherited by his sons like movable property. It was a mark of dishonour for any man to have a daughter, and many preferred to bury alive their female children rather than face social opprobrium. It was Islam and the teachings of the Holy Prophet which dispelled the prevailing idea that women were inferior to men or that female children deserved any treatment different from that meted out to male issues. The Qur'an asserted the dignity of women by declaring:

> They are an apparel for you and, you are an apparel for them (ii. 188).

Social Equality

Here, again, the Qur'an lent support to the basic equality of women and men by declaring that each sex complements the other, and neither is inferior in status and dignity. The word 'apparel' may be interpreted to mean either 'protection' or 'dignity and beauty'. The verse would mean, therefore, that men and women protect each other from sin and dishonour or it may mean that woman lends dignity and adds beauty to the existence of man, as, man does to that of woman. Similarly, the Qur'an heaped scorn on the Arabs' traditional attitude towards the female sex in the following verses:-

And when a daughter is announced to one of them his face becomes dark and is full of wrath. He bides himself from the people, because of that which is announced to him. Shall he keep it with disgrace or bury it (alive)- in dust? Now surely evil is what they judge.

(xvi. 58-59).

With a view to contradicting the notion that women have no rights, the Qur'an came out with the plain and unambiguous declaration:

> They have rights similar to those against them,
> in a just manner. (ii. 228)

In consonance with this spirit of equality the Prophet of Islam constantly reminded his followers that female children should be treated exactly in the same manner as male issues. Prior to Islam, daughters were looked upon with disfavour and as a kind or economic and social burden. The result was that male members of the family enjoyed a respect which was denied to those of the fair sex. There were marked differences, in the treatment and upbringing of sons and daughters. All this was discouraged by the Holy Prophet (peace be on him) who upheld the rights of female children and insisted on their being treated on a footing of equality. For example, according to a report of Ibn 'Abbas, the Prophet's cousin, he is said to have declared: 'If a daughter is born to a man and he brings her up affectionately, shows her no disrespect and treats her in the same manner as he treats his sons, the Lord will reward him with paradise' (Kanz al'Ummal, p. 277). According to another report from Anas b. Malik, the Prophet said: 'Girls are models of affection and sympathy and a blessing to the family. If a person has one daughter, God will screen him from the fire of the hell owing to his daughter; if he has two daughters, God will admit him to paradise, if he has three, God will exempt him from the obligations of charity and Jehad' (ibid). Abu Hurairah, a revered companion of the Prophet, says: 'The Prophet of God said that if a person has three daughters whom he provides for and, brings up, God will surely reward him with paradise.' According to 'Abdullah ibn Mas'ud, the Prophet is reported to have said: 'If a daughter is born to a person and he brings her up, gives her a good education and trains her in the arts of life, I shall myself stand between him and hell-fire' (ibid.). Not content with moral exhortations intended to assert the equal rights of free women, the Prophet went so far as to declare. 'A person who has a female slave in his charge and takes steps to give her a sound education and trains her in arts and, culture, and then frees her and marries her, he will be doubly rewarded' (Bukhari, Sabih, Kitab al-Nikah).

The Holy Qur'an has at more than one place made it plain that in regard to moral and spiritual development, men and women stand on a level of perfect equality. There are no limits to the moral progress of a woman as that of a man. For example, the Holy Qur'an says:

> Men shall have the benefit of what they achieve and acquire and -women shall have the benefit of that which they similarly achieve and acquire (iv. 32).

And again:

> And whoever does good deeds, whether male or female, and he or she is a believer, these shall enter the garden and they shall not be dealt with a jolt unjustly. (iv. 124)

Religious Duties

In regard to religious duties, the Qur'an recognises no distinction between men and women. Their obligations towards God and man are similar in many respects, and, therefore, their position and status in the eyes of God are also not dissimilar. Says the Qur'an:

> And as for the believing men and the believing women they are guardians of each other; they enjoin good and forbid evil-and keep up prayer and pay the, poor-rate, and obey Allah and, His Apostle; (as for) these, Allah will show mercy to them, surely Allah is Mighty, Wise.
>
> Allah has promised to the believing men and the believing women gardens beneath which rivers flow, to abide in them and goodly dwelling in gardens of perpetual abode; and the best of all is Allah's goodly pleasure; that is the grand achievement. (ix. 71-71)

It follows that if men and women have equal, duties in regard to prayers, the payment of Poor-tax and, most of all, in the enjoining of good and the forbidding of evil in all their social, economic and political forms, it is necessary that they should have equal educational opportunities. How can a woman enjoin the good in politics or forbid men from bad politics, how can she raise her voice against ruinous economic policies or advocate, beneficial economic reforms, if she is not mentally and spiritually well equipped for the supreme religious duty? It should also be remembered that Islam makes no distinction between secular duties and religious duties. According to the teachings of Islam all duties, whether they concern politics, economics or social well-being in general, are religious duties, in no way different from prayers, fasts and the organisation of social charity. It is, therefore, a plain deduction from the above verses that men and women should be regarded as equal in the fields of politics and education, etc., and, consistent with the discharge of their special responsibilities in their particular spheres, they should receive equal rights in all these fields of action.

General Doctrine

The Prophet not only enunciated this general doctrine of sex equality involving equal educational opportunities but also practised it. Innumerable are the traditions of the Prophet which show that women like men, used to come freely in the presence of the Prophet for putting questions and addressing inquiries on all sort of social, religious and economic matters. The Prophet used to answer their queries and enlighten them on all live issues. Arabia, in particular and the world in general, was so backward in those days that there were no organised educational institutions even for boys, not to speak of girls. So the Islamic attitude towards female education can be studied only from the casual remarks of the Prophet and his permission to women to approach him freely for inquiries on matters of religious, economic and social importance. There is no doubt that the Prophet encouraged women in the spirit of understanding and inquiry. His wife, 'Ayeshah, was herself a very learned woman, and during the reign of the first four Caliphs her advice, even on political matters, was eagerly sought by the rulers of Islam. On Islamic jurisprudence she was and is still regarded as a great authority. In his collection of traditions, Muslim reports that Ayeshah praised the women of Ansar for their spirit of inquiry and learning, saying, 'How praise-worthy are the women of Ansar that their modesty does not prevent them from attempts at learning and the acquisition of knowledge'; (Muslims, Sahih, Kitab al-Taharat). This statement was occasioned by the fact that the women of Ansar were more eager than others to learn from the Prophet and they used to address frequent inquiries to him. Instead of discouraging them, the wife of the Holy Prophet characterises as highly praise-worthy their eagerness for learning and inquiry.

The Holy Qur'an further stresses the equality of women, in regard to the possibilities of spiritual progress by quoting from history the examples of women who reached spiritual eminence by their own efforts:

> And Allah sets forth an example to those who believe the wife of Pharaoh when she said: My Lord, build for me a house with Thee in the Garden and deliver me from Pharaoh and his doings, and deliver me from the unjust people.
>
> And Mary, the daughter of 'Imran, who guarded her chastity, so we breathed unto her of Our inspiration, and she accepted the truth of the words of her Lord and His Books, and she was of the obedient one.
>
> (lxvi. 11-12).

The Holy Qur'an further declares that women have been the recipient of special gifts from God so that nothing stands in the way of their reaching the highest pinnacle of spiritual progress:

> And We revealed to the mother of Moses. (xxviii. 7)

> And (remember) when the angels said: O Mary, surely Allah hath chosen thee and purified thee and selected thee (for His special blessing) of all the women of the world. (iii. 41)

Despite the great stress it has laid on the essential and fundamental equality of men and women and their equal rights in all matters, of vital concern, the Holy Qur'an does not believe in that conception of sex equality which ignores the natural differences, special aptitudes and specific powers and faculties of men and women with the resulting of men for some kinds of work and the equal fitness, of women for other types of activity. On the whole, the Holy Qur'an regards men and women as complementary to each other, one sex making up what the other lacked. This is evident from the following verses of Holy Qur'an which underline the purposive nature of sex differences:

> He it is Who created you from a single being, and of the same (kind) did He make his mate, that he might incline to her. (vii. 189)

> And one of His signs is that He created mates for you from your selves, so that you may find quiet of mind then and He put between you love and compassion. (xxx. 21)

> Men are the maintainers of women because of that excellence which Allah has given to some of them over others and because they spend out of their property. (iv. 34)

> And they (women) have rights similar to those against them in a just manner and the men are a degree above them. (ii. 228)

The main points to be noted here are, first, that the female sex must be a source of comfort and peace of mind to its male counterpart; secondly, that men and women excel each other or are superior to each other in some respects and that in the general affairs of life men are partially, but not absolutely, superior to women. These general statements involve certain indirect conclusions which are of the greatest importance to social happiness. The Qur'an, it seems, first sets forth a general doctrine of sex equality and then qualifies and defines it with the assertion that this is not a bald and undifferentiated equality but one involving special rights and duties both for men and women, within the framework of their special responsibilities: both sexes are absolutely equal to each other.

Now, what are the conclusions to be drawn from the qualifications mentioned by the Holy Qur'an? It is emphasised by the Holy Book that the female sex is a source of comfort and quietness of mind to the male sex. This can happen only if men and women are united in a more or less permanent based of interests which finds expression in a life planned and based on some idea of the future which requires them to co-operate and not to compete, and integrates them as complements in an ordered whole. These considerations involve a pattern of life of which Marriage, Family and Children are the most important factors because there can be no other abiding interest to hold together two individuals of different sexes. A mere community of intellectual interests or identity of special aptitudes is an insufficient bond even for that microscopic minority to whom, these things matter most. For the large majority of men and women these can hardly provide any link unless they are supported and strengthened by the desire for family life and children. It is obvious, therefore, that Islam does not envisage any social pattern from which family and children have been excluded, and since these two factors involve special functions for women and special responsibilities for men, equality of rights in Islam means an equality which is adjusted to and qualified by the special duties and responsibilities of each sex.

Again the Qur'an recognises the superiority of both sexes over each other in some respects. To the extent that men are superior to women and women to men in certain matters, the doctrine of equality must be, qualified with due regard to natural, facts. About the special position of men, the Qur'an makes two statements. First that men are the supporters or sustainers of women in a sense. But it must be noted that this implies no natural superiority on the part of men, nor any inherent inferiority of women, because it is a purely, economic arrangement dictated by natural necessities. The Qur'an, however, accords a slight superiority to men, in general by saying that men are a degree superior to women. This superiority of men relates both to the domestic and political fields. In domestic life, final authority must rest with one sex or the other. There cannot be two co-equal authorities here as elsewhere. Similarly, in the political field also final decisions should rest with men in general, because men are by nature gifted with a wider vision and also because their comparative freedom from certain natural limitations, which absorb a considerable amount of female time and energy, enables them to devote more attention to political affairs.

Having stated the Islamic conception of sex equality, we shall examine whether the qualifications made by Islam to the general doctrine of sex equality find any support from modern writers on the subject of sex. The question ultimately resolves itself into one of differences between men and women in regard to their faculties, powers, aptitudes and temperaments. If there are such differences and dividing lines, then the doctrine of perfect sex equality can be true only with the qualifications set forth by the Holy Qur'an and to the extent of these qualifications there ought to follow a scheme of life in which men and women, apart from general and equal rights and duties, must be assigned special rights and exclusive responsibilities. Many modern writers on sex, would generally agree with the above proposition. For example, Dr. Alexis Carrel, a French Nobel Prize winner, says in his famous book, *Man, the Unknown:*

Fundamental Nature

The differences existing between man and woman are of a mere fundamental nature. They are caused by the very structure of the tissues and by the impregnation of the entire organism with specific chemical substances secreted by the ovary. Ignorance of these fundamental facts has led the promoters of feminism to believe that both sexes should have the same responsibilities. In reality, woman differs profoundly from man. Every one of the cells, of her body bears the mark of her sex. The same is true of her organs and, above all, of her nervous system.

Women should develop their aptitudes in males. Their part in the progress of civilization is higher than that of men. They should not abandon their special functions.

There are a large number of equality enthusiasts among us now who are either unwilling to recognise such radical differences between the two sexes or accepting them grudgingly, insist on their removal and obliteration by conscious efforts. What these people fail to note is that the peace of mind and comfort on which the Qur'an has laid stress in the relation between the two sexes is the outcome of these very differences. If they could possibly be removed, sex life and marriage would lose much of their charm. On this point we would quote the American writer, Margaret Mead, who says in her book, *Male and Female:*

Our tendency at present is to minimize all these differences in learning, in rhythm, in type and timing of rewards, and at most to try to obliterate particular differences that are seen as handicap on one sex. If boys are harder to train, train, them harder; if girls grow faster than boys, separate them, so the boys would not be damaged; if women have a little less strength than man invent machines so that they can still do the same work. But every adjustment that minimizes a difference, a vulnerability, in one sex, a differential strength in the other, diminishes their possibility of complementing each other, and corresponds symbolically to sealing off the constructive receptivity of the female and the vigorous outgoing constructive activity of the male, muting them both in the end to the duller version of human life, in which each is denied the fulness of humanity that each might have had. Guard each sex in its vulnerable moments; we must protect and cherish them through the crises that sometimes are harder for one sex than for the other. But as we guard, we may also keep the differences. Simply compensating for differences is in the end a form of denial.

This sound advice of a writer who herself happens to be a woman and belongs to an advanced country of the West must serve as an eye-opener to those extremists who, in their blind enthusiasm for sex equality, are advocating all sorts of ridiculous reforms and denying the beneficial effects of sex differences as well as the complementary position of man and, woman in respect of each other.

This same American writer, commenting on the increasing entry of women in professional field (of course, under a wrong conception of sex equality) further remarks: 'It is of very doubtful value to enlist the gifts of women if bringing women into fields that have been defined as male frightens the men, unsexes the women, muffles and distorts the contribution the women could make, either because their presence excludes men from the occupation or because it changes the quality of the men who enter.'

It would seem, then, that the doctrine of sex equality cannot be pushed to a point where it means that men and women are equally, fit for all fields of employment or that the indiscriminate entry of women in the professional fields would have no undesirable social effects.

In regard to the Quranic statement that men and women excel each other in some respects and are, therefore, unequal to that extent, we shall quote another American woman writer, Mary B. Bread, who gives a very interesting account of the discussions held on this point by American psychologists, in her book, *Woman as Force in History*. She writes:

At its ninth spring meet the Eastern branch of the American Psychological Association held-sessions on the attitude of men and women towards men.

The meeting lasted for two days and nearly one thousand persons were reported attending its session. The main discussion revolved round the results of a questionnaire submitted to an equal number of men and women. By means of this survey designed to explore opinions of men and women about women, the conclusions was reached by its promoters, that both sexes were in a remarkable agreement in favour of equal social rights for both sexes and a wide disagreement in evaluating the emotional stability and originality of women.

In the discussion which followed, a statement of the survey's findings, men and women participated and according to newspaper accounts, 'seven out of every ten men, and an equal proportion of women, believed that men were less influenced by emotion than women in their judgements.' To the statement that 'women are more interested in the trivial things of life than men,' 91.7 per cent of the men and 92.1 per cent of the women gave their assent.

The discovery or assumption that women differ from men governed discussions of the subject by members of the Psychological Association which assembled at Palo Alto a, few years ago, and much importance was attached to glandular differentiations.

'What is the psychological difference between a boy and a girl?' was the question on which they attempted to focus their remarks. The question had been put before the members of the Association for meditation in advance of this meeting. Indeed, a report, framed by two men and one woman of Stanford University, was ready for the guidance of the discussion. Its burden was that the 'original constitutional' equipment of girls and boys differs. And in women, it asserted, the whole glandular system is 'more precarious' than in men. But mental balance is 'superior in the male'. Whys and where-fores of the divergence in mental balance were 'probably' traceable to the basic physical differences, some speakers averred. As the discussion was reported in the Press, its upshot was the consensus that 'women in general have made no relative progress against mental irregularities since they began throwing off conventional restraints at high speed.'

Now, if the above conclusions are true, it means that men, being less amenable to emotional influences and possessing a more stable mental balance, are better fitted for political activity which requires calm reasoning and lesser susceptibility to emotional influences. Similarly, these conclusions also establish the fact that, being mentally more stable, men are bound to remain superior in intellectual pursuits which require persistent and continuous work. These facts make it clear that the ideal of sex equality cannot be accepted without important qualifications and reservations based on the ultimate facts of the psychology and nature of the two sexes.

Let us now see what Havelock Ellis, one of the greatest modern authorities on the, psychology of sex, has to say about the special nature and characteristics of woman. In *Man and Woman*, Havelock Ellis has considered impartially a great amount of available data as to the intellectual and other capacities of the two sexes. He says that abstract though a woman is, on the whole, marked by a certain docility, and receptiveness. Even in trivial matters, he says, the average woman accepts statements and opinions more easily than a man; and in more serious matters, 'she is prepared to die for a statement or an opinion, provided it is uttered with such authority and action that her emotional nature is sufficiently thrilled'. Further, Ellis points out that woman craves more for sympathy than man and that she has not the same sturdy independence like him. This is a statement which leads support to the Quranic view that men are the maintainers of women, because even if it were possible for all women to become economically independent of men, their emotional nature and craving for sympathy would involve most of them in partial dependence on men. In man, on the other hand, there is no such gravitating force to incline him towards the fair sex, unless it, be sexual attraction or the bond of children. Ellis illustrates his statement on this special characteristic of women'by giving a list of famous women of genius who have put forth their best efforts only in sympathetic and intimate association with another person of the nude sex. Thus Madame Curie, the most distinguished woman of science in modern times, was the wife of a distinguished scientific man who shared in her investigations. Mrs Browning wrote her finest poems after she knew Robert Browning. The whole of George Eliot's fiction and other imaginative work was written in the company of a man (J.H. Lewis) who shared her scientific as well as literary tastes.

Qualities of Intelligence

Taken as a whole, Havelock Ellis considers that the qualities of intelligence in men and women are not of identical character or value; but there is no question of superiority or inferiority. Their respective intellectual qualities fairly balance each other. Thus men, he says, are better able to apply what they have leamt; they are much more inclined, to support what they have learnt; by reflection or further investigation. They have a precise knowledge in their own department, are without doubt more apt to supplement the prescribed course of reading by independent scientific research, take more interest in scientific pursuits and have greater power of observation. Women, on, the other hand, dislike the essentially intellectual process of analysis, because, says Ellis, they instinctively feel that 'analysis may possibly destroy the emotional complexes by which they are largely moved and which appeal to them' This is, why women do not favour rigid rules, principles and abstract propositions. They are more impulsive and believe in its rightness. There are not all defects of the feminine mind, says Ellis; they are innate sexual differences pointing to the ineptitude of women for science, however numerous and, brilliant the exceptions.

Those characteristics, in his opinion, are 'probably correlated with instinctive and emotional qualities which may fairly be regarded as organic'. Ellis then proves that emotion is not, as popularly supposed, a purely mental phenommon. It has its reactions upon man's vascular and muscular system, however self-controlled a man may be. 'No amount of self-control on coarser expressions of emotion alters the case, for even to unscientific inspection the passion of the self-controlled man reveals itself by some quiver of muscle, some quickening, of the heartbeat.' Here he lays down an important truth that emotion depends on physical organisation. Woman's heart, is easily excited under the influence of stimuli by which man's heart in a state of health is unaffected. And he gives a proof of the greater, excitability of woman's heart by pointing out that there is a distinctly greater increase in the number of pulsations on awakening from sleep in women. Even the complex phenomenon of hysteria is due to weakness of resistance of the vaso-motor system. And the special tendency of women to be affected by the disease of the eye called 'glaucoma' is, he says, accepted by all authorities to be due to the disturbances which emanate in generative organs.

He then points out that woman is more liable than man to convulsive manifestations. It is based on an.abnormal readiness or, in other words, an undue affectability. Frequent appearance of blushing in women is due to the greater affectability of their vaso-motor system. Convulsive tendency of women is testified by the facility with which they yield to tears and laughters. Tears are not produced by pain even when amounting to agony, but occur when 'sympathetic nervous system is most developed and most impressionable'.

Irritability, which Ellis calls 'irascibility,' is another form of affectability which 'has been quite legitimately attributed to women.' How far is this affectability in women, their, greater emotionality, organic and, therefore, ineradicable, and how far is it the product of external circumstances and, therefore, capable of modification? Ellis says that affectability in women may be decreased to some extent, but that 'there is, however, a limit to this sexual equalisation of affectability, remains extremely probable.' And he further emphasises that the comparatively large extent of the sexual sphere in women and of the visceral regions generally, the physiological tendency to anaemia, the existence of inevitable periodicity of function in women, conspire to famish a broader basis for the play of emotion, which no change in environment or habit could remove. And he quotes Hymen that-'all the most characteristic features of women's nature are correlated with emotionality, and half of women's psychic nature would remain unexplained if we struck out this factor.' Affectability in women, therefore, is an innate quality which, according to Havelock Ellis, may be reduced to finer and delicate shades but can scarcely be brought to the male standard.

It is not only Havelock Ellis who holds this opinion on the differences between men and women. There are other psychologists who think almost in the same terms. Thus, Bloch says that 'psychologically also man and woman are different beings;' and Forel expresses a similar opinion. Kisch who has made an elaborate and deep study of woman's sexual life remarks: 'The intellectual changes undergone by the girl at puberty are no less extensive and characteristic than the physical. In brief, the girl is transformed into a young woman endowed with all the attributes, mental and bodily, characteristic of femininity.' Dr. Winge, a Norwegian physician, quoted by Weith-Kundsen, says: 'The difference of sex is fundamental. Both bodily and mentally the difference between the typical woman and the typical man is all-pervading-the difference is by no means confined to sexual organs.' And Weith.-Kundsen himself remarks: 'Man and woman are not equal; they have never been equal and they never will be. On the contrary, the difference of sex is so deep-going that two men of different civilized races are much more nearly similar in their nature than are men and women belonging to the same race.' Dr. Lambrose Gina writes in her book, *The Soul of Woman*, that not only man and woman are different in height, in structure of the bones and in the muscular system, but they are also different in the quality and quantity of air and food that they absorb, that they are subject to different sicknesses, their desires are different and finally they differ in their mental and moral tendencies. She further remarks, 'Progress, evolution and life are possible only through differentiation.'

After quoting these authorities, the author of *Whither Woman* - V.M. Rege writes: 'There is, therefore, no escaping of the fact that there are certain inherent psychological differences which sharply distinguish man and woman. Here there is no question of their relative superiority or inferiority. They only point to the fundamental differences of the sex in their function and mission. In their zeal to show equal educable capacity and intelligence, the English and American women are utterly misguided in demanding the same education for girls as for boys. It is now proved beyond doubt that woman has as much intelligence as man in, pursuing the highest possible education. And this is exactly what has misguided the modern woman. She has misunderstood her own nature, needs and functions. She has allowed herself to be exploited by male-like ideals. She has come to conceive in womanliness something inferior and lacking, so that she has held before her as model all that the male is doing. She has become ashamed of her womanliness and wishes it better if she had been born a male. These ideas have created a false standard before her, and consequently she has identified her personality with that of man. She has ignored that she has an independent personality, quite different and entirely equal to man and which, if she developed, would develop into perfect womanliness.'

In the sphere of sexual morality, it has been observed by modern protagonists of sex equality that it is unjust to apply two different standards in respect of men and women; that if sexual laxity in men is not regarded as a very serious offence, there is no reason why it should be so regarded in women. This is true up to a certain limit and Islamic teachings have never made any discrimination in this respect between males and females. Thus adultery, according to Warn, in both men and women, is legally an equal offence punishable with equal penalties. But even in this sphere unalterable facts of nature tilt the balance in favour of men. Discussing this question, Dr. Westermarck says in *The Future of Marriage in Western Civilization:*

> But even if public opinion would, in the future, grant complete sexual freedom to the unmarried of either sex, the indulgence of it by girls would still be attendant with serious disadvantages already pointed out. There would undoubtedly be exploitation in women by men; girls who remained virgins would still be preferred as wives, and the others would run the risk of being used for temporary purposes. Feminists advocating equal freedom for men and women

> seem to overlook the benefits that the men would derive from it; they would find it easier to gratify their desires in a more agreeable manner than through intercourse with prostitutes, and at the same time to acquire sexual experience is considered useful for their future marriage. When speaking of the 'injustice' of different moral demands on men and women, those advocates also fail to notice that this difference is ultimately due to a difference in the sexual instincts of the two sexes.

The ideas expressed above are more or less in line with the Islamic conception of sex equality; As we have shown in the beginning of this chapter, Islam upholds the essential human dignity and fundamental equality of the two sexes, but, along with the common rights and duties of men and women in which both are equal, it concedes some separate rights and prescribes some separate duties for men and women, in accordance with its view that each sex has its specific functions in society and is charged with an independent mission for the preservation and advancement of the human race. Within the limits of their special mission and functions in society, both men and women will have different rights and responsibilities and neither sex should feel jealous of the other if this involves lesser rights for one sex against the other in a strictly limited sphere and on easily understandable terms capable of adjudication in law-courts. This is the meaning of the Quranic verse:

> And do not covet that by which Allah has made some of you excel others; men should have the benefit of what they earn and women shall have the benefit of what they earn. (v. 32)

According to Islam, there is a specific sex individuality in man and woman which they must preserve and cherish, because it is this individuality which gives them honour and dignity and enables them to fulfil in an effective manner their specific role in society. Where this specific sex individuality, instead of being regarded as a source of honour and dignity, is sought to be pulled and effaced, as if it involved an inferiority in men or women, it produces a dead and colourless equality which is, in effect, a denial of real equality, as it makes for less differentiation and, therefore, for less progress. There are clear instructions of the Holy Prophet on this point which stress the need for preserving sex individuality. Thus Abu Dawud records it on the authority of Abu Hurairab, a companion of the Prophet, that the Prophet uttered a curse on men who imitate women in their dress and manners and similarly on women who abhorred their femininity by trying to dress and act like men. Similarly, at another place, Abu Dawud has recorded that the Prophet severely condemned those women who tried to appear and behave in the form and likeness of men.

Consistent with the exercise of their specific individuality and of the special functions flowing therefrom and involving special rights and responsibilities, both sexes have equal rights and are looked upon by Islam as distinct legal personalities. A wife, even after having come in partnership with her husband, is a separate legal person in Islamic law capable of suing and being sued in her own individual capacity and entitled to sue her own husband for any infringement of her just rights. This is a position which was not accorded to the female sex in Europe and America until the nineteenth century and this too after a great deal of agitation against the existing legal disabilities of women. Blackstone, who was the greatest exponent of the English Common Law and has profound influence on legal theory and practice both in England and America, maintained that the legal position of a married woman was one of unity with husband. In *The Legal Rights, Liabilities and Duties of Women*, Professor Mansfield summarised the Blackstonian thesis as follows:

> The first great principle of Scripture, the unity of husband and wife, is repeated by the law. They are, in law, one person ....Upon it, as observed by Blackstone, depend nearly all legal rights, duties and disabilities acquired by marriage.

Commenting on Blackstone's dictum, Mary B. Beard says in her book, *Woman as Force in History*:

> When Blackstone spoke of the husband's rights over the real and personal property of his wife and of her disabilities in law, he was technically

> correct, within fixed limits. On its face, the statement meant that, in case of litigation, the husband asserts certain rights over the real and personal property of his wife, and if the wife contests them or the said rights are drawn in question at Common Law, the Common Law Courts will enforce the husband's Common Law rights, unless the husband and wife have made agreements to the contrary before and after the marriage, or a relative of the wife has safeguarded the wife's rights by the creation of a trust or otherwise, which agreements or trusts made in due form are valid in equity and will be enforced by courts of equity. In other words, in the absence of valid agreements and actions to the contrary, the husband may, if he so desires, or his creditors and other litigants may assert a husband's rights over the wife's property and within the limits set by the specific rules of Common Law, the Common Law Courts will enforce them in case of litigation.

This was the position of a married woman in Europe and America until about 150 years ago. She could lose her rights on her own property, if the husband wished to deprive her of them because the law did not recognise her as separate legal personality. Islam, on the other hand, from its very inception, gave the married woman a separate Legal status with full property rights. Little wonder that a wrong conception of sex equality and extremist stand in respect of female freedom resulted from the sense of utter frustration generated by such great social and legal disabilities. But how could the Muslim women be justified in going to the same extreme length and preaching a conception of sex equality which lacks all scientific and natural basis as evidenced by latest researches on sex psychology.

In the 6th century the greatest event of the history of mankind which shook the very basic ideals and concepts of man and brought about a complete revolution in his thoughts and views and a total change in his character, was the high-spirited and high-hearted proclamation of the Prophethood of Hazrat Muhammad (peace and blessings of Allah be upon him). The result of this revolution was that it not only took a different turn in man's thought, but also gave a new direction to his life. One significant aspect of this new trend of thinking was the 'concept of woman' which underwent a complete change and thereby established the relationship between man and woman on entirely new grounds.

Before the advent of Islam and the arrival of Prophet Muhammad (peace be upon him) and his proclamation of Prophethood, the history of woman was no doubt the history of subjugation and oppression. She was underestimated and condemned as a low and mean creature and was regarded as the root cause of all evils and disasters. Instructions were given to be careful about her and to avoid her like snakes and scorpions. She was bought and sold like animals. She did not enjoy any absolute or independent position in the society and was made subservient to man. She was denied all rights and had to live on the pity and mercy of man. In such a dark period of the history of woman, Islam raised its voice so vehemently that the whole world reverberated with it. Today no one dares say that her previous position was correct and real. It was loudly proclaimed:

> O mankind! Reverence
>
> Your Guardian Lord,
>
> Who created you
>
> From a single soul
>
> Created, of like nature
>
> His mate, and from them twain
>
> Scattered (like seeds) Countless men and women:
>
> Reverence God, through Whom
>
> Ye demand your mutual (rights).
>
> And (reverence) the wombs
>
> (that bore) for God
>
> Ever watches over you. (4:1)

It was declared that the discrimination which the world has made between one man and the other is false, absurd and baseless. The whole mankind is the offspring of the single human soul. Originally all have the same descent. No one is noble or mean, or low or high by birth. All are equal and enjoy equal position. Any kind of distinction between them on the grounds of family status, race, colour, tribe, region, language, occupation or nationality is null and void.

Differences and Discrimination

It was thus a repudiation of the age-old differences and discrimination between man and woman. It brought into light the fact that the very companion of the first man was not of some other kind but belonged to the same species. No different kind of creature was taken for his companionship, rather she was taken from him alone. This first pair gave birth to numerous men and women and among them some or the other kind of relationship existed and thus the whole human generation got spread far and wide. Hence to differentiate and discriminate between man and woman is in fact to differentiate and discriminate between one side of mankind and the other and is the division of the two parts of a single whole. There can be no better elucidation than this for the expression of the equality of man and woman and their equal status.

It is also stated that all human beings are the servants of one God and the children of one and the same father and mother. Therefore on the one side they should worship and obey God and lead their life in fear of Him and on the other, give due respect to the relationships which exist between them. Here, with the honour of man, the honour of woman is also emphasised.

Islam totally repudiated the notion that man is dignified and honoured merely because he is a man and woman is low and mean simply because she is a woman. Both man and woman are equal in the eyes of Islam. Neither the inferiority of anyone nor superiority of anybody is written down for eternity. Whoever is adorned with faith and fair practice emerged successful here and in the hereafter and whoever is devoid of such qualities fails in this as well as in the eternal world:

Whoever works righteousness,
Man or woman, and has faith,
Verily, to him will We give
A new life, a life
That is good and pure, and We
Will bestow on such their reward
According to the best
Of their actions. (16:97)

Islam assigns different spheres of activity for man and woman. The field of work of woman is her own house and of men is the world outside. What the Qur'an instructs the honourable wives of the Holy Prophet (peace be upon him) holds true for all such women as believe in Allah and His Messenger.

Generally, two objections are raised against the position of woman in Islam. First, that the great responsibility of household affairs which is imposed upon her, would debar her from participating in the economic and social development. For this reason it is assumed that her position in the society would not be definite, but would be weak and unstable.

Regarding this, it needs to be clarified, that Islam has not barred woman from economic activities, rather it has given permission while imposing on her a few appropriate limitations. Although it is doubtless that her involvement in family affairs affects her economic struggle, Islam offers its own solution to it. Islam has held man legally responsible for the maintenance of his wife and children.

The second objection is that since the great responsibility of the house is vested in woman, she is confined to the four walls of the house. It is conceived that since she is completely engrossed in the home affairs, neither the society would be benefited from her abilities nor would she get any opportunity to contribute her potentialities to society.

This objection is also incorrect and without any substance. Islam has not forbidden woman from other activities which stand beyond the household activities. What Islam virtually intends and emphasises in this regard is that a woman is mainly a queen and fore-runner of her house. Hence, she should not bear the outward burden of the work at the risk of her indoor work. She is allowed to participate in the economic struggle with man while performing her role in the family affairs. Furthermore, she can take interest and contribute her abilities in different fields of life while keeping into consideration her condition, social environment and her own interest. History bears witness to the fact that the Muslim women have manifested their abilities, skill and talent in different fields of life and have left a tremendous impact on the age.

The most important thing is, Islam has assigned woman a prominent position at social level. Hence, she can lead an honoured and dignified life without becoming a victim of any inferiority complex. She can, in fact, offer her fullest cooperation to man in building up a chaste and virtuous society while contributing her potentialities and abilities which she possesses.

Distinguished Areas

There are two important reasons for which Islam assigns different spheres of activity to man and woman. First, it helps them guard their chastity. When both of them perform their work in the same sphere, it will become difficult for them to lead a life of chastity and modesty. If man and woman mix with each other in educational institutions to pursue education and participate in sports and games, and other recreations in parks and picnic spots and engage themselves openly in markets and in business centres without any checks and balances and meet each other without any restriction and this process of intermingling continues not for a day or two but for years together and in this way all the stages from childhood to youth and from youth to old age will be crossed, it is certain that their physical urges will get excited and flared up and will become uncontrolled and unchecked and ultimately they will become victims of indecent sexual anarchy.

In the present age, wherever free mixing of man and woman has been granted, it has resulted in a disaster. Chastity and honour are ravaged and modesty and decency are crippled. It gives rise to vulgar and ignoble sexual lapses which like an epidemic disease goes to such an extent that it becomes difficult to cure and correct it. And now it is taken as an inescapable social evil. Also all the evil results of it are willingly or unwillingly tolerated.

Chastity and modesty are apparently moral values, and it is on this basis that the direction of the whole society is determined. In a society where no importance is given to these values, man from every direction is taken to debased and evil acts and adultery. It gives rise to a particular kind of culture, civilisation, association, manners and literature, each element of which ignites fire in the sexual emotions of man. Contrary to it, the society which realises the importance and value of chastity and purity is erected entirely on a different standard. Each act of such a society reflects the purity of character, modesty and decency, and piety and purity fills the whole environment.

Islam is very sensitive to the chastity and purity of a man. It forbids free mixing and unrestricted meeting between man and woman. Islam considers it wrong to let man and woman mix with each other in their fields of work and let themselves involve in a severe test from where it is difficult to return. Islam not only forbids the acts of adultery but also prohibits man and woman to go near it.

The Qur'an says:

> Nor come nigh to adultery:
>
> For it is a shameful (deed)
>
> And an evil, opening the road,
>
> (to other evils). (17:32)

The second reason to assign different fields of work for man and woman is that their abilities and potentialities differ with each other. It is a fact that a woman is physically weaker than a man. She cannot bear hardship and strains.

Woman passes through such stages of life which restrict her from performing heavy work constantly. Her menstrual period begins from her youth and continues until she steps into the old age. Moreover, she passes through the most difficult and arduous stages like pregnancy and delivery. All these conditions and stages affect her health, strength and manner and stand as obstacles on the way of constant and laborious work. Now, it is the question of justice that she should not be given any tedious and wearisome works. Islam, therefore, assigns the work which requires more strength and valour to man and the work which is not hard and tedious to woman. Islam solves the problem thus that woman should look after the house while man should perform outside duties.

The very nature, interest and the psychology of woman demands the same sort of work. Woman in herself possesses the qualities of grace, love, patience, devotion and sacrifice more than a man. She fills the whole atmosphere of the family with happiness and order, peace and tranquility and love and affection. But to face the hardships and difficulties of life and to march forward firmly on all ups and downs, strong determination, bravery and intrepidity are the qualities which are required. Man possesses all these qualities far more than woman. The home and the family, however, provide a peaceful environment. The abilities of woman distinctively appear more sharply in the house from which full advantage can be derived. Man can face the complications and problems of life. For this reason man should be given such responsibilities as require more courage and valour.

It is no fairness to woman that she should be taken out from her natural field of work and be pushed into an unnatural field of work. It is not advantageous for her, rather a great loss.

The pains of menstrual period, pregnancy and delivery are unavoidable. Man can hardly assist her in all these difficulties and complications. It is, therefore, not a fair play if she is also given the responsibilities of man.

The woman is the queen of the house. She gets all the love and affection from her father, brother and husband and all the members of her family and all her rights are protected in the house. If woman does not bear the responsibility of the house, she cannot claim her rights. Thereafter she will have to work in such a field to pass her life which will not be in fact her own field and where she will have to face such a partner at every step who will be stronger than her. Then, it can be hardly expected that she will surpass man.

The place of honour and dignity of a woman is her own house, not the market. But in the present age, the importance of house and family is not fully recognised. It is the reason that the important role of woman in the house is interpreted as an injustice to her or that it gives her a low and mean position in the society or to deny her rights which she possesses or to condemn her constantly to the lowest position though a family is the basic unit of every society. The importance and significance of the house stands far ahead than of an office or a bazaar. The service which a woman renders in building the inner environment of her house is more important than the service which she can render outside. Here some aspects of her work are mentioned.

Contribution of Women

1. Today, man is engrossed in innumerable political, social, cultural and other problems. Other factors like health, diseases, poverty, difficulties also coincide with these problems. Sometimes for earning and living, man struggles too severely, bears all kinds of pains and faces innumerable difficulties. For maintaining and uplifting his family, he overcomes insurmountable hardships. In such a state of affairs, he deserves mental peace and content. It is the home which can provide him with all this peace and rest. If he does not get peace even at his own home, it becomes too hard for him to live: Islam teaches that a woman should make her home a 'peaceful dwelling' so that man should forget all his tensions and complications after reaching his home and prepare himself for a fresh struggle after breathing an air of gratification.

2. It has become an established fact that there is no better nourishment for a child than the milk of his mother. If a mother does not stay at home and engages herself in outside activities, she cannot set herself for breast-feeding. In this way the proper nourishment of the child for a considerable period even after the age of breast-feeding depends on mother. For the proper bringing up of the child, it is not just enough to give him proper nourishment but the child abundantly needs the love and affection, sympathy and an earnest devotion of his mother. If he is devoid of love and emotions from his nearest environment, his whole personality gets affected and even if his personality blossoms it will develop in a very wrong direction. It is the heart

of mother which is the source of inspiration for the child. Nobody else can take the place of woman for playing a decisive role. If the mother remains outside the home, the child would yearn for the love of his mother and he will not get it.

3. For the basic education and training of the child, mother is most suitable. For the purpose of education of the child, it is necessary that his teachers should be very loving and devoted to him, and should be acquainted with the nature and psychology of the child, and tolerate all his mischiefs and check him with love and patience. The most important thing is that the child should also love the teacher and consider even the bitterest scolding of the teacher to be good and beneficial for his well-being and tolerate even the harshness of the teacher. These sorts of feelings do not prevail between any two persons other than between mother and child. Let us look at another aspect. From educational point of view, it is extremely important that there should prevail an intimate and cordial relationship between the teacher and the child. The stronger this relationship, the better and beneficial it would be for the child. Perhaps, because of this reason, classes of higher standards are not much liked in schools because there the relationship between the teacher and the child is weaker in most of the cases. Comparatively, the classes of the lower standards are liked much because here this relationship is found to be stronger. In this manner the mother can provide basic education for her children which they cannot possibly acquire even at school.

Most of the children do not obtain proper education because they do not get better tutors at home or their parents are not able to afford tutors for them. Furthermore, most of the parents do not get proper tutors for their daughters. If the mother is capable enough to educate her children and even feel that it is her responsibility to give proper education to her children, the expenditure which is incurred on education will also get curtailed and help solve many other problems.

Here, one important point from the Muslim outlook on education is that today little attention is being paid to religious education. Very few children obtain religious education. Consequently, the child is sent to school when he has reached the age of school going. He does not get any opportunity even the preliminary religious instructions. Therefore, even the children of some good and God-fearing people remain ignorant of the basic religious tenets. The reason behind all this is that the father does not get time to give them religious instructions and the mother either herself lacks such education or does not take interest in education. If the mother is thoughtful enough and also capable of giving education to her children, they will not be ignorant of their religion, even after obtaining education in schools.

Even for training the children, the role of the mother is most important and significant. It is the mother who stands as an ideal for a child. The child observes the morals and etiquette of his mother day and night and moulds his behaviour noting the behaviour of his mother. The child maintains the same sort of relationship between himself and others on the mode of the relationship which his mother maintains between herself and others. Mother is his virtual model in this aspect and plays a decisive role in moulding the character of her child.

The fact is that the construction of a society depends upon the construction of a house. This is the reason that Islam has completely relied upon woman to construct her house. Islam does not wish to thrust on her other burdens along with this responsibility. The woman is freed even from the financial responsibilities. In the light of Islam, the construction of their house is no less important than Jihad. Hazrat Anas related that once a group of women asked Prophet Muhammad (peace be upon him) that men perform some acts and attain the reward of Jihad, what we should do to get such reward which men get through Jihad in the way of God? Prophet Muhammad (peace be upon him) replied that woman who sits at home receives the reward of Jihad in the way of God.

8

High Position

Dignity and Honour

The sum total of Islamic teachings is to raise human dignity and honour. It relieves mankind from disgrace and provides higher and honourable place in human society. It imparts the lesson of human dignity. Islam directs humanity to prostrate before Allah alone for the achievement of—superiority over other creations. Mankind is the masterpiece creation of Allah. The following verses of the Holy Quran testify this fact :

> Verily We have honoured the children of Adam. We carry them on the land and the sea, and have made provision of good things for them, and We have preferred them above many of those whom We created with a marked preferment. (17 : 70)

> Surely We created man of the best stature. (95 : 4)

> "When thy Lord said unto the angels : Lo : I am about to create a mortal out of mire. And when

> I have fashioned him and breathed into him of My spirit, then fall down before him prostrate. The angels fell down prostrate, everyone save Iblis; He was scornful and became one of the disbelievers." (38 : 72-75)

Right Practice

In Islam the welfare of mankind depends upon right thinking and right practice. It is sheer ignorance to degrade woman simply because she happens to be a woman, and man is considered a heavenly creature simply because he happens to be a man. Islam has explained it in very clear words that human dignity rests upon piety and virtue. Hence, who is more honourable, man or woman? This question is well answered by the Holy Quran :

> "Whosoever doeth right whether male or female, and is a believer, him verily We shall quicken with good life and We shall pay them recompense in proportion to the best of what they used to do." (16 : 97)

> "Lo! Men who surrender unto Allah, and women who surrender, and men who believe and women who believe, men who obey and women who obey, and men who speak the truth and women who speak the truth, and men who persevere (in righteousness) and women who persevere, and men who are humble, and women who are humble, and men who give alms, and women who give alms, and men who fast, and women who fast, and men who guard their modesty, and women who guard (their modesty), and men who remember Allah much and women who remember Allah hath prepared for them forgiveness and a vast reward." (33 : 35)

> "And their Lord hath heard them (and He saith): Lo! I suffer not the work of any worker, male or

> female, to be lost. Ye proceed one from another. So those who migrated and were driven forth from their homes and suffered damage for My cause and fought and were slain, verily I shall remit their evil deeds from them and verily I shall bring them into gardens underneath which rivers—flow a reward from Allah, and with Allah is the fairest of rewards." (3 : 195)

The Holy Quran distinctly explains the characteristics of the Momineen (The faithful followers of Islam) who submitted their lives, property and desires to the Will of Allah:

> "(Triumphant) are those who turn repentant (To Allah) ' those who serve (Him), those who praise (Him), those who fast, those who bow down, those who fall prostrate (in worship), those who enjoin the right and who forbid the wrong, and those who keep the limits (Ordained) of Allah, and give glad-tidings to believers! " (9 : 12)

At another place, the pious wives of the Holy Prophet (S.A.W.) have been 'commanded to develop such qualities in them without which they would not be able to remain in his Nikah. And the Holy Prophet (S.A.W.) would easily find such wives who would possess such virtuous qualities.

> "It may happen that his Lord, if he divorces you, will give him in your stead wives better than you, submissive (to Allah) believing, pious, penitent, inclined to fasting, widows and maids."
> (66 :5)

Now, it becomes crystal clear that according to the Holy Quran, piety and virtue are the only criteria for the achievement of successful life in the Hereafter. None, whether man or woman can accomplish his or her goal without fulfilling this condition.

The Holy Quran points out that man and woman both have helped and cooperated with each other in the development of human life. Both have equally shared the burden of life. Their union has brought the civilization into existence. No nation or movement of the world can neglect either of them. If man and woman are responsible for the establishment of the authority of Truth and its enforcement, they are equally responsible for the spread of vices in the world, The Holy Quran says:

> "The hypocrites, both man and woman, are one and the same. They enjoin the evil, and forbid the right; and they withhold their hands from spending in the cause of Allah. They have forgotten Allah and so He hath forgotten them. Indeed, the hypocrites, are the transgressors." (9 : 76)

> "And the believers, men and women are protecting friends one of another; they enjoin the right and forbid the wrong, and they establish the prayer and they pay the poor-due, and they obey Allah and His Messenger, as for these, Allah will have mercy on them. Lo! Allah is Mighty Wise." (9 : 71)

Since it is admitted that the revolutions in the civilization of the world are brought about by both, man and woman, no logical argument can degrade one and upgrade the other. Besides, it will be foolish to eliminate either of them from the civilization and march forward. No person can play any role in life after having paralysed one half of the body.

Before the advent of Islam, the world had degraded the woman and had almost outcast her. She was thrown in such deep abyss that there seemed no hope of her redemption. Islam boldly remonstrated against this injustice and emphasised that life needed both man and woman. Woman is not created to be derided and cast aside. Like man, woman also has her purpose and right to exist. And the Nature is achieving its aim with the help of man and woman both. As the Holy Quran says:

> Unto Allah belongeth the Sovereignty of the heavens and the earth. He createth what He wills. He bestoweth female (offsprings) upon whom He will, and bestoweth male (offspring) upon whom He will; or He mingleth them, males and females, and He maketh barren whom He will. Lo ! He is Knower, Powerful. (42 : 49-50)

Islam lifted woman from the abyss of disgrace and granted her rights and facilities. Abdullah-bin-'Umar (R.A.A.) relates:

> During the life time of our Prophet, Muhammad (S.A.W.) we did not talk to 'our woman freely because we feared revelation against us. When the Holy Prophet (S.A.W.) passed away, we became frank with them.
>
> (Bukhari, and Ibn Majah)

Whereas, all other religions deprived woman of right even to live.' Islam granted her rights almost on a par with man. It also warned that all those who strive to snatch her rights away, will surely be, accountable to Allah on the Day of Judgment.

> And when the girl-child that was buried alive, is asked For what sin she was slain? (19 : 8-9)

The Holy Prophet (S.A.W.) has issued numerous instructions in favour of woman, the favour which she could not receive even from the so-called modern upholders of the woman's rights. The Holy Prophet (S.A.W.) has said :

> Allah has forbidden you, disobedience unto your mothers, refusal to sanctioned rights, accumulation of wealth from all sides and burial of living daughters. (Bukhari)

The Prophet of Islam (S.A.W.) has also said:

> "A man who has a daughter and he neither despises her nor buries her alive nor prefers son to daughter, Allah will admit him in Heaven."
>
> (Abu Daud)

Abu Sayeed (R.A.A.) relates that the Holy Prophet (S.A.W.) said:

> "Whoever brought up three daughters and treated them well, the Heaven is for him."
>
> (Abu Daud - Tirmizi)

The world condemned woman, but Islam honoured her. The Holy Prophet (S.A.W.) raised her status and assigned her respectable place in the human society. He (S.A.W.) said :

> "In worldly things, I like woman and perfume, but coolness of my eyes lies in salat (Prayers)".

Once the Holy wives were travelling on camels, the Holy Prophet (S.A.W.) said to the camel driver.

> "Carry these glasses very carefully."

About Fatimah (R.A.A.) the Messenger of Allah (S.A.W.) has said :

> "My daughter is my flesh, any trouble to her will cause pain to me."
>
> (Bukhari, and Muslim)

Once Hazrat Aisha (R.A.A.) was asked whom did the Holy Prophet (S.A.W.) love most? She replied, Fatimah (R.A.A.).

On another occasion, somebody asked the Holy Prophet (S.A.W.), 'Who is your most beloved person?' The Holy Prophet (S.A.W.) replied,' Aisha (R.A.A.).'

Thus we see that the Holy Prophet (S.A.W.) loved his wife Aisha (R.A.A.) and his daughter Fatima (R.A.A.) most. And the sayings of the Holy Prophet (S.A.W.) explicitly explain the aim of Islam with regard to the treatment of fair sex.

The teachings of Islam revolutionized the thinking of those men who buried their daughters alive and felt no shame in doing so. They began to love and nourish their daughters, those who refused to shelter their own daughters, became the guardians of other's daughters. Those who were devoid of love and affection for women, now loved and cared for them.

> On the occasion of the Battle of Uhud, Jabir's father told Jabir (R.A.A.), "My Son! I may be martyred in the forthcoming battle, so I advise you to look after my daughters." Consequently, Jabir (R.A.A.) who was still young, married a widow owing to the responsibility of his sisters. The Holy Prophet (S.A.W.) asked him, "Why did you not marry a young woman?" He replied, "O Prophet of Allah (S.A.W.) My father was martyred in the Battle of Uhud and he has left behind his nine daughters who are my sisters. Therefore, I chose such woman for my marriage, who could look after them well." The Messenger of Allah (S.A.W.) replied, You did a good deed." (Bukhari)
>
> It is related that after the martyrdom of Hazrat Hamza (R.A.A.), three persons claimed to have the right to look after his daughter. The first was Hazrat Ali (R.A.A.) who claimed his right to look after her because she was his cousin (sister). The second person was Hazrat Jafer (R.A.A.) who said that his claim was better than that of Hazrat Ali (R.A.A.) because she was not only his cousin (sister) but her maternal aunt

> was his wife. Hence, she could be brought up in better way. The third man was Hazrat Zaid (R.A.A.) who filed his petition on the ground that she was his brother's daughter and that none else can have better claim than her own uncle. (Bukhari, and Muslim)

These are the examples which the history of other nations cannot present. Islam is the only religion that raised the status of woman to such extent in the world.

According to Islam, society is responsible for the protection of human rights and maintenance of law and order. Its duty is to chop off the hands of the oppressors and unjust. The Quran says:

> "And there is life for you in retaliation, O men of understanding, that ye may ward off (evil)."
>
> (2 : 179)

The law of Shariah awards death penalty to murderer whether he has murdered a man or a woman, because the life of woman is as sacred as that of man. The laws given to the people of Yaman by the Holy Prophet (S.A.W.) included the death penalty to the murderer of woman also.

> "Undoubtedly (men) murderer of a woman shall be sentenced to death."
>
> It is stated that a Jew crushed the head of a girl and killed her. The Holy Prophet (S.A.W.) ordered him to be put to death in the same manner (Bukhari and Muslim)
>
> Once, all those men who murdered a woman, were put to death by the order of Hazrat 'Umar Farooq (R.A.A.)
>
> (Al-Ahkam-ul-Quran, Jassas)

If a woman pardons a murderer of her relative, the other relatives have no authority to nullify her consent for forgiveness. Not only this, she can offer protection to an enemy during the emergency of war and this act of her cannot be considered unlawful. The Holy Prophet (S.A.W.) has said

> "Undoubtely, a woman can shelter an enemy for the benefit of Muslims." (Tirmizi)

On the occasion of the conquest of Holy Mecca, Umm Hani said to the Holy Prophet (S.A.W.), "O Messenger of Allah (S.A.W.), I have provided protection to Ibn Hera, but Ali (R.A.A.) says that he will kill him under any circumstance."

> The Holy Prophet (S.A.W.) replied, "Umm Hani Whomsoever you have protected, he is under my protection too." (Bukhari)

Similarly, Islam permits woman, within the limits of Shariah, to participate in the financial affairs and derive benefits.

No man can interfere in this matter. Even her husband has no right to make use of her personal wealth. Likewise, woman has no right to enforce her will for the use of the wealth of her husband. There is a distinct injunction of the Holy Quran :

> "And covet not the thing in which Allah hath made some of you excel other. Upto men a fortune from that which they have earned and unto women a fortune from that which they have earned. (Envy not one another). But ask Allah of His bounty. Lo ! Allah is Ever Knower of all things." (4:32)

According to the Holy Quran the Law of Inheritance is:

> "Unto the men (of a family) belongeth a share, of that which parents and near kindred leave, and unto the women a share of that which parents and near kindred leave, whether it be little or much a legal share." (4 : 7)

The ancient religions were not prepared to give equal status to man and woman. Therefore, they formulated separate laws for them. But Islam does not make this distinction. In Islam, man and woman both are equal before law. The Holy Quran says:

> "Lo ! We offered the trust unto the heavens and the earth and the hills, but they shrunk from bearing it and were afraid of it. And man assumed it. Lo ! He hath proved a tyrant and a fool. So Allah punisheth hypocritical men and hypocritical women, and idolator men and idolator women. But Allah pardoneth believing men and believing women, and Allah is Forgiving, Merciful." (33 : 72- 73)

> "And it becometh not a believing man or a believing woman when Allah and His Messenger have decided an affair (for them), that they should (after that) claiming say in their affair, and whoso is rebellious to Allah and His Messenger, he verily goeth astray in error manifest."
>
> (33 : 36)

Islam has granted equal rights to both, man and woman. It provides equal opportunity to both of them for the progress and prosperity of life. It guarantees the protection of their lives, property and honour.

The spouses are equally inter-dependent. Therefore, there is no question of honour for man and dishonour for woman. In Islam both are equally honourable. There is no distinction on the basis of sex. In fact they are created for each other to live in harmony and co-existence. As the Holy Quran says :

> "They are raiment for you and ye are raiment for them." (2 : 187)

The relation between man and woman is not of hatred but of love. Man is incomplete without woman and woman is incomplete without man. They are the source of peace and harmony to each other.

According to the Holy Quran

> "And of His signs is this : He created for you help-mates from yourselves that ye might find rest in them, and he ordained between you love and mercy. Lo ! herein indeed are portents for folk who reflect." (30 : 21)

Control for Safety

Allah Has endowed mankind with charm and beauty. Mankind is also fond of beautiful things. Therefore, man seeks beauty in every thing of the world. He despises ugly and awkward things and he is never tired of seeking beauty in the Nature.

Indeed, it is natural urge of mankind, hence it is essential to fulfil it. But this admiration of beauty is worthwhile so long it is within the limits of Shariah. If it crosses the limits then it opens the door to evil practices which spoil the society. Therefore, Islam restricts the observation of the opposite sex, because, if the sight is not controlled, then it will be difficult to control the sexual desire.

The Holy Quran. says:

> "Say to the believing men that they should lower their gaze and guard their modesty that will make far greater purity for them and Allah is well acquainted with all that they do. And say to the believing women that they should also lower their gaze and guard their modesty."
>
> (24 : 30-31)

According to the Holy Qur'an, it is necessary for a man to control his eyes to keep his character blameless. The Holy Prophet (S.A.W.) has said :

> "O Ali ! Do. not have a second look-the first glance may be by chance, but the second view is not justified." (Abu Dawood -Tirmizi)

> This Hadis means that the first (casual) sight is pardonable, but the second and deliberate looking is not proper because they are Satanic acts which destroy the human character. , Hazrat Jabir-bin-Abdullah says, "I asked the Holy Prophet (S.A.W.) if I happen to look at the stranger by chance what should be done?" The Holy Prophet (S.A.W.) replied, "Turn your face at once." (Mushm- Tirmizi-Abu Dawood)

Hearing also leaves profound impression on human feelings and emotions. This impression can be harmful or beneficial. It is the aim of the good law to clarify the lines of loss and gain. Hence, Islam lays down the rule that a Muslim can hear any beautiful song for the satisfaction of his interest. However, it prohibits the kind of hearing which leads to sexual incitement and immorality, because Islam wants a man to be of finest character. There is nothing wrong in listening to sweet melody but it is a sin to listen to anything that is morally harmful. Therefore, music or musical instruments are not allowed in Islam. The reason for the ban is explained in the best way by Hafiz Ibn Jauzi (R.A.):

> "It should be known that there are two kinds of harms in listening to the music; the one is that it makes man negligent in his duty towards Allah, and secondly it inclines his thinking towards the worldly pleasures only. He strives to satisfy his material wants only particularly the sexual desire which is on the top. And it is not possible to satisfy these wants without having new contact. Such possibilities could not be found in the lawful area of life. Music also incites man for unlawful sexual pleasure. If music is the food of soul, the sexual pleasure is the food of the body. It is related in a Hadis that music leads to sexual pleasure."
>
> (Naqdul Ilm-wal-Ulema)

The man has been proved very careless in respect of the use of his tongue. Whatever a man utters, it effects the people and the environment. The effects of the tongue are stronger than those of seeing and hearing. The tongue is the means of expression of human thoughts which may be good or bad and accordingly these thoughts leave their impression on the people around. The speaker tries to influence the listener with his power of the tongue. If his speech is liked and appreciated by the listeners then his thoughts grow stronger and this process leads to collective listening and thus his influence grows stronger day by day.

The fact cannot be denied that the power of speech can create chaos if not controlled and allowed to be used wrongly. Hazrat Sohail bin Sa'd relates that the Holy Prophet (S.A.W.) has said:

> "If a person gives me guarantee for the protection of (his or her) tongue and sexual organs, I shall guarantee Heaven for him (or) (her)."
>
> (Bukhari)

On another occasion the Holy Prophet (S.A.W.) said :

> "A person who is saved from the evil of the tongue by Allah, shall enter Heaven."(Tirmizi)

Today the greatest evil of the world is the, nudism, which has greatly influenced the human mind and provided the unlimited means of sensuality. The fair sex is already attractive and charming in appearance and if nudity is added, the mischief is greater, making it difficult for the man to control his passions. Therefore, Islam condemns all means and sources of evil which lead to immorality and destroy the human society. The purpose of clothing is to ward off the evil consequences of nudity and maintain decency in the society.

It is the sign of utter ignorance to think that nudity is the call of modernization. In fact, the nudism is the imitation of Western culture. It has nothing to do with the term, 'Modern.' Islam is the most modern 'Deen'. It, not only allows the advancement in modern science and technology but also encourages all efforts intended to attain knowledge from any part of the world.

The concept of dress in Islam is to cover the-body, specially those parts, which must not be exposed to others. It also emphasises decency in dressing. Therefore, Islam has given certain guidelines for the dresses of the man and the woman and both have to follow these instructions strictly. Hazrat Ayeshah (R.A.A.) says that she has heard the Holy Prophet (S.A.W.) saying:

> "A woman who removes her clothes in a house other than that of her husband, violates the command of Allah." (Musnad Ahmad)

It is a very dangerous idea for a woman to meet a stranger in loneliness. Logically speaking there is no sense in meeting a stranger when a woman has no relation with a man. In such circumstances she cannot be sure of protecting her chastity from the attack of the stranger. Therefore '. Islam strictly prohibits woman from meeting a stranger in loneliness. This is done for her own safety and protection of her honour. Hazrat Jabir (R.A.A.) relates that the Holy Prophet (S.A.W.) has said :

> "The women who have no company of their near relatives, should not visit strangers, because nobody knows when the devil inside man incites him for the commission of sin."
> (Muslim-Tirmizi)

9

Special Rights

Sometimes dower is mentioned sarcastically as the price paid by the husband for the bride. That shows ignorance about the nature of *mahr*. To Islam woman is not a commodity which can be purchased and sold. She has an independent identity of her own. She is not the property of the parents or any other guardian who can sell her. If she had been their property and they could sell her with mahr as her cost, the amount coming from the would-be groom would have accrued to them whereas according to the Law of the Islamic Shari'ah mahr is the due to the bride herself. Nobody can claim it or even a portion of it. Again, if the husband had purchased her, she would have been his property when the 'nikah' or wedlock against mahr, does not make the husband her master having proprietary rights over her. After marriage too she retains an independent identity of her own.

The Dower

Let us now examine how the Quran presents dower. After mentioning the totally forbidden women in Surah Nisa', in detail, it declares :

> Thus hath Allah ordained (Prohibitions) against you : Except for these all others are lawful, provided you seek (them in marriage) with gifts from your property, desiring chastity, not fornication, give them their dowry for the enjoyment you have of them as a duty; [14]
>
> —Al Quran IV: 24

We learn the following lessons from this verse :

□Barring the forbidden women others can be sought in marriage. □For this purpose it is necessary that their hand should be sought by man against his substance. □This seeking a woman should be with the purpose of nikah (clean and chaste relationship in sanctified wedlock and not fornication or illicit sex, outside wedlock). The difference between the two lies in the fact that in fornication, man after casual gratification of his lust, leaves the woman to fend for herself when its dreadful consequences come to the surface in which predecament he remains aloof and totally unconcerned. As against this dastardly selfish and cruel attitude, nikah is with the intention that husband and wife are bound in a stable relationship which shall be abiding. Both shall meet the mutual obligations and responsibilities of conjugal life. □The context of the verse also reveals that it is mahr that differentiates between nikah (lawful wedlock and Safah (illegal gratification of lust), since one of the financial responsibilities of man to the woman is mahr which is her lawful right, and man must pay it to her. In case of momentary pleasure of illicit sex man undertakes no such responsibility. □Mahr is the return of the benefit man derives from the woman through the bond of nikah.

The Quran says:

> Give them their dowry for the enjoyment you have of them as a duty. [15]
>
> (Al Quran IV: 24)

Zamakhshari says that the Quran has called mahr the return for man's deriving benefit from the woman. Because the mahr is the return for the sexual gratification of man with the woman.

In the Hanafite jurisprudence mahr has been defined in these words :

Mahr is that amount of man's substance which in case of nikah falls due on the husband for the gratification of his sex urge. This may become due on fixation of mahr or after nikah.

This makes it evident that mahr entitles man to and makes lawful for him to gratify his desire but it does not make her his property (purchased with mahr). Undoubtedly woman too derives sexual pleasure from the sex act, but that does not make her liable to anything like mahr, because Islam does not like to throw the burden of any financial responsibility on the woman. It has kept her free from all such obligations.

Expression of Integrity

Mahr has been termed return or the wages since she gets it against nikah which denotes her legal position. But the Quran has used for it the words "Sadaqat" and "Sidaqah" and "Sidaq" also for it, which interprets its spirit. The Quran says :

> And give the women (on marriage) their dower as an obligation. [16] (Al Quran IV: 4)

The words "sadaqah" and "Sadaq" have been derived from "Sidq" which is an Arabic word with very wide sense including sincerity, love, friendship, sticking to one's word, to come up to the expectations of people, to prove one's mettle in trial, etc.

The word sadaqah being used for mahr is very meaningful. Allamah Savi says : Sadaqah is a derivative of sidq which is the antonym of 'kizb'. It (sadaqah) has been used for mahr since its existence between the husband and the wife is proof of the fact that they are at heart bound by the Shari'ah.

Mulla Jeevan says :

> This is proof of the sincerity and truth in the husband's love.

The fact is that dower is a token of the husband's sincerity and love and to declare it the price of the bride is an insult to that sincerity. Through payment of mahr the husband proves that he will come to the woman's expectation of her good faith in him and shall not deceive her.

And also the word 'Nihlah' in the original Arabic text is just as meaningful expressing the passion behind the payment of dower in a much better way. This word literally has three meanings according to the lexicologists and there is room for all the three to fit in here all together.

> □The first sense is Faith and religion meaning thereby that the dowers of women must be paid as a religious duty binding on you legally with answerability Here and Hereafter. □Paying it cheerfully, meaning that it should be paid without the express demand for it from the wife. There should be no dilly-dallying in this payment, For, in that case it does not remain "Nihlah" (something paid cheerfully as a religious duty). □To pay as a gift in the sense that the husband does not take anything in return for it. As for the benefit of sexual enjoyment, they both derive it and stand on an equal footing with no obligation on either side. This sense has been brought out in the following words:

Allah has made enjoyment derived from the sexual act and producing offspring common to the husband and the wife. (Neither is benefited alone). Along with that He commanded the husband to pay dower to the wife. It is, as it were, a gift from Allah at the commencement of conjugal relations of a man and woman.

The above mentioned meanings of the Quranic term "Nihlah" have been commented upon by Allamah Ibn-e-Katheer in the following words :

The sum total of these expositions is this that it is the bounden duty of man to pay to his wife her mahr cheerfully just as one offers a gift to somebody.

Not withstanding the fact that the dower of a woman is her due, the way it has been put up as a "Nihlah" or a gift. Her maintenance likewise has been termed "sadaqah" though it too is of a binding nature. Commenting on the meaningfulness of these terms. Allamah Ibu-ul-Munayyar says:

'Nafqah' or maintenance has been called sadaqah for reasons similar to those in case of giving the mahr the name of 'Nihlah'. Since for the sake of sexual gratification, affection and love modesty and chastity and the natural urge for offspring, just as the woman needs man, so does a man stand in need of the woman. When both enjoy an equal status in this respect, nothing ought to have been due from man. But Allah has conferred this superiority on man that he is her caretaker and hence a degree of ascendancy in his position. For this reason calling mahr "Nihlah" and maintenance as sadaqah is justified.

Legal Imposition

Some people may be led to think that mahr or dower might have been regarded as a token of love in a particular period and it might also have had some importance and utility at that time. But the circumstances and social trends differ from time to time. The present day social values regard it as a negation of conjugal love. And practically also mahr has lost its importance in view of the fact that woman is an earner of livelihood in her own right and does not look to any one for support.

This can be considered from two aspects. Firstly what importance the Islamic Shari'ah attaches to mahr? Was it a provisional ordinance or it is of the nature of abiding laws and ordainments? Secondly, was the importance of mahr transitory which has become ineffective with the passage of time or it persists even today?

Where the Shari'ah comes in, it has presented it as an ordainment of importance and utility. Some Quranic verses have already been quoted earlier. They are definite about its binding nature and not conditioned by time and the changing circumstances. The Quran has also ordained mahr definitely and with great stress, and in detail elsewhere too. But there also there is not the least hint to their being provisional. For, in that case there would hardly be any Quranic injunctions which could be called an abiding law.

The jurist are one on the issue that nikah without mahr is strictly prohibited, no matter even if that woman might have gifted herself to him. Only the slave girl in one's lawful possession is an exception. Ibn Hajar R.A. says :

> It is not permitted to any one to have conjugal relations with any woman without mahr except the one his right hand possesses. There is concurrence of ulama on this issue.

Ibn Rushd says :

> Among the conditions laid down for the nikah to be regular and lawful mahr is also one and binding too. Concord on its abolition is not permissible. The jurists have consensus on this issue.

The nature of mahr is such that if a person imposes a condition at the time of nikah that he would not pay mahr or that he does not mention it at all, even then it must fall due according to the Hanafites, since nobody has the right to decide whether he will pay it or abstain from it, being a divine injunction, a bounden duty or promise that he has to fulfil. Imam Malik R.A. has gone so far that the nikah in which the man has expressed the condition of non-payment of mahr will not be valid.

Let us now consider its utility. If nikah makes lawful the private parts of a woman, mahr denotes its value. It induces in man the feeling that the permission of the Shari'ah by which he is benefited, he had to spend his substance on it. And this feeling does away with the impression of denigrating the woman and nursing the erroneous notion that his acceptance of her as life-partner and establishing relations with her was a boon granted to her.

Mahr is also a means of keeping the conjugal relations intact. For, it is a psychological fact that he is not prepared to lose something on which he has spent his substance. Rather it is his endeavour to maintain it. Moreover, it is also a deterrent to divorce, since in case of divorce he will not only lose mahr of the divorced wife but will have to pay it afresh to the newcomer as his life-partner.

There is also an aspect of woman's comfort and satisfaction as well as financial aid. She can benefit thereby in meeting her needs, can spend it for a noble cause or invest it profitably in business.

As for the statement that in the world of today the avenues of economic effort are open to her and hence payment of mahr to her is hardly necessary, the question arises whether such facilities in the form of earning propositions are freely available to her to a degree where she has become totally independent of man? And taking for granted for the sake of argument, if it is really so, will it be beneficial to her to deprive her of the right of mahr because of earning facilities? And then the utility of mahr is not only economic but moral and psychological also. Can it be overlooked?

The Fixation

The quantum of mahr is also an issue that comes time and again for consideration. Here we shall take it up for exposition. The Islamic Shari'ah has not fixed the quantum of mahr, leaving it to the social and economic condition of the husband and the wife, their familial traditions, mutual relations and trust. They can keep it very low if they are so pleased. And they are also permitted to keep it very high under their particular circumstances.

> But if you want to take one wife in place of another, even if ye had given the latter a whole treasure for dower take not the least bit of it back: Would ye take it by slander and a manifest sin? [17]
>
> (Al Quran IV:20)

It has been reported that 'Umar R.A.A., the second rightly guided Caliph, once harangued to the Muslim gathering about not fixing very high mahr and wanted it to limit it to four hundred dirhams. A woman in the audience raised the objection to his suggestion, saying that he had no right to any such decision as it went against the definite teaching of the Quran. Then she quoted the relevant Quranic verses. On hearing this from her 'Umar R.S.A. remarked that a woman was right and 'Umar's decision was erroneous.

The traditions have not prevented people from fixing higher quantity of mahr, but people have been persuaded to keep them low or moderate. One such tradition says :

> The most blessed nikah is that which does not involve heavy burden.

It is a historical fact that mahr was kept low during the period of the Prophet S.A.W. So we find Abu Hurairah R.A.A. reporting that during the Prophet's time it used to be ten ooqiyah or four hundred dirhams.

The mahr of the wives of the Prophet S.A.W. was 121/2 ooqiyah or five hundred dirhams.

Umar R.A.A. says : Do not fix large amounts as mahr. For, it had been a symbol of honour and prestige in this life and of piety in that to come, the Prophet S.A.W. ought to have been foremost in fixing vast amounts as mahr. But none of his daughters or wives had more than 12 ooqiyah as their mahrs.

An Ansari gentleman fixed four ooqiyah or 200 dirhams as Mahr and the Prophet S.A.W. said:

> It appears this mountain consists of silver and
> you cut out pieces for yourselves.

Now the question is what is that minimum which can be fixed as mahr for nikah? Whether the Shari'ah has prescribed any limit for it or not? The jurists are one on the norm that only such things as have any substantial value can become mahr. So something useless, with no substantial worth, cannot become mahr, and nikah is not permitted against it, since the Quran has declared it in clear terms :

> Except for them, all others are lawful, provided
> ye seek (them in marriage) with gifts from your
> property. [18] (Al Quran IV: 24)

The Quran has decisively used the word 'property'. Therefore, a group of jurists are of the opinion that the way it can be a very large amount so can it be very meagre also. Unless it gets reduced to a limit where its value as property is nullified, it-shall be tenable as mahr. Imam Navavi has written that this is the opinion of Ulama of all the past ages and those of the recent times. This list includes Yahya bin Sa'eed, Abuz-Zannad, Rabia', Ibn Juraih, Muslim bin Khalid, Imam Laith, Imam Thauri, Ibn-e-Abi Laila, Imam Shafi'i, Da'ood Zahiri, jurists of Ahle-Hadith, Ibn-e-Wahab Maliki and others.

As against this Imam Abu Haneefah, Imam Malik, Sa'eed bin Jubair, Imam Nakha'i, Ibn Shibramah and others are of the opinion that the Islamic Shari'ah has fixed a minimum for mahr and it is not proper to reduce it further. However, they are divided on this minimum of the Shari'ah. Imam Abu Haneefah puts it at ten dirhams. Imam Malik says it is quarter of a dinar or three dirhams. Ibn-e-Shibramah has put it at five dirhams. Imam Nakha'i is reported to have fixed it at forty and according to other reports also at ten dirham.

Imam Shafi': and those subscribing to his view offer a Quranic verse as an argument in support of their opinion :

> Give them their dowry for the enjoyment you
> have of them as a duty. [19]
> (Al Quran IV: 24)

This shows that mahr is a return which becomes due from man for enjoyment they have of them (women). This should be settled by mutual consent or it will not be in order. If the amount of mahr is prescribed before any mutual agreement the concept of return shall be no more and Quran's purpose shall be defeated.

The other argument put forth by this group is a report quoted by Bukhari and Muslim in which it has been said that a woman came to the Prophet S.A.W. and submitted that she was prepared to gift herself to him, meaning thereby that he should accept her by entering a marriage tie. She remained waiting for a sufficiently long time but he (the Prophet S.A.W.) did not respond to her. Seeing him quiet, somebody in the audience said to him that in case he (the Prophet S.A.W.) himself did not want her let her be given in marriage to him. The Prophet S.A.W. asked him if he had anything to offer her as her dower in this contract. He replied that he had nothing except the sheet around his loins. The Prophet S.A.W. remarked that if he would give his loin cloth to her, he himself would be left without one. He should, therefore, go home and see if he can find anything to offer him. Let it be an iron ring if there is nothing else. He tried to get something but failed, admitting to the Prophet S.A.W. that he could find nothing. The Prophet S.A.W. then asked him if he knew any portion of the Quran. He named some surahs (Chapters of the Quran) that he knew. The Prophet S.A.W. then pronounced his decision saying that in return for that much of the Quran (to be imparted to her) he gave her to him in wedlock.

From this tradition it has been argued that there is no limit to minimum amount of mahr. A whip, a pair of shoes, an iron ring or some such thing can be offered as mahr by mutual agreement.

However those scholars who think that there is a bottom line and Mahr can not be less than that; have countered the above argument. We will present the Hanafite stand below.

The Ulama of the Hanafite school have said that the nature of mahr (dower) is not merely that of mutual agreement between the husband and the wife. It has also an aspect of a devotional act in it. For any contract can be nullified by mutual agreement. Not so mahr. The parties concerned cannot cancel it even by mutual accord.

Several explanations have been given for this report. Firstly, 'Let it be an iron ring' does not mean that an iron ring can become the dower of a woman. Rather, it is a style of expression denoting that what ever can be given as mahr should be given, the minimum quantum of which is, however, specified. The other rejoinder to those shielding themselves with this tradition is that the deferred quantity of dower (mahre-Mu'ajjal) has been mentioned here. One should pay whatever is possible immediately and the rest remaining a liability. In support of this argument a custom of that period, deferred payment of mahr has been mentioned to which great importance was attached. The third explanation offered is that the permission was specifically for that person and not a general rule. A tradition of the Prophet has also been quoted in support of this statement. But it is not in order. The fourth explanation is that witnessing his poverty but with his knowledge of several Quranic Surahs he gave that woman in marriage to him and did not pronounce the quantum of mahr. But the deferred mahr becomes automatically due from him which he might have paid later. But all these interpretations are weak and are not duly applicable to the subject matter of the Hadith.

The basis for the stand of the Hanafite school is a report by Baihaqi :

> Mahr cannot be less than ten dirhams.

It is also supported by another report by 'Ali, quoted both by Dar Qutni and Baihaqi:

> The quantum of mahr cannot be less than ten dirhams.

Those who believe in the quantum of mahr to have been specified have also conjectured it on the quantum of (property stolen) fixed for cutting off the hand of the thief. According to Ahnaf it is ten dirhams. Therefore, they argue that the quantum of mahr should also be ten dirhams, since this quantum points to the fact that any thing less than that cannot justify waste of a useful organ (which is normally immune like one's life, But on the one hand this quantum for cutting off the hand is not unanimous. On the other conjecturing enjoyment of a woman on cutting off the hand of a thief is a far-fetched anomaly, rather a baseless conjecture. Cutting off the hand is a punishment for a crime and causes a defect in man. But in the use of the private parts of a woman for the gratification of sexual urge there is no concept of punishment inflicted in the act on the woman, nor does she come by any harm or defect. Rather, it is a means of mutual love and the gratification of a particular passion. There is no common basis of conjecture between the two.

This tradition clearly brings out the fact that the quantum of mahr has been less than ten dirhams also. So it would not be proper to fix it at a minimum of ten dirhams. Below we have furnished two examples of it :

Abdur Rahman bin Auf R.A.A. married an Ansari woman against one nawat of gold as her dower. When the messenger of Allah S.A.W. received information of it, he said:

> May Allah bless you! Throw a walimah feast
> even if it is just one goat you can slaughter.

Nawat is the stone inside the date fruit. This word is used for five dirhams also.

'Amir bin Rabi'ah reports that a certain person married a woman of Fazarah tribe and gave her a pair of shoes as her dower. The Prophet S.A.W. asked the woman whether she was satisfied with that mahr and had given her consent to enter wedlock with him? When she replied in the affirmative he declared that match lawful. Jabir R.A.A. reports the Prophet S.A.W. to have said, "If a person gives his would-be wife a handful of grain and she assents that nikah is permitted."

The first of these reports is to be found in all the six most authentic collections of hadith (Sihah-e-Sitta) and hence its authenticity is unquestionable. The latter are rather weak, but still they are more reliable than the reports put forth in support of fixation of mahr. Moreover, they are supported by other reports also which tell us that the principle parties concerned have the right to fix the mahr, more or less as they are pleased. Whatever, they agree upon is proper and lawful, however, meagre.

The irrefutable fact is that the Shari'ah has not fixed the quantum of mahr but left it to the circumstances of every age, the economic and social status of the man and woman, their family traditions, mutual relations and trust of one another and the needs of the woman. If the intending principal parties so desire they can reduce it to a bare minimum. But they have also the option to keep it high depending on their financial status. The Quran also provides the same guidance. At one place it says:

> Wed them with the leave of their guardians, and give them their dowers, according to what is customary. [21] (Al Quran IV: 25)

Here in this verse the word 'ujoor' in the original Arabic text has been taken to mean mahr and it has been conditioned by 'ma'roof' or common usage (but of the reasonable type). Certainly mahr that has come for mention here is that of the slave girls and not that of free noble women. And according to our 'ulama, they, poor girls are not deemed to be the owners of their dowers. It is their masters whose property it becomes. But this clarifies the point that the Shari'ah aims at assigning the matters relating to mahr according to usage, which are the customs of any period that are likable and not conflicting with the general temperament of the Islamic Shari'ah. That means the quantum of mahr which may be considered suitable and reasonable is the proper mahr. The status of man and woman and the trend of times must be kept in view if it is desired that it should not be looked upon with disfavour.

Another point of interesting discussion relating to mahr has been what is property and to what commodities or substances it is applicable? The Hanafite school has taken to mean cash or things that have some value. It is not used for profit. Abu Bakr Jassas says that the Quranic verse, 'seek them with your properties' clearly points to two things : Firstly mahr can only be that commodity which can be called property and which the woman can take possession of. Secondly, mahr should be handed over to woman so that she can make use of it. In profit both these things are not possible. It is neither entrusted to her nor does she become its possessor. There is another Quranic verse relating to mahr:

> And give the women (on marriage) their dower as an obligation : but if they, of their own good pleasure, remit any part of it to you, take it and enjoy it with right good cheer. [22]
>
> (Al Quran IV: 4)

The words "Give the women their dower" indicate that it is not benefiting the woman in any way but giving her some material object. Benefiting is not the same as giving anything. Again, the words "you can enjoy it," clearly indicate that mahr should be something that can be enjoyed or in return for which something enjoyable can be obtained. For example, if somebody fixes his wife's mahr teaching the Quran, this mahr shall not be proper. And for that matter 'ulama of the Hanafite school of the early days regarded any material return for the teaching of the Quran improper.

Imam Shafi'i R.A.A. says that accepting anything as wages for the teaching of the Quran is permissible and it can also become mahr. His argument is that the tradition mentioned earlier in which the Prophet S.A.W. is reported to have said :

> Rest assured. I have given her in marriage to you for (teaching her) the Quran that you have (know).

And there is also another report :

> I have given her in marriage to you. Teach her some portion of the Quran.

In some other reports there is to be found detail of this affair that he should teach her so many verses. The latter day 'ulama of the Hanafite school have adopted the stand taken by Imam Shafi'i. They regard wages for teaching the Quran in order and its fixation as mahr also proper. Thus the issue is one of unanimity among the 'ulama. It means that mahr can be in the form of cash, land, garden, a house or any other thing having value. And if the woman so desires she may opt for being educated or taught some professional skill in lieu of things material.

After Divorce

Some issues of mahr are related with divorce also. Divorce is possible after proper conjugal privacy or before that. In both these situations either the mahr will have been fixed or its fixation deferred. Thus divorce becomes possible in four different situations, and they are governed by different ordainments.

In case of divorce after proper conjugal privacy and fixation of mahr, full amount of mahr will have to be paid. The Quran says:

> Give the women (on marriage) their dower as an obligation. [23]
>
> (Al Quran IV: 4)

At another place it has been said:

> It is not lawful for you (men) that you should take back any of your gifts (from your wives). [24] (Al Quran 11 : 229)

Divorce after proper conjugal privacy but without previous fixation of mahr also entails payment of mahr, since its payment becomes compulsory after enjoyment of the woman:

> Give them their dowry for the enjoyment you have of them as a duty. [25]
>
> (Al Quran IV: 24)

If the mahr has not already been fixed man and woman can do so by mutual consent. If they are in conflict about its quantum, it will be "mahr-e-mithl" or the quantum in vogue in case of other women of the family.

Imam Razi R.A.A. says that the argument in support of it is that in case of cohabitation with any woman erroneously (mistaking her for his wife), the erring man becomes liable to 'mahr-e-mithl' (like that of the women of the victim's family). On this basis the woman regularly entering wedlock is all the more entitled to 'mahr-e-mithl'.

Divorced before actual cohabitation but after fixation of mahr entiles the woman to half of the fixed amount of mahr.

The Quran has explicitly pointed it out in these words :

> If you divorce them before consummation, but after the fixation of a dower for them, then half of the dower (is due to them), unless they remit it, is the nearest to righteousness. And do not forget liberality between yourselves, for Allah sees well all ye do. [26]
>
> (Al Quran II : 237)

Divorce before consummation, but mahr not fixed entitles the divorce *to mata*' (a suitable gift). The Quran says nothing about the mahr :

> There is no blame on you if ye divorce women before consummation or the fixation of dower, but bestow on them (a suitable gift), the wealthy according to his means and the poor according to his means, - A gift of reasonable amount is due from those who wish to do the right thing. [27] (Al Quran II : 236)

Besides these four situations, there is the fifth one also, that in case of man's death before consummation, and mahr also not being fixed, Imam Malik and Imam Auza'i are of the opinion that the woman shall not get her mahr, and only *mata'a* will accrue to her. The underlying reason being that mahr is the return of the enjoyment of man from her. And since no such relationship comes into existence, the question of mahr does not arise. However, she will get her share from the inheritance of the husband. Imam Shafi'i's well known opinion is also the same.

But Imam Abu Haneefah and Imam Ahmad and some others are of the opinion that the woman shall get *mahr-e-mithl* as well as inheritance. This is supported by a Hadith. Abdullah Ibn Mas'ood was questioned about this very issue — man dying before consummation and fixation of mahr—to which he replied that she will get her dower like that of the other women of her family, neither more nor less than that. She will have to observe iddat and she will also be entitled to her share in the husband's inheritance. Ma'qal bin Sinan Ashja'i said in support of the verdict of Abdullah Ibn-e-Mas'ood, that a woman of his own tribe, Baru' binte-Warshiq had an identical case and the Prophet S.A.W. had pronounced exactly the same decision upon it. This information gladdened Abdullah Ibn Mas'ood very much.

This hadith has come in for critical examination also. But it is not in order. Imam Shafi'i's disciple Imam Mazani says that if this hadith gets proof of authenticity, nothing else shall be accepted but this. Since the Hadith is in order Imam Abu Haneefah's stand appears to be stronger and preferable.

If the woman dies before consummation with mahr unfixed, Hanafite jurisprudence has the same verdict for it.

Full Control

The Quran has on the one side declared that mahr is her right and she has the right to make use of it as she is pleased. And in the first place this right of her is to be recognized. Then she can have it in full if she likes, can make some concession in it or remit it altogether. On the other side man has been told that if she gifts a part of it to him of her own free will, he is permitted to enjoy it :

> But if they of their own good pleasure remit any part of it to you, take it and enjoy it with right good cheer. [28] (Al Quran IV: 4)

This Quranic verse clearly indicated that mahr is the property of woman. She cannot be compelled to forgo her claim to it. She can also utilize it freely. If she remits any portion of it, the husband can enjoy it cheerfully. But if she is remitting it in full or a portion of it under coercion or fear of oppression or tyranny on his part, it would not be lawful for him to be benefited by it. Some 'ulama are of the opinion that if after remission of mahr the woman later changes her mind and demands it she can do so, since it is a pointer to the fact that she had not cheerfully remitted it.

Sha'bi says that a woman came to Qazi Shuraih with her husband. She had given him (husband) some gift which she now wanted to be returned to her. Qazi Shuraih directed the husband to give it back to her. The husband with reference to the verse (quoted above) said that after giving it away she had no right to demand its return. Qazi Shuraih told him that the Quran has laid down the condition of her cheerfully gifting it and only then it can be enjoyed. Now in your case, if she had cheerfully done so, she would not have demanded its return.

It is reported about 'Umar R.A.A. that he wrote to the Qazis that women remit mahr cheerfully as also under coercion. So if the woman wants to go back upon her earlier plighted word, she may be allowed that freedom.

For that matter none of the jurists of the well-known schools of jurisprudence approve of either party, husband or wife taking back the gift once given. But this is a legal issue. What is accepted on all hands is that whatever a woman gifts should be of her own free will having no element of compulsion in it.

At an other place it has been said :

> But if after a dower is prescribed, ye agree mutually (to vary it) there is no blame on you.
> [29] (Al Quran IV : 24)

By the mutual consent of man and woman mahr can be reduced as well as increased. Payment can be immediate or deferred at will by mutual agreement. Total remission allowed just as a change after fixation by mutual negotiation is also possible. For example, a grove was offered in the first instance and later changed to a house.

All these issues depend upon the relations of the husband and the wife, their mutual trust and their circumstances. It is for this reason that the Quran has left it to their mutual accord. In meeting this obligation the pleasant atmosphere created by the facility and freedom in the social life can be easily appreciated.

10

Men's Upperhand

Islam has discussed in detail every aspect of the conjugal life and presented a broad and comprehensive picture of the family. An objection raised against it is that man has been given extraordinary rights and powers, thus curtailing woman's freedom. Man is in authority and rule and can drive her as he is pleased so long as she is shackled through marriage tie. She can in no way take the offensive against him.

This picture of the woman's aggrieved state and helplessness is as far from truth as it is horrible. In painting this dreadful portrait of her, perhaps greater time and effort have been devoted to distortion of Islam than trying to understand its teachings.

Let us take up first of all the religious and moral aspects of this problem which have the basic importance in the Islamic version of familial life. According to Islam the real and basic relationship of the husband and wife is that of affection and love in which both of them in their own spheres and each in his or her own turn tries to please and meet the requirements and provide ease and comfort to the other. The Quran declares this love and affection as one of the Signs of Providence. It says :

> And among His Signs is this, that He created for you mates from among yourselves, that ye may dwell in tranquillity with them, and He has put love and mercy between your (hearts) : Verily in that are Signs for those who reflect. [11] (Al Quran XXX - 21)

At another place, the spouses have been likened to garments for one another :

> They (the women) are your garments and you (men) are their garments. [12]
>
> (Al-Baqarah 2: 187)

This characterisation has a deep significance. Dress has certain attributes. The Quran wants, the same attributes to characterise the relationship of husband and wife. One aspect of the dress is that it is next to one's body and nothing intervenes between the dress and the body. Similar is the relationship of husband and wife in a world of materialistic relationships, the closeness found in conjugal relationship is unique. Secondly, dress protects a person from climatic hardships. Husband and wife are also expected to help one another in overcoming various hardships, in achieving peace and solace and in not letting life become uncomfortable. Thirdly, dress covers those parts of body whose exposure is shameful. Similarly, husband and wife should hide each other's weaknesses and drawbacks and not let them be exposed. Fourthly, dress is a means of adornment. Similarly, husband is adornment for wife and wife for husband. The beauty of this world rests on the harmony of this relationship. Otherwise life will become dull and barren. This particular similie of "dress" is pointing towards many such sublime realities.

And in the tradition of the Prophet (S.A.W.), it has been explained from various angles. In one of his sayings :

> When the husband looks at her she should gladden his heart; if he suggests something she should accept it cheerfully and whichever item of expenditure trait of behaviour, the husband

> disapproves of; she should (abstain from it) and not displease him by insisting on it.

Similarly, a polite husband has been called the best person in the tradition. 'Ayesha (R.A.A.) reports the Prophet (S.A.W.) to have said :

> The better person among you is one who is kindly disposed to his family and I am the best among you in benevolence to my family.

There are many traditions on this theme. If the moral standards stated therein were adopted by the husband and the wife, the family would become the haven of peace and blessings and an ideal society can on those lines, be easily built.

Taking up now directly the problem of man's guardianship and supervision of the family, we notice that every institution big or small needs the services of a supervisor to run it smoothly and maintain perfect discipline in it. It is his responsibility to keep in view the interests of the institution foremost, recognize the right of its members and treat them with love and kindness. Those associated with the institution should also obey the supervisor cheerfully.

So long as he keeps in view the interest of the institution they should not resort to headstrongness and rebellion against him, and in controversial issues his decision should be the last word, to be accepted on all hands. The position of leadership can be the privilege of only one person. In case of more than one person trying to handle its affairs, each one insisting on his or her own opinion, the organisation of the institution will go topsy-turvy. The family too is an institution and a complicated one at that. Its organisation can be maintained only when only one person is at the helm of affairs to manage it. If the authority is duplicated the organization will cease to function. Rather, its very existence will be in peril. The only question that needs consideration is : who is to be the head of the family, man or woman? The following Quranic verse provides answer to this question:

> Men are the protectors and maintainers of women because Allah has given the one more

> (strength) than the other and because they support them from their means. [13]
>
> (Al Quran IV: 34)

Here in this verse two reasons have been advanced for appointing man as the head of the family. Firstly he has superiority over woman and secondly that he spends his substance on her. That means that the Quran has selected man as the head of the family not on the basis of any prejudice but in consideration of his capabilities and his financial responsibilities. Let us now ponder over these two arguments seriously.

Basis of Strength

The physical and mental make-up of man and woman point to the fact that man is better equipped physically and mentally to bear the burden of a family. He is capable of greater effort in seeking the livelihood, his own and that of the family, and can undertake difficult and labour consuming efforts in agriculture, industry and other fields. In the matter of facing the hardships of life and in overcoming them also he manifests better capability. But this marvellous fact can also be witnessed that the jobs that are considered exclusively the woman's fields of activity and she has been at them since the dawn of man's birth, like cooking, tailoring and washing, etc., in these jobs too man exhibits superior skills and powers. The breast of a woman is the centre of finer sentiments and delicate feelings. Both happy and sad events leave her worse than man. Therefore, it occurs to us at first sight that she should be able to express these impressions much more effectively than man. But it is a historical fact that in literature, poetry, art and fine arts, the height of perfection (in both imagination and skill) the level attained by man, woman could not dream of. Man has presided over all the fine arts through the ages. It can be asserted that man had the monopoly in all these departments and woman had no occasion to exhibit her capabilities in them. But this further raises a question: How did man come to have a monopoly here? And how was woman left behind in this race for perfection and superiority in skills? (And there is hardly any answer to this question). So it will have to be admitted that man can furnish better proof of his capacity for perfection in skills as well as put in greater energy and has done so in every age.

When experience furnishes evidence that man is capable of putting in greater amount of energy and superior capabilities, he must naturally be the head of the family. Not to acknowledge man's superiority and trying to put woman on a par with man in every respect is a sort of reaction or prejudice which may sound logical in discussion and debate, but in the battlefield and bivouac of life it cannot go far enough in our support. Here, the hard facts and realities of life have to be admitted.

Now let us consider the financial responsibilities of man. Under the Islamic Law man must pay the woman her dower, accept the responsibilities of her maintenance and provision of her lodging with all the amenities of life. And along with them he has to arrange for the wife's education and training, looking after the religious and moral supervision and undertaking the responsibility of the protection of her life, property, honour and dignity.

Man accepts this burden with the expectation, that under his supervision, his wife shall manage the house, shall provide him peace, shall educate the children and thus co-operate in building up a healthy family.

To meet these different types of financial and administrative responsibilities properly man has been endowed with certain rights, privileges and powers. But they are not absolute and unlimited. There are certain limits beyond which he cannot go in the exercise of those powers and privileges. Undoubtedly in practical life there is a possibility of man's overstepping the prescribed limits and make wrongful use of his powers and woman may become the victim of excesses. Islam does not overlook or disregard this possibility. The woman under these conditions can compel man to abide by the limits through legal action. Under inevitable circumstances she can obtain her freedom through Khula' (legal divorce at the request of the wife) or separation from the husband.

Who is Supreme ?

In their zeal to overreach themselves in championing the cause of woman's lib some persons went to the extent of stripping man totally of the rights, privileges and power devolving on him normally in familial life to meet his onerous responsibilities. But obviously enough in course of being deprived of all authority in his own family and home he cannot be expected to meet his financial responsibilities as the head of the family. So the only feasible solution that presents itself under the changed situation is that woman, who is now in saddle, is the new protector and maintainer and all the rights and powers associated with that position have been vested in her, she must also take upon herself all the responsibilities that formerly used to be man's headache. So long as she does not accept and meet those responsibilities, there can be no justification for transferring the important and difficult job of protecting and maintaining the family to her.

It is usually asserted that under the changing social conditions, woman's maintenance is no more a problem since she has already started making economic efforts, doing jobs and rendering utility services to the society which are remunerative, thus attaining economic independence. But apart from the fact that such working and economically independent women are a negligible minority in our society, the problem is not really one of her own maintenance and independence alone. It also involves bringing up children, their up keep, education and training, liabilities of their marriages and multifarious other problems relating to other members of the family in a wider sense. The question arises weather woman along with her own support can meet fairly and squarely all the other problems devolving on her as the head of her family.

Undoubtedly there have been exceptional women in every age with a sound economic position and, they were also capable of managing family affairs satisfactorily. Such individuals of the female sex are there in our existing society and shall also be there in future. But a gigantic problem is not solved by a microscopic minority, since it concerns along with them the untold millions, each one by herself a problem crying for solution. Apparently enough, notwithstanding the counselling and support of her so-called well-wishers, the champions of the cause of woman's lib, she does not appear to forgo her time-honoured well-recognized right of maintenance, nor is she prepared to shoulder the onerous responsibilities of the familial organization as an independent charge.

11

Property Claims

The chapter of the Qur'an called 'The Woman' (al-Nisa) details in a just manner the share of inheritance that is due to each individual, male and female. According to this chapter, women are not only no longer allowed to be inherited like chattels but, as individuals, they have a legal right to inheritance. 'Men shall have a share in what their parents and kinsmen leave; and women shall have a share in what their parents and kins men leave; whether it be little or much, it is legally theirs'.

This verse was revealed when an Ansari lady came to the Prophet and complained that after her husband's death she and her daughter were prevented from inheriting any of his property. Her husband's brother justified the action by stating that, 'Women do not mount horses, do not endanger themselves and go .into battle', therefore they could not be allowed to inherit.

Right to Inheritance

Before Islam, women were not only deprived of their right to inheritance, but also had no impact over their own destiny, which was a matter between the men of the husband's clan or her own relatives.

During the Jahiliyya, when a man lost his father, brother, or son, and that person left a widow, the heir, taking advantage of the fact that her dowry was paid by the dead man, rushed to the widow, covered her with his cloak, thus claiming (unjustly) to himself the sole right to marry her. When he married her, he denied her of her right to the part of the inheritance constituted by the dowry. But if he decided, for one reason or another, not to have her as a wife, he could then ask another person to marry her in return he would take (for himself) her dowry. However, if the widow (at the time of her husband's death) managed to get to her own clan before the arrival of the heir, he would lose his rights over her in favour of the males of her own clan. New laws regarding women challenged the social structure of a society that had given males the upper hand over females in matters related to inheritance. Therefore, it was inevitable that it would create an uproar among sections of the male population who felt threatened by them and questioned the validity of granting women a share in the inheritance. So, they decided to ignore these laws and continued to apply the customs of the Jahiliyya, hoping that as time went by the Prophet would change them. But the matter was brought to the surface by women themselves who continued to suffer from the Jahiliyya mentality.

For pre-Islamic Arabian society, it was outrageous to allow fatherless children who could not fight or earn a living to have shares in the inheritance. Therefore, they were denied any rights to inheritance. Moreover, they were mistreated and not looked after well, especially young girls who were also the object of sexual abuse. For example, the guardian very often decided to marry the prettiest ones thus securing two things for himself. (1) controlling their share of inheritance; (2) setting away from or escaping: paying a dowry for them. If a fatherless girl happened to be ugly or not pretty enough to persuade him to marry her he would use her ugliness, to oppose any marriage for her. In doing so, he did not have to pay her share of inheritance. If a fatherless girl was ugly, her guardian did not give her her share. He forced her not to marry and waited for her to pass away so that he would assume control over her inheritance. Islam, would not tolerate such inhumane practices, with its egalitarian message which aimed at redressing the injustice of society. It began by affirming the legal right of fatherless children to have a share in their own inheritance and ended by cautioning against depriving them of their due.

Although Islam granted woman the right to inheritance, her share is by no means fair and equal to that given to man. The critics refer to the verse that allows the brother to take twice as much as the share of their sisters. Therefore, they view this as detrimental to the dignity of women. By giving women half the share of men, they say, there is a clear implication that women are inferior to men. This argument has been used by both Muslims and non-Muslims. But it is based on a fallacy. If it happens for one reason or another that one sex receives a greater or lesser share than the other, this does not mean that the recipient of the lesser share is regarded as inferior. The whole issue of inheritance in Islam depends entirely on the social and economic context, and the role or function of a particular sex within it. If this crucial contextual factor is borne in mind, a proper understanding of the verses related to inheritance in the Qur'an would ensue.

The Qur'an has ensured that women could get their shares of inheritance not only as daughters, but also as mothers and wives. The fact that women have been given half the share of male heirs has to be looked at within its social and economic framework. In Islam the wife is to be cared for by her husband, even if she is wealthy enough to maintain herself. By law she is entitled to claim maintenance from her husband. At the same time she is not obliged to spend any of her wealth on the household.

In addition a Muslim woman receives at the time of her marriage a considerable sum of money. This money, which the husband is obliged to pay, constitutes her dowry, or Mahr, which belongs to her alone. She is free to use, spend or invest it in any way she likes. Therefore, as a wife she adds to whatever she receives through inheritance in her capacity as daughter and that, too, without any legal commitment to support either herself or her children.

The position of women is secure as far as inheritance is concerned. Although women have been given half the share of men, their financial situation in the long term is guaranteed. This is due to the fact that the marriage contract gives her the right to ask for Mahr as well as claim maintenance, both of which entail no legal commitment to anybody including herself.

But it may be objected, what about women who cannot marry for one reason or another? What about the ones who cannot work and earn a living, especially in the rural areas where women have been denied the chance to gain a decent education? How would they live and maintain themselves?

Quranic Injunctions

The Quranic injunctions make it clear that male relatives, especially brothers, have the obligation to care for women and meet their financial needs. At the moment, in most Muslim countries this issue has been left to the individual conscience, which has led to many cases of abuse and desertion. Therefore, in order to secure and protect these women, governments need to legislate and make it legally binding on those male relatives to pay for the upkeep of their needy women.

The Qur'an makes it clear that a person is entitled to make a will. Indeed, it is highly recommended by the Prophet that a person should prepare a will as early as possible and not wait until it is too late. Contrary to the misconception held by large sections of the Muslim public that a person has no right to make a will, both the Qur'an and the Sunnah encourage people to do so. There are even some misguided jurists who argue, contrary to clear principles in the Qur'an, that Islam does not recommend the making of wills. This negative attitude advocated by a small band of jurists has confused ordinary Muslim people and has led many to abandon the idea of making wills.

The Qur'an, on the other hand, has specifically asked for the distant relatives, the needy people and the orphans to be treated kindly and to be helped if they are present at the time of the division of inheritance:

> If relatives, orphans, or needy men are present at the division of an inheritance, give them, too, a share of it, and speak to them in kind words.

The Virtues

So, if the Quran is so kind even to distant relatives and needy people by virtue of the fact that it encourages people to give them some share of the inheritance, we see no problem, in keeping with this spirit of Divine Justice, that a bequest be made in favour of a needy person, particularly if this person is a close member of the family. The point here is emphasised that if parents think that their daughter is unable to get married for whatever reason and she is in a disadvantaged position, they can write a will in her favour in order to secure her future. This accords with the spirit of the Qur'an and the Sunnah.

The position of Muslim women as far as inheritance is concerned is secure and guaranteed by the Islamic Law. But in practice this is not the case. Constantly, the Divine instructions concerning women's rights to inheritance are violated and overlooked by Muslim societies. Social, political, economic and cultural factors play a major role in determining who does and who does not take a share. In such situations the weak have always been kept at bay when it comes to their right to inheritance. This takes place in both the cities as well as the rural areas.

Very often, strong social pressure is applied on women to renounce their shares for the benefit of the immediate male members of the family. This is particularly the case when women are well off or married to wealthy men. Their due is automatically written off and transferred to their male relatives. Whether they like it or not they are all too often forced to accept the loss of their shares; if they refuse, they are accused of being selfish, greedy, inconsiderate and irresponsible.

Often this has led to tension, friction and conflict of interests among the members of the family, shattering the whole concept of caring and sharing which lies at the heart of the Islamic faith. Here are a few examples which illustrate the evident disregard for the Divine decrees regarding women's right to inheritance.

Islamic Concept

The Islamic concept of broad and equitable shares which take into consideration the interests of all persons concerned has been transferred into a prerogative for males, outrageously disregarding the Divine Will. There is no doubt about the fact that in most parts of the Muslim world the Islamic Law concerning women's rights to inheritance is not in operation; instead it is the social and cultural rules which dominate. It is crucial that something has to be done to rectify this situation, and women themselves have an essential role to play in the process of any such change.

12

Goodness of Faith

Due to these very reasons 'modesty' is a part and parcel of the faith of Islam and Allah's Messenger (peace and blessings of Allah be upon him) has laid special stress on these virtues and has exhorted his followers to inculcate these virtues. Allah's Messenger (peace and blessings of Allah be upon him) once heard an Ansari saying to his brother:

Do not be much ashamed. He forbade him from saying this:

> Because modesty is half of Faith. (Mishkat)

'Modesty' as defined in the Shari'ah is a virtue which prevents a man from doing all such deeds as are abhorrible in the Shari'ah.

> Modesty brings only goodness. (Mishkat)
>
> Shame and modesty are laudable virtues in human life.
>
> They must be reflected in one's conduct, behaviour, and speech. He who is devoid of these virtues is easily led astray.

> If you have no shame you can do what you like. (Mishkat)

Due to this very reason, Allah's Messenger (peace and blessings of Allah be upon him) once said:

> Modesty is a part of faith and faith would lead to Paradise and rudeness would lead to Hell fire. (Mishkat)

After explaining the importance of shame and modesty, the detail of all such things as lead to immodesty and immorality and the remedial measures suggested by Islam are given in the following pages. We can judge how far it is necessary to act upon these principles if we want to lead a pious and healthy life.

In this category first comes 'evil gaze' which is the mother of all evils and their main-spring. Islam has first of all blocked this avenue of sin and has called evil gazing as an adultery of the eyes. Every one is aware of the arrows shot by the eyes. While defining love, it has rightly been said that it is an unseen thing which enters the heart through the eyes. Poets have written volumes about them and have said: How many eyes there are which dart arrows which pierce into the hearts. The poets of every time and every age agree on this point that the eyes move the hearts. It has been said in the Holy Quran:

> Tell the believing men to lower their gaze and be modest. That is purer for them. Lo! Allah is aware of what they do. (24:30)

Islam by imposing this restriction has blocked the way to sin and vice. It teaches its followers not to do anything deliberately or inadvertently which may ultimately lead to evil act. The eyes have been called by the pious men of the past as transmitter of messages of love and, therefore, Islam lays stress on keeping the eyes under control. It exhorts its followers to keep their eyes downward and avoid immodest stray glancing. This would be helpful in maintaining the purity of heart and soul. To keep the eyes downward is the demand of nature and has been ordained by Allah as women have an irresistable fascination for men. It has been said in the Holy Quran:

> Beautiful for mankind is love of the joys (that come) from women. (3:14)

A further probe into the matter would reveal that evil of the eyes is the basis of all mischief. Imam Ghazali has written: You must restrain from evils of the eyes as these are the cause of all mischief

In the first part of the verse there is an admonition that even if it is permissible to look at any one, he should obey Allah and avoid gazing. Secondly, there is a warning in the verse and the result of turning away the eyes would be that his soul would be purified and his interest and fervour would be increased in the *ibadah*. If he would not act upon these instructions, he is bound to go astray. His peace of mind would be shattered and his heart would become a store-room of devilish insinuations. In the concluding lines of the verse there is a warning that if the people did not care for these instructions, Allah, the Exalted is all aware.

The Holy Prophet (peace and blessings of Allah be upon him) has observed:

> I have not left any mischief more harmful for men than women. (Mishkat)
>
> Be afraid of the world and women as the first mischief of Bani Israel started in women. (Mishkat)

Allah, the Exalted, keeping in view the human nature and the sexual instinct ingrained in him not only permitted him to marry, but also ordained marriage. Thereafter He taught him how to control his passionate nature. He imposed restriction on free, loose sexual behaviour and allowed sexual gratification within the limits prescribed by Him. Thus, the humanity was saved from moral degradation, hatred and discord.

Whereas Islam has given the lesson of piety to men, it has not overlooked women as both are by nature alike. The difference is only that of degree. Woman is not divested of sexual desire and its natural demands. It has been mentioned in the Holy Quran:

> And tell the believing women to lower their gaze and be modest, and to display their adornment only that which is apparent. (24:31)

It is clear from the above verse that unrestricted and immodest gazing stimulates the sexual desire. There is such an allurement in the eyes that it hardly takes any time to entice the heart and mind.

As far as the sexual instinct is concerned there is little difference between the two sexes and the feminine eyes make more mischief. Woman is by nature more sentimental and is easily carried away. Because of her capricious nature, she must be more careful in controlling her eyes lest a handsome man should captivate her heart. It is also possible that the man might be already burning in the fire of her love without her being aware of it.

Sometimes the woman is not affected; but her careless wayward glances disturb the peace of mind of man who, blinded by the passion, does all in his power to get her by hook or crook. Sometimes he tries to play with her modesty by force. A letter of a girl was published in the Siddq Jadid of 21st March, 1951:

> "When I go to school, five or six boys pursue me."

Rules and Regulations

> In view of the above verse and many other verses of the Holy Quran, there is consensus among the Ulama (scholars) that it is not lawful for a woman to gaze at a stranger the gaze may be lewd or not. The Ahadith also support this view. Hadrat Umm Salarna (Allah be pleased with her) has reported: I and Maimuna (may Allah be pleased with her) were in the company of Allah's Messenger (peace and blessings of Allah be upon him) when a blind man entered for some need. Seeing Ibn Maktum, Allah's Messenger (peace and blessings of Allah be upon him)

> asked us to go behind the veil. I said: O Allah's Messenger! Is he (Ibn Maktum) not blind. He said: Are you both too blind and do not see him. (Mishkat)

This incident occurred after the revelation of instructions regarding purdah (veil). It is clear from this Hadith that women are not permitted to look at men. Sa'id b. Jubair while explaining the meaning of the verse 24:31 has said that believing women have been ordained to abstain from all indecencies. Qatadah and Sufyan say that women should guard against all unlawful and forbidden acts. Hadrat Maulana Ashraf Ali Thanvi writes:

A woman is not permitted to cast a lewd glance deliberately at any one except her husband. As far as looking without lust is concerned, a woman can look at the body of another woman except the portion between navel and knees and it is strictly forbidden for her to see that portion of a man's body. So far as the other parts of his body are concerned, there is divergence of cpinion among the 'Ulama. According to the Shafi'ites it is forbidden but according to Hanafites it is not forbidden to see without lust but it is against the way of the ancestors. There is a Hadith in Tirmidhi, Nasa'i and Bayhaqi that when Ibn Makturn requested to see the Holy Prophet (peace and blessings of Allah be upon him), the latter asked Umm Salama and Maimuna to go behind the curtain. They said: He is a blind man. He won't be able to see us.

Thereupon the Holy Prophet (peace and blessings of Allah be upon him) said: Are you too blind, would you not see him? It is, however, permitted to see if there is need of the Shari'ah. If any one happens to cast a glance he should turn away his look, there being no sin in it. The word which has been used in the verse implies that on some occasions it is permitted to see while on others it is forbidden.

Hafiz Ibn Qayyim has observed: The eye conveys the messages of love and stimulates the lust. By controlling the stray glances one can guard one's modesty and chastity. He who does not restrain his look ruins himself. It is the root-cause of all devilish thoughts which badly affect the heart and mind, and arouse sexual passions. The intention to gratify the sexual urge is born out of these devilish thoughts and when a man determines to commit this evil deed he commits it as and when he finds an opportunity for it. (Al-Jawab Al-Kafi) If the arrow shot by the eyes hits the heart of a person once, its wound is never healed. The sting of its pain is felt every now and then. He knows no rest and heaves deep sighs; the pangs of separation are unbearable for him. The life becomes hard for him. The Holy Prophet (peace and blessings of Allah be upon him) has warned against this: Glance is one of the poisoned arrows of the Iblis. (Al-Jawab, Al-Kafi) The Holy Prophet (peace and blessings of Allah be upon him) observed in a lengthy Hadith:

> The fornication of the two eyes is (evil) glance; the fornication of the two ears is the hearing, (obscene) talk is the fornication of the tongue and fornication of the hand is (evil) touch and grasp, and the fornication of the foot is the steps (taken for committing evil) and the heart desires and longs and the private parts either accord with or does contrary to it. (Mishkat)

Some learned people have observed:

> The glance is an arrow which injects poison into the heart.

One must, therefore, take care in casting a glance and it may cause great mischief. It has ruined the moral character of many people and nations and created enemities among many families. It is the root cause of moral corruption.

> Due to the above reasons the Holy Prophet (peace and blessings of Allah be upon him) has instructed us to keep our eyes downward and has impressed upon us the importance of this commandment by explaining the various aspects of this problem. He once said to Hadrat 'Ali (Allah be pleased with him): " O'Ali! After casting one glance, don't cast a second as you are permitted to glance only once and not after that." (Mishkat)

> If any one suddenly casts a glance at a woman, it is not a sin as he is helpless in the matter; but he is not permitted to cast a second glance. This does not mean that there is permission to see for the first time. Hadrat Jarir bin 'Abdullah Al-Ba ali has reported that I asked the Holy Prophet (peace and blessings of Allah be upon him), What is your commandment about a sudden glance. He ordained: You should turn away your glance. (Mishkat)
>
> According to a tradition, the Holy Prophet observed: Cast your glance downward.
> (Ibn Kathir)

There are different ways in which one can turn away one's glance. The main object behind this action is that one should avoid this sin by turning away one's gaze or by gazing downward or by fixing gaze on something else. Once the Holy Prophet (peace and blessings of Allah be upon him) questioned in the company of his followers: Which thing is good for a woman? No one answered and all of them kept silent. Hadrat 'Ali (Allah be pleased with him) said: I too was present in this company and could give no reply. When I came home I asked this question from Hadrat Fatimah (Allah be pleased with her): Which thing is good for women? She at once answered: The best thing is that they should remain immune from the glances of (strange) men.

Hadrat 'Ali (Allah be pleased with him) was so pleased with this reply that he told it to the Holy Prophet (peace and blessings of Allah be upon him). He too was glad and said: Fatimah is my daughter.

It is prohibited to form a gathering and sit in the street as every kind of men happen to pass there. It is possible that some irresponsible glance may accost you and cause a mischief. Once the Holy Prophet (peace and blessings of Allah be upon him) said to his Companions: Avoid sitting in streets and thoroughfares. The Companions said that sometimes they are compelled to do so. Thereupon he observed: In that case you must fulfil the right (abide by the rules and regulations) of the way. The Companions asked: What is this right. He answered: To keep the glance downward, to refrain from molesting (anyone), to respond As-Salam and to enjoin good and forbid evil.

> Once the Holy Prophet (peace and blessings of Allah be upon him) observed: You take the responsibility for six things, I assure you of Paradise: When you speak with anyone do not tell a lie. When something is entrusted to you, you do not deceive. When you promise, you do not back out. You keep your gaze downward and hold your hands (from aggression) and guard your chastity. (Ibn Kathir)
>
> Those six things include gazing downward and protection of modesty and chastity. One can easily understand the importance of guarding the glance. There is a Hadith in Musnad Ahmad that the Holy Prophet (peace and blessings of Allah be upon him) said: If any believer happens to cast his first glance at the beauty of a woman and then turns his sight away, Allah the Exalted, creates sweetness for him in his 'Ibada (prayer, worship etc). (Mishkat)
>
> It has been mentioned in Tabrani that the Holy Prophet (peace and blessings of Allah be upon him) said: You should keep your glance downward and protect your modesty and chastity. (Ibn Kathir)
>
> Once the Holy Prophet (peace and blessings of Allah be upon him) said: A glance is one of the poisoned arrows of Iblis. He who guards it for fear of Allah, he would turn it into sweetness of Faith and the believer would relish its taste in his heart. (Ibn Kathir)

It is mentioned in Sahih al-Bukhari that the Holy Prophet (peace and blessings of Allah be upon him) said: Whosoever determined to maintain chastity, has glad-tidings of Paradise from Allah.

> He who takes the responsibility (of guarding) what is between the beards and the feet, I assure him of Paradise. (Ibn Kathir)

> Ibn Kathir has mentioned a Hadith that the Holy Prophet (peace and blessings of Allah be upon him) said: On the Day of Resurrection, all eyes would be weeping except a few which would be happy. The eye which remained immune from seeing what has been forbidden to see; the eye which remained awakened in the cause of Allah and the eye which shed tears out of fear of Allah. (Ibn Kathir)

From the above details it is easy to understand that along with many other preventive measures it has also been ordained to keep the eyes under control as irresponsible behaviour might ultimately lead to sin and vice. Great emphasis has also been laid on guarding the private parts. Modesty and chastity are the valuable assets which build up the character and morale of the people. It is the duty of an honourable nation to adopt all lawful ways and means to protect them, otherwise, there would remain no law and order and sins, crimes, hatred and discord would be rampant everywhere.

In this connection separate instructions have also been given to women. As a matter of principle, the address to men also holds good for women but by addressing the women separately more emphasis has been laid on this point. It has been said in the Holy Qur'an:

> Beautiful for mankind is love of the joys (that come) from women. (3:14)

Due to the above reasons great restrictions have been imposed on women and the Shari'ah has imposed limitations on their going out freely. It is common experience that free mixing of women with men gives rise to many evils. It has been mentioned in the Holy Qur'an:

> And stay in your houses. Bedizen not yourself with the bedizenment of the Days of Ignorance. (33:33)

This revelation has a special purpose; but the instructions contained therein are applicable to all.

Allah, the Exalted has asked the women to forsake the custom of the Days of Ignorance and live within the limits prescribed by Him.

During the Days of Ignorance, the women devised all ways and means to decorate themselves in order to look more attractive in the company of men. They wore necklace, earrings and all sorts of ornaments. They covered their breasts with dupatta in such a way that they looked more prominent. Men were carried away by emotions. The women used to walk briskly waving their bodies. Their beauty and coquettishness was irresistible. When Islam came, it forbade the women from these habits of the Days of Ignorance. It taught them piety and modesty and told them to stay in their houses. However, if they came out in case of necessity, they must discard their embellishment.

> It would not be out of place to mention here that purdah was not enjoined during the first days of Islam; but it was enjoined during the fifth year after the Hijrah. Hadrat 'Umar (Allah be pleased with him) desired from the core of his heart that the believing women should observe purdah and he expressed this desire on several occasions. Purdah is one of the heart-felt desires of Hadrat 'Umar which Allah, the Exalted fulfilled. There is a Hadith in Sahihain that Hadrat 'Umar reported: I said to the Holy Prophet (peace and blessings of Allah be upon him) O Messenger of Allah! All sort of persons, good and bad come to your house. Would that you keep them (your wives) in purdah. Thereupon, Allah, the Exalted, revealed the verse Al-Hijab. (Bukhari)

It happened so at the time of marriage of Hadrat Zainab hint Jahsh that the Holy Prophet (peace and blessings of Allah be upon him) arranged the marriage feast (Walima) and invited the people to it. As a rule, all people were required to leave after dinner; but three persons did not move from their seats and remained busy in talking. The Holy Prophet (peace and blessings of Allah be upon him) would not ask them to go out of courtesy; but he was annoyed at their stay for such a long period. On that occasion Allah, the Exalted, revealed complete instructions regarding veil (Hijab). It is permitted to ask anything from women in need; but in a reasonable and decent way:

> And when ye ask of them (the wives of the Prophet) anything, ask it from behind a curtain.
>
> (33:53)

Although the above instructions were revealed on a specific occasion, yet they are applicable to all. It has been ordained that if you need anything from women, ask it from behind the curtain so that both men and women should not face each other. This is a more proper way to protect one's modesty and chastity and to guard against doubts and misconceptions.

It is an admitted fact that when strange men and women meet there is every chance that some of them might be led astray. Moreover, it provides an opportunity to the devil to spread rumours and scandals. We do not at all mean that women cannot be relied upon or that men are devils. Both are good and reliable. History bears out the fact that wicked persons and the enemies have slandered many a pious and chaste women and every one is fully aware of its evil consequences. It is, therefore, necessary that all ways and means should be adopted to put an end to this evil practice of free mixing of men and women. The history of Western morals has exposed the evil consequences of free contacts of men and women. Our co-educational institutions are also not immune from the evils of this freedom. It would be a blessing for the Muslim community if it observes purdah in the strict sense of the Shari'ah.

Meeting Points

A woman expresses her feelings and sentiments in the following words:

> "As regards the moral character of women who come out of co-educational institutions, I can

> say that co-education destroys their inherent modesty and chastity. They acquire masculine habits which render them quite unfit for home-life. The education which is being imparted in our Universities on the Western pattern is not necessary for our womenfolk."

Let us see the condition of the countries where co-education is in vogue. The judge Lindsay writes about the co-educational institutions of America:

> Four hundred and ninety-five girls of teen age studying at the high school level confessed before me that they had sexual experience with boys.

He further adds:

According to an estimate at least forty-five percent of girls studying at the high school lose their modesty before leaving the schools.

A Western woman Mrs. Dowan has written in her article "Hurdle in Female Education":

> The last point which I want to emphasise is how much do we extol co-education, the sentimental nature of adolescence period cannot be overcome and in some cases, it creates hurdles in whole-hearted application to work. Daily mixing up of boys and girls not only develops sentimental attachment between them but also it is destructive for education and discipline. Most harmful effect is that sometimes the students develop sentimental and illicit relations with their teachers. What we have said above has been taken from the writings and experiences of modem educated men and women. We have given above the deplorable

> condition of educated persons and educational institutions. You can well judge the condition of the general public.

Believe that the Islamic teachings are based on immense prudence, wisdom and human insight. If we want to uplift the general moral, standard and protect human modesty and chastity, we must propagate its golden principles and adopt them as part and parcel of our Faith.

There is no denying the fact that there are different categories of men and women in every age. Where there are pious and noble persons there also live evil and wicked persons who are always on the look out for an opportunity to commit evil. They go about casting ugly and evil glances. They are recognized by their conduct and behaviour. These wicked persons try to tease the women about whom they come to know as belonging to the other tribe. Allah, the Exalted, has ordained in the Holy Qur'an to observe the following instructions in such circumstances:

> O Prophet! Tell thy wives and thy daughters and the women of the believers to draw over them their Jalabib (when they go abroad); this will be more proper that they may be known, and thus they will not be molested. (33:59)

It has been enjoined in the above verse that believing women should cover themselves with Jalabib so that they could be recognized as pious and chaste ladies so that the wicked and evil minded persons may not dare tease them.

It is common experience that the women who wear fantastic dresses and display their decoration and beauty are not held in high esteem in society. The people cast glances at them and try to entince them. On the contrary, no one can dare tease a pious and chaste lady. Maulana Shabbir Ahmad 'Uthmani has added the following comments on this verse:

That is, along with covering the bodies with Jalabib, parts thereof should remain hanging on the faces. On receipt of this revelation, believing women went out covering their bodies and faces in such a way that their one eye remained uncovered to enable them to see. The face is, therefore, required to be covered by a free woman if there is fear of being molested by the wicked men.

The Manners

In the Holy Prophet's time some wicked Jews and hypocrites used to tease women and even pious and chaste ladies did not remain immune from them. By ordering Jalabib distinction was made as to the dress of the believing women. It has been mentioned in the Holy Qur'an:

> If the hypocrites, and those in whose heart is a disease, and the alarmists in the city do not cease, We verily shall urge thee on against them, then they will be your neighbour in but a little while. (33:60)

He who still annoyed any believing woman despite the fact that she wore special dress, was liable to punishment and in the Holy Prophet's time (peace and blessings of Allah be upon him) a number of Jews were expelled.

In other words, according to the Holy Qur'an it is not permissible for a woman to go out except in the case of necessity as has been ordained in the first verse. There is a clear Hadith:

> A woman is required to maintain purdah. When she comes out, the devil stares at her. It is a blessing that she should remain within her house. (Ibn Kathir)

If, however, she is to go out, in the case of need, she must keep her gaze downward. She must avoid such sex-stimulating functions, societies, clubs, theatres, cinemas, dancing and singing parties where men and women mix up freely as the believing women have been ordained:

> And tell the believing women to lower their gaze. (24:31)

Then they have been ordered that if they go out in need they should cover their bodies and the purdah is for the whole body of a free woman except the palms of her hand and her face as is evident from the verse:

> And to display their adornment only that which is apparent. (24:31)

Moreover, if they go out or come across any one they should cover themselves in dopatta in such a way that the outlines of their bodies are not visible as has been ordained in the above mentioned verse:

> O Prophet! Tell thy wives and thy daughters and the women of the believers to draw over them their Jalabib. (33:59)

It has been said in another verse:

> And tell the believing women to draw their veils over their bosoms. (24:31)

Dopatta means head-covering. A woman is required to cover her head and bosom with dopatta in such a way that the outlines of her body are not visible. In the Days of Ignorance, dopatta was used in such a way that the outlines of the body and bosom became most prominent. Islam ordained the woman to observe complete purdah. It has been observed by Hadrat 'A'isha (Allah be pleased with her):

> May Allah have mercy on women who migrated first. When dopatta was enjoined, they tore out their coverings and made dopatta out of them. (Bukhari)

Ibn Kathir has quoted many other Ahadith from which it is clear that the above instructions were fully observed in the days of the Holy Prophet (peace and blessings of Allah be upon him) and those of his Companions.

If they go out, they should not display their beauty and decoration nor try to attract others openly or secretly. Their outer self and inner self should be free from evil and sin. Allah, the Exalted, knows best what is in the hearts:

> He knoweth the traitor of the eyes, and that which the bosoms hide. (40:19)

As regards the outward behaviour, Allah, the Exalted, has ordered:

> And let them not stamp their feet so as to reveal what they hide of their ornament And turn unto Allah together, O believers, in order that ye may succeed. (24:31)

Women generally wear many kinds of ornaments. In some of them bells are set which give melodious sounds at the time of walking. Such ornaments are absolutely prohibited in the Islamic Shari'ah. Some ornaments give sounds when they strike with the other such as rings and bangles. It is permissible to wear them; but care should be taken by a woman that they should not give sounds when she is walking. Care should also be taken that the glare of these ornaments should not be dazzling others' eyes as the sound and glare of ornaments can cause mischief.

Character Supreme

Anyone who has some experience of this world or grain of sense cannot deny the wisdom behind these instructions. The people who do not act upon these instructions are bound to err. One has just to turn over the pages of the newspapers to find the news of moral crimes.

There is no denying the fact that a young man is easily wounded by the arrow cast by the Cupid of love and sacrifices his all for the sake of his love. Islam fully realizes the significance of this fact and suggests measures to block all the ways leading to moral turpitude. It has thus saved the humanity from being soiled with the filth of immorality.

This is not all. Islam has ordained that if a woman is required to speak to a stranger, even from behind the curtain, her tone should not be soft so that the visitor should have no misconception and he should remain within limit. It has been mentioned in the Holy Qur'an:

> If ye keep your duty (to Allah), then be not of soft of speech, but he in whose heart is a disease aspire (to you), but utter customary speech. (33:32)

The specific feminine style of talking sweetly is meant only for the husband. This style is forbidden to be used for any one else. The way of talking with a stranger should be customary and to the point. Ostentatious and coquettish way of talking should be avoided as it may lead to misconception and evil. The scholars of Islam are of the view that a woman is allowed to talk with a stranger in need; but according to some scholars, the voice of a woman also comes under the items of purdah which implies that her tone should not be sweet and melodious. Moreover, she is forbidden to talk with men without need. The author of *Dur Mukhtar*, has written on the authority of Allama Muqaddasi:

> No one should interpret as containing the meaning that woman is prohibited to speak with strangers. We are of the view that a woman is allowed to talk with a stranger in need; but we are against her talking in a sweet, melodious and fascinating style to attract men and to excite their passion. Women are, therefore, forbidden to call Adhan as it is generally called in a sweet, melodious voice.

Islam has forbidden the woman to display her decoration or to come unveiled before strangers or to speak to them in a sweet, melodious tone except her some very near relatives for whom she always entertains good and noble sentiments such as her father, her son, her nephew, etc. It has been mentioned in the Holy Qur'an:

> And tell the believing women not to reveal their adornment save to their own husbands or fathers or husband's fathers, or their sons or their husband's sons, or their brothers or their brother's sons, or their women, or their slaves,

> or male attendants who lack vigour, or children
> who know naught of women's nakedness.
>
> (24:31)

The word 'brother' used in the above verse means full brother. It does not mean cousins or brothers by relation i.e. uncle's son, maternal uncle's son, father's sisters' son and others by relationship with whom marriage is allowed do not come under the definition of 'brother'.

The term Mahram used in the Holy Qur'an means the persons with whom marriage is disallowed and a woman is allowed to come before them without veil. She need not cover her decoration before them. The practice of not observing purdah before cousins which is in vogue in India, Pakistan and other countries is against the Shariah as the term 'brother' implies full brother and not brother by relation. 'Your women' means your believing women purdah is also required to be observed from the disbelieving women as they also fall under the category of strangers. However, purdah is not required to be observed from the maid servants. The servant also comes under the category of a stranger. If he is of matured age, it is necessary that purdah should be observed from him.

It is not necessary to observe purdah from boys of immature age or men who have no inclination for women or insane persons who have no distinction of men and women. Purdah, however, is required to be observed from all the remaining persons whether they are old or impotent or without sexual organ.

Even before whom there is no purdah of decoration, a woman should not display her decoration unnecessarily. However, if it is exposed by chance, there is no harm in the Shariah. The only parts of the body the exposure of which is permitted in the Shari'ah are palms of hands, and face and at the most the parts of the body i.e., ears, arms, neck on which ornaments are worn can be exposed before a Mahram. It is, however, not necessary to hide any part of the body before the husband although etiquette demand that they should avoid seeing each others private parts. Even a eunuch is not allowed to enter the women's apartment.

According to the Shariah, a boy of adolescence is not allowed to go near the women folk nor are the women permitted to display their decoration before him. It has been observed by the Holy Prophet (peace and blessings of Allah be upon him):

> Refrain from going to the company of women.
>
> (Mishkat)

The practice of not observing purdah from the husband's relatives and playing jokes with them which is in vogue in our country is against the Shari'ah. Husband's brothers and all other relatives except his father come under the category of Ghair Mahram. It is therefore better to keep aloof from them as they may cause more mischief due to their easy access.

Islam forbids all such acts which are hazardous for piety and morality and ultimately lead to ignominy and disgrace. The evil consequences of meeting of men and women in solitude are best known to every one. The slander and disgrace which such meetings bring to the family are also not hidden from anyone. So the Holy Prophet (peace and blessings of Allah be upon him) has strictly forbidden the meeting of men and women in solitude:

> Man and woman do no meet in solitude except
> when the third person, devil, is among them.
>
> (Mishkat)

In this state (of loneliness), the devil tries to excite their lust by infusing evil and lewdness in their hearts. If he fails to do so, he induces some one else to spread rumours and scandals against them and cast a slur on their fair names.

The main cause of the social evils in the modern society is that men and women mix freely and discuss their feelings and sentiments without any qualms of conscience.

It has been forbidden to visit the houses of women whose husbands are away. The reason for imposing this restriction is that the devil rushes through us like the blood rushing through our veins. There is every possibility that he succeeds in dragging us into sin and vice by exciting our lust.

> The devil rushes through the individual like the circulation of blood. (Mishkat)

It has been mentioned in the above Hadith that the narrator enquired from the Holy Prophet (peace and blessings of Allah be upon him) about himself. He observed: The same was the position with me but due to Allah's grace and mercy, I overcame the devil and now I am quite immune.

> The same was the position with me; but Allah helped me and now he has surrendered.
> (Mishkat)

The irresistible charm and attraction which man and woman possess for each other can be judged from the above Hadith. No one can deny that much of the evil and mischief prevalent in the world today is due to free mixing of the two sexes.

Hadrat Safiyya, the wife of the Holy Prophet (peace and blessings of Allah be upon him) said: Allah's Messenger (peace and blessings of Allah be upon him) was observing 'Itikaf. One night I went to see him. I had a talk with him. Then I got up to return. The Holy Prophet (peace and blessings of Allah be upon him) accompanied me to my house. On the way we came across two respectable men of Ansar. Seeing the Holy Prophet (peace and blessings of Allah be upon him) they quickened their footsteps. Thereupon he said: Here with me is Saffyyaya bint Hye. They said: Glory be to Allah! OAllah's Messenger! How can we have any doubt about you. He replied:

> Verily, the devil rushes through the son of Adam like blood and I fear lest he should put something evil in your hearts.
> (Riyad Al-Salihin)

So far we have discussed this subject in the light of the Holy Qur'an, the Ahadith and from purely intellectual point of view; but some people are not convinced unless they are given the arguments of the West. We reproduce here some excerpts from the *Encyclopaedia Britannica* for these people. The Western writers also support our views:

In the Roman empire, which was the mainspring of Western culture and civilization and which stood at the highest pinnacle of progress and prosperity, the women observed purdah and they had nothing to do with outside activities. It has been mentioned in the nineteenth century Encyclopaedia:

> Roman women took interest in works like men. They remained busy in domestic works. Their husbands, fathers and brothers were warriors and laid down their lives in the battle-field. After household work, the other important jobs for women were to spin cotton and to weave after cleaning wool. Roman women strictly observed purdah. Even the nurses among them when they went out used to cover their faces with thick veils and their bodies with thick covering which went upto their knees. Then they put on big cloaks over them so that none, could see their faces or the construction of their bodies.
>
> (Musalman 'Aurat)

It was the time when the country and its people stood at the highest pinnacle of progress and prosperity. They excelled in all spheres and departments of life; but just then they began to revel in joyous, voluptuous and lewd parties. Women were invited to these jolly parties and without them these were considered to be quite useless and incomplete. The result was that purdah was discarded and the women became immodest and flirts and moved in the clubs and night parties. They began to participate in singing and dancing parties. The result was that the Roman empire and all its pomp and show was razed to the ground. If the women were not given undue freedom this would not have happened. 'Allama Farid Wajadi writes in the light of historical facts:

> It happened that when purdah was discarded by women, men were naturally drawn towards them fascinated by their beauty and charm. They began to cut each others throat. No one can deny this great political fact.
>
> (Musalman 'Aurat)

Allama Luis Parol has written an article "Political Evils" *in The Review of Reviews*. He says:

> Woman is responsible for sapping the foundations of excellent morals and behaviours.

He further says:

> In the last days of the romantic Roman empire the governors and rulers very much liked the company of delicate, passionate women who were found in large number.(Musalman 'Aurat)

Luis Parol proceeds

> You will have to go through the pages of history to understand the downfall of the nations. The expenditure and burden on the exchequer rose; the moral of the people became low and there was rapid increase in crimes and raping and moral values lost their significance and hatred and discord prevailed everywhere.

He further writes:

> Due to this free contact of men and women, the Romans were addicted to such despicable habits as cannot be explained. Their spirit and morale became low: their courage and aspirations were gone and their temperament became mean and avaricious Hatred and discord overcame them and they began to shed each others blood with the result that they lost all sense of morality and humanity. (Musalman 'Aurat)

We have given above a historical fact. Even the Western scholars have supported the Islamic rules and regulations concerning purdah. They have been compelled to do so in the light of their day to day experience.

A scholar of physical science, Xzol Siman writes in an article:

> "A woman must always remain a woman. Yes, she must always remain a woman; herein lies her salvation. It is this character of hers which can make her happy and, successful. It is a law and directive of nature. A woman who is nearer to this law would command respect and honour and whosoever would deviate from this law would suffer and add to her worries. Some philosophers consider that life is devoid of piety; but I am of the view that life is beautiful, it is noble and pious, very pious provided every man and woman is conscious of the status and duties assigned to him/her by nature and fulfils them conscientiously.

The western scholars are constrained to say that a woman who does not fulfil her conjugal duties cannot be called a woman. Xzol Siman mentions:

> "A woman who goes out for job may perform the duty of the vast world stretched before her; but loses her feminine traits."
>
> (Musalman 'Aurat)

In the present day many Muslims argue against the institution of purdah in Islam under the influence of western civilization but they have never cared to study the view of the western scholars regarding purdah. We give below an excerpt from the writings of August Count. He says:

> "In the absence of husband or any relative, it is the duty of the people to provide means of sustenance to the woman by spending out of their wealth lest she should have to do a job outside under the stress of need because as far as possible the activities of a woman should be restricted to her house. We should try to save

> her from outside hardships and difficulties and her sphere of work should be restricted to her household and she should not be compelled to go out.

You have seen that the people are bound to act upon the principles of Islam. According to Islam the poor and helpless women are paid from Baitul Mal to fulfil their need and the western scholars are compelled to say that this burden should be borne by the society.

(Musalman 'Aurat)

Every one knows that the freedom of women is disastrous for themselves. It eats into the vitals of a nation. It takes the women to the Hell-Fire. Women are happy over the rights given to them. They can get employment in every department; but perhaps they do not know that they are being driven like cattle. They know no rest. They have become quite indifferent to the duty assigned to them by nature. They come on the screen and work in films in order to amuse and entertain men. They sing and dance for the sake of men and sometimes they go half-naked to the clubs and theatres to satisfy their lust; but still she thinks that she has got freedom.

Men do not understand as to how the freedom of woman is extremely harmful for her. How many pious and noble women are doing jobs in films and theatres. How many brides and daughters belonging to noble families have adopted this wretched profession and how many are there who have lost their respect and honour. Every one knows what is happening in the coeducational institutions and universities.

Islam has laid great stress on piety and chastity so that our cultural values should not be spoiled and both men and women could be able to perform their specific duties smoothly and efficiently. Where there is mixed gathering of men and women, the devil finds ample opportunity to lead them astray. Hatred and discord spoil the healthy atmosphere and none is able to perform the duties with concentration.

We agree with this view of Mahir ul Qadri: The longing to discard purdah and display charms is not satisfied by merely discarding the purdah of face. With it the modest and downward gaze becomes bold and arrogant. Then the dress undergoes a radical change and it becomes brief and thin. The psychology behind decoration is that a woman should look pretty and charming and everyone should admire her beauty and that she should be a cynosure of every one. Thus begins the life of sin and vice and it knows no end. The woman who hesitated to expose her face is degraded to such an extent that she feels no qualms of conscience in dancing with the strangers in clubs.

Those who are of the view that purdah weakens the nerves and that it stimulates the sex and stands in the way of education are badly mistaken. The increasing number of cases of suicides committed in the West, and their lusty and lewd lives have belied these charges. As regards the education, history shows that there was no dearth of educated women in Islam. The allegation that marriage with purdah observing women is not successful is falsified in view of the alarming number of divorces in the western countries.

There is no denying the fact that modesty and chastity can be guarded only by observing the purdah. Many western countries have begin to recognize the importance of purdah and have started a strong movement in favour of it. In Germany the movement, "Woman should go back to their houses" was started. In America about one Lac of people try to commit suicide out of which only seventeen thousand succeed. This number include a majority of women who commit this act due to frustration in love.

Islam has discouraged all such acts as are deliberately or inadvertently harmful for moral conduct and behaviour. The Holy Prophet (peace and blessings of Allah be upon him) said: When a woman should see and meet another woman, she should not describe her person to her husband. Just possible her virtues and beauty should captivate the heart of her husband and he should have a longing to possess her. The Holy Prophet (peace and blessings of Allah be upon him) has observed:

> A woman should not have such a direct contact with another woman that she should describe her person to her husband as if he is looking towards her. (Bukhari)

It may lead to evil exciting the passions of her husband.

Similarly, the Holy Prophet (peace and blessings of Allah be upon him) has forbidden the man to divulge the secrets of his wife before another man:

> The most wicked of men in the sight of Allah is one who comes to his wife (for sexual intercourse) and then divulges her secret.
> (Muslim)

Just as a woman is not permitted to describe the person of another woman in the same way, man is also not permitted to divulge the secrets of his wife. Besides other things, the wisdom behind these instructions is that it is not permitted to excite the passions of others as description of such details stimulates the sexual instinct. So one must refrain from such absurd and obscene talk as excites the sex.

Imam Nawawi observes: It is abhorrent to discuss the sexual act without any purpose. One may talk about sex only in case of need; but to go into its detail is, however, forbidden and is an act of indecency.

All such acts and deeds as stimulate the sexual passions and lead to sin and vice are prohibited in the Shari'ah. The Holy Prophet (peace and blessings of Allah be upon him) has instructed to exercise utmost vigilance in this matter and to abstain from all such acts. He once observed:

> No man should see the private parts of another man and no woman should see the private parts of another woman. (Muslim)

There is no denying the fact that looking at the private parts of the body stimulates the sexual desire. When any man sees the private parts of a man or any woman sees the private parts of a woman or a woman sees the private parts of a man or vice versa, the sexual instinct is excited which is hazardous for chastity and morality. Devilish insinuations overcome the heart. Sometimes man is inclined to homosexuality which is a great sin.

Sometimes the sexual urge compels him to love a woman. The same is the position of a woman. Sometimes she begins to love a woman of her own sex or desires that some one should love and adore her. These things lead to sin and vice. Moreover, hiding of the private parts of the body is ordained in Islam and social rules stress upon it. It is disgraceful to act against these rules.

Keeping in view the human nature and the sexual instinct, Islam has prohibited that two men or two women should lie together. It has been mentioned in the last lines of the Hadith:

> No man should lie with another man under one covering and no woman should lie with another woman under one covering. (Muslim)

Psychology has proved that it is harmful for two men or two women to lie together. Its results are not good. Hadrat Shah Waliullah has rightly observed: This act stimulates the sex and it sometime leads to sodomy which is an extremely detestable act.

The *satr* for man is from navel to the knees. He is not permitted to expose these parts of the body except before his wife. The *satr* of a free woman is for her whole body except her face and the palms of her hands. For a woman the satr of a woman is also from the navel to the knees. This portion of her body should not be seen even by a woman except at the time of child-birth. This concession is allowed as there is no other alternative. This concession is, however, allowed for her husband.

It is the inherent nature of man that his sexual instinct is sometimes excited to see his own sexual organs. Therefore, Islam has prohibited nudeness even in loneliness. It is also against canons of morality. The Holy Prophet (peace and blessings of Allah be upon him) has described:

> Beware of nakedness as along with you are those (angels) who never leave you except at the time of answering the call of nature and during sexual intercourse. So be ashamed of them and respect them. (Hujjatul Baligha)

In another Hadith the Holy Prophet (peace and blessings of Allah be upon him) said to a person:

> Guard your satr except from your wife or maid-servant. He asked: If someone is alone. He (the Holy Prophet) observed: To be ashamed of Allah at that time is your rightful duty.
>
> (Hujjatul Baligha)

One should ever remember Allah and the esteemed angel; so we should not be immodest and shameless. Moreover, nudeness excites the sexual desire. So wisdom lies in maintaining the satr strictly except under very exceptional circumstances. Once the Holy Prophet (peace and blessings of Allah be upon him) observed:

> No one should spend a night with a married woman except in presence of her husband or her mahram. (Muslim)

Islam has pin-pointed all such acts and deeds as ultimately lead to sin and vice and instructed its followers not even to go near them.

Islam has guaranteed the protection of female piety and chastity. If she has to travel, proper arrangement should be made for her protection and chastity. So the law of Islam does not allow a woman to travel alone. She should take with her a *mahram*. She cannot even perform Hajj, one of the obligatory duties in Islam, unless she is accompanied by a mahram. Islam has laid stress to adopt all such precautions as are necessary to guard female piety and chastity. It has been observed by the Holy Prophet (peace and blessings of Allah be upon him):

> It is not permissible for a believing woman that she should go on a journey of one day and one night alone without mahram.
>
> (Riyad as-Salihin)

Mahram is a person with whom it is unlawful to marry, such as father, brother etc. or she should go with her husband. It is forbidden for a woman to travel alone. Shariah is not in favour of taking any ghair mahram as Shariah does not recognize him as reliable. It is an admitted law that one comes across all sorts of persons good and bad during the journey. Women are physically weak and delicate. They have no experience of life. So they cannot be let alone to face the danger. On such an occasion the woman should take her father or brother so that they would defend her in need and guard her against any temptations. The Holy Prophet (peace and blessings of Allah be upon him) once said:

> No man should meet a woman unless a mahram is with her. No woman should travel without a mahram. A person asked: O Messenger of Allah! My wife is proceeding on Hajj and I intend to participate in battle. Then (the Holy Prophet) said: Do proceed on Hajj with your wife. (Riyad as-Salihin)

It is clear from the above Hadith as to how much stress is laid by Islam on female chastity. Instead of ordering the husband to proceed on Shad (an extremely important duty), he was asked to proceed on Hajj with his wife. The reason for giving priority to the latter action is that Islam attaches great importance to moral conduct and behaviour. A woman is not permitted by Islam to travel without a mahram.

Travelling Time

When the husband proceeds on journey, he is anxious for his women-folk. He provides for their needs; prays for their safety and their righteous conduct. According to the Sunnah of the Holy Prophet (peace and blessings of Allah be upon him) he should supplicate to Allah for their health and safety. The Holy Prophet (peace and blessings of Allah be upon him) himself recited the following prayer when he proceeded on journey:

> O Allah! Thou art (our) companion in this journey, and representative in (our) household. O Allah! I seek refuge in Thee from the toil of this journey, from beholding a sad sight and a bad reverse in my wealth and household.
>
> (Riyad as-Salihin)

He advised the people to recite this prayer at the time of proceeding on journey and beside all other things to pray to Allah for the safety of his family and seek refuge in Him from beholding any sad sight and a reverse in wealth and household. Thus a believer entrusts his household to the special safety of Allah. Allah is always the Protector. The Holy Prophet (peace and blessings of Allah be upon him) has said: When you come back from the journey, go to your household at once.

> Journey is a sort of infliction. It prevents an individual to eat, drink and sleep, when the journey is ended return to your household at once. (Riyad as-Salihin)

The wives of the fighters of Islam who are left behind demand more respect and honour than other women. They are considered as the most valuable assets of the Muslim Uirmah. The Muslims have been instructed to guard their respect and honour under all circumstances. The Holy Prophet (peace and blessings of Allah be upon him) has ordered:

> Those who remain sitting in the houses should respect the wives of the Mujahidin like their mothers. If any one of them is disloyal to the household of any Mujahid, that Mujahid would be asked to take as many of the virtues of that person as he would like on the Day of Resurrection till he would be pleased.
>
> (Riyad as-Salihin)

13

Good Moral Character

According to Islam, the main aim and object of marriage is that it is a means of protection of modesty and chastity and great stress has been laid on this aspect of marriage. There are numerous verses of the Holy Qur'an in which the believing men and women have been exhorted, in an eloquent, charming style, to guard their moral character. It has been mentioned:

> "And men who guard their modesty and women who guard (their modesty), and men who remember Allah much and women who remember Allah much, Allah hath prepared for them forgiveness and a vast reward." (33:35)

In short, the people who protect their modesty and chastity and gratify their sexual urge by lawful means, without transgressing the limits imposed by Allah, have been promised forgiveness and immense reward in the Hereafter! In another verse of the Holy Qur'an, pious men and pious women who maintain piety and chastity have been given the glad tidings of salvation and success in the Hereafter. It has been said in the Holy Qur'an:

> "And who guard their modesty save from their wives or the (slaves), that their right hands possess, for them they are not blameworthy, but whoso craveth beyond that, such are transgressors." (23:5-7)

There are only two lawful means of gratifying the sexual lust. Firstly, sexual intercourse with the wife whom you have married. Secondly, sexual intercourse with your female slave. Besides the above two means, any other method to gratify the sexual lust would be deemed as deviation from the limits prescribed by Islam.

The importance of piety and modesty can be judged from the fact that all the Prophets were pious and chaste. These are the essential qualities of Prophethood. Whenever any mischief maker or slanderer levelled any false accusation against the moral conduct of any Prophet, Allah, the Exalted. Himself rejected it and furnished a proof of his piety and chastity.

We have already narrated the story of Hadrat Yousuf (Joseph) (peace be upon him). Zulaikha, the wife (if the Aziz of Egypt fell badly in love with him. She tried her utmost to allure Hadrat Yousuf (peace be upon him) into an evil act; but Allah, the Exalted saved him at the critical moment. Although, Zulaikha first accused Hadrat Yousuf (peace be upon him) of having an evil intention against her, in a fit of shame; in the end she testified to his piety. The Holy Qur'an has said:

> "I asked of him an evil act, but he proved continent." (12:32)

Allah, the Exalted, has explained this reason for protecting Hadrat Yousuf (peace be upon him) from this evil act:

> "Thus it was, that We might ward off from him evil and lewdness. Lo! he was Our chosen slave." (12:24)

Praising Hadrat Yahya (peace be upon him) Allah, the Exalted, says:

> "Allah giveth thee glad tidings of Yahya to confirm a word from Allah, lordly, chaste, a Prophet of the righteous." (3:39)

When the Jews levelled a false accusation against Christ (peace be upon him) Allah, the Exalted, Himself repudiated it. It has been mentioned in the Holy Qur'an:

> "And Mary, daughter of 'Imran who guarded her chastity." (66:12)

Allah, the Exalted has mentioned in another verse:

> "And she who was chaste, therefore We breathed into her (something), of Our Spirit." (21:91)

It has been said about the Prophet's family:

> "They are innocent of that which people say: For them is pardon and a bountiful provision." (24:26)

The above verses of the Holy Qur'an which speak highly of the piety and chastity of Allah's Messengers (peace be upon them) and their families, furnishes irrefutable proof of the fact that Islam attaches paramount importance to piety and chastity is an essential quality of a believer that his moral character is spotless.

Greatness of the Faithful

While commenting upon the pious men and pious women, the Holy Qur'an says:

> "Vile women are for vile men, and vile men for vile women, good women are for good men and good men for good women." (24:26)

The position of an evil-doer cannot be equal to that of a pious person. Both are poles apart and have no resemblance to each other.

The evildoers from one group and the pious belong to another group. While explaining the virtues of the pious men, it has been mentioned that their greatest quality is that they shun vices:

> "And those who cry not unto any other god along with Allah, nor take the life which Allah hath forbidden save in (course of) justice, nor commit adultery." (25:68)

It is clear from the above verse that modesty and chastity are excellent virtues, the essence of respect, honour and morality. When a man associates anything with Allah, he commits Polytheism and negates Tauhid (Oneness of God). He is guilty of disbelief. By killing a man unlawfully a person commits the heinous crime of putting and end to life, and by committing fornication, he spoils his moral character and loses respect and honour.

Womenfolk under Pledge

One of the points on which it was allowed to take Bai'at (Pledge) from women, related to their chastity, that they would not commit adultery nor allow any stigma to be attached to their hitherto spotless character. It has been said in the Holy Qur'an:

> "And will neither steal nor commit adultery nor kill their children, nor produce any lie that they have devised between their hands and feet." (60:12)

It often happens that in the case of an illegitimate child, the woman has an abortion. Infanticide was also in vogue among some tribes of Arabia and this evil practice was required to be put to end. The Arab women were also in the habit of making false accusations. They gratified their sexual lust with some person and then attributed the child (as a result of this sexual intercourse) to anyone whom they liked. We have already written in the foregoing pages that one of the practices in vogue in Arabia was that a woman had sexual intercourse with many people and on the birth of a child attributed the child to whoever she liked, and he could not refuse. Some women were in the habit of attributing the children wrongly to people to whom they did not actually belong.

The Holy Prophet (peace and blessings of Allah be upon him) exhorted the people in various manners to guard their modesty and chastity. Islam aims at establishing a social set-up wherein these virtues are held in high esteem. The Holy Prophet (peace and blessings of Allah be upon him) once observed: 'O young men of Quraish! guard your modesty and do not commit adultery/fornication. Lo! for him who guards his modesty there is Paradise.' (Hakim & Baihaqi)

In the above Hadith, the young men of Quraish have been exhorted to guard their modesty and lead a pious life and have been warned against all acts of debauchery.

Dignity of the Pious

When Heracle (Caesar) the king of Rome, asked Abu Sufyan about the Holy Prophet (peace and blessings of Allah be upon him) as to what he preached, Abu Sufyan had not yet embraced Islam. He said to him: 'He (the Holy Prophet), asks us to offer prayer, to give charity, to guard chastity and to unite blood relations.' (Bukhari).

Modesty and chastity are such valuable qualities, that the Holy Prophet (peace and blessings of Allah be upon him) has laid great stress on them from the very beginning. He never was indifferent to them.

Once the Holy Prophet (peace and blessings of Allah be upon him) said: On the Day of Resurrection when there will be no shelter except that of Allah, He will grant shelter to seven people; one among these will be the pious person whom a beautiful lady tempted to evil but he refused her saying: 'I fear Allah.' (Bukhari)

The Holy Prophet (peace and blessings of Allah be upon him) has guaranteed Paradise for a person who does not let his radiant face become besmeared with the stigma of ignominy and disgrace by committing fornication. He has observed: 'He who assures to guard his private parts and his tongue, I assure Paradise for him.' (Bukhari)

The Holy Prophet (peace and blessings of Allah be upon him) narrated an event: Three people were travelling. They took shelter in a nearby cave for fear of rain and a duststorm. They thought they were safe; but just then a heavy stone slid and shut the mouth of the cave. These three people were imprisoned in the cave. They consulted each other and decided that they should pray to Allah to avert this calamity for any good action of theirs. Each of them repeated his good action and Allah removed the stone from the mouth of the cave for the sake of the virtues; one of them prayed; O' Allah! I had a cousin whom I loved very passionately. I loved her more than any man can love a woman. I requested my beloved to have sexual intercourse with me. She put me off saying: Bring one hundred coins of gold before you touch me. Hearing this I became busy in collecting one hundred gold coins. At last I was in possession of one hundred gold coins which I took and put on her feet. She was constrained to fulfil her promise. I sat in front of her making myself ready for the act. Just then she uttered: 'O Allah's servant! Fear Him and do not commit this act without legal right.' I abstained from this sin. 'O Allah, the Exalted, You are aware that I did so merely for Your pleasure. I beseech You to remove this stone from the mouth of the cave.' The stone turned aside and there was light.

(Bukhari)

You have read about the blessing of piety and chastity and studied how the fear of Allah saved the people at the critical moment. The Holy Prophet (peace and blessings of Allah be upon him) said: He who wants to meet his Lord pure and chaste should marry a pious lady.

(Bukhari)

The sum and substance of what we have said above is that a person should not intend adultery nor cast a slur on his or her natural and lawful fair name. He should resort to marriage means of gratifying his sexual desire.

Once the Holy Prophet (peace and blessings of Allah be upon him) observed: 'It is a charitable act to have sexual gratification from one's wife.' The Companions said surprised: 'O Allah's Messenger! Is this also an act of reward?' He said; 'Yes, why not, is this not a sin, that one should gratify one's sexual urge in an illegal manner? Thus every act which keeps one away from sin and vice has its reward.' And why should this not be so?

The Holy Prophet (peace and blessings of Allah be upon him) has observed: 'The Lord of the worlds would not speak with three persons on the Day of Resurrection nor purify them nor look at them, but inflict severe punishment on them. An old man who indulged in unlawful sex despite his old age; a king Who tells a lie despite his being a king and a destitute person who is proud despite his poverty. (Riyad Al-Salihin)

Fair Character

These are not only lessons of piety and chastity but the Prophet's illustrious Companions and set practical examples of piety and morality. It was due to the teachings of Islam that the Companions of the Holy Prophet (peace and blessings of Allah be upon him) showed marvellously good moral character in the face of all sorts of temptations and allurements. A Companion, namely Ma'iz bin Malik Aslami (Allah be pleased with him) was guilty of fornication. His conscience pricked him so much that it became impossible for him to conceal his guilt. He bore the punishment of stoning to death of his own accord, and was stoned to death.

At the time of migration, the duty of bringing the people who lagged behind and those who were weak rested with Murthad bin Abu Murthad al-Ghanavi. Hadrat Murthad (Allah be pleased with him) came to Makkah for this purpose. Before embracing Islam, he had relations with a prostitute, namely Ghanaq. He happened to pass by the house of that lady. She recognized him, welcomed him cordially and requested him to spend a night with her. Hadrat Murthad (Allah be pleased with him) flatly refused the offer on the plea that Islam has forbidden unlawful sex. She threatened: 'I will make a noise and get you arrested.' But Hadrat Murthad (Allah be pleased with him) did not agree. He ran away from the clutches of that woman and saved his life by hiding himself.

Someone tried to touch a woman who was previously a prostitute before embracing Islam but she said: 'Be off, the time of debauchery is gone. Now we are bound by the tenets of Islam.'

Everyone knows the story of the maid servants of 'Abdullah bin Ubayy bin Salul, the leader of the hypocrites. After the advent of Islam when he ('Abdullah bin Ubayy), ordered his maid servants to earn money through prostitution, they went to the Holy Prophet (peace and blessings of Allah be upon him) and told their sad story. Thereupon, the following verse was revealed:

> "Force not your slave-girls to whoredom."
> (24:33)

Hadrat Abu Musa Ash'ari (Allah be pleased with him) said that he would prefer an obnoxious smell in his nose to the smell of the body of a strange woman.

We have told you about the pious and chaste lives of the Holy Prophet's Companions. You will be deeply impressed to read that the Last of the Prophets (peace and blessings of Allah be upon him) who led an exemplary, pious and innocent life, never forgot even for a moment to pray for modesty and chastity:

> 'O Allah! I beg of Thee the right guidance, righteousness, piety and freedom from want.'
> (Mishkat)

Sometimes he prayed from the core of his heart:

> 'O Allah! Suggest to me my right course, and save me from the mischief of my soul.'
> (Tirmidhi)

Sometimes the following prayer was on his sacred lips:

> 'O Allah! I seek refuge in Thee from evil morals, deeds and desires.' (Tirmidhi)

The above prayers of the Holy Prophet (peace and blessings of Allah be upon him) reflect deep fear of Allah and longing to maintain piety and chastity. He was never forgetful in this respect.

The above prayers teach a definite lesson of piety and chastity to all the people. We should always try to keep our moral character free from all sorts of evils.

Sanctions

The measures adopted by Islam to guard modesty and chastity are not without wisdom. Islam aims at eradicating vice and sin. It teaches good morals and excellent conduct. A stern warning of severe punishment in this world and in the Hereafter has been administered to all such people. As regards the worldly punishment, the details thereof will be given in the next pages. We give below only a glimpse of the punishment prescribed for these wretched creatures in the Hereafter.

During Mi'raj (Ascension), the Holy Prophet (peace and blessings of Allah be upon him) was shown the punishment which would be inflicted on the sinners. He saw an oven of burning flames. There was much hue and cry. He peeped to know what was happening. To his great astonishment, he saw naked men and women from whose private organs there arose burning flames. When the fire lashed their bodies all of them began to cry loudly. He was told that it was a group of men and women who committed adultery in this world. (Riyad Al-Salihin)

An Evil

Islam has suggested the remedy for the moral uplift of the people so that they may remain immune from the Fire of Hell:

> "Marry of the women who seem good to you,
> two or three or four." (4:3)

The gratification of sexual desire is permissible through legal means only and one is allowed to marry four women at a time, provided he has the high moral sense to maintain equity and justice among them and is able to support them.

Polygamy is permissible in the case of the people who possess a strong sexual desire but it does not mean that the keeping of four women has been made compulsory. Islam does not insist on keeping more than one woman. Nowhere in the verse is there any such persuasion or commandment. The Holy Qur'an has clearly mentioned:

> "And if ye fear that ye cannot do justice (to so many), then one (only), or the (captive), that your right hands possess. Thus it is more likely that ye will not do injustice." (4:3)

The criticism of the enemies of Islam on the institution of polygamy does not hold good as it is permissible provided a person can maintain equity or justice among his wives. If he is unable to fulfil this essential condition he is not allowed to marry more than one woman despite his need. Allah, the Exalted says:

> "But turn not altogether away (from one), leaving her as in suspense."
> (4:129)

The word 'Adl (justice) implies the fulfilment of the rights and obligations which the husband owes to his wife. He should do justice in matters under his control i.e., in providing food, clothing, spending time with wives, etc. So far as human feelings and sentiments are concerned, these are beyond one's control. The Shari'ah exhorts us also to try to do justice in this respect but if in spite of that the heart is fascinated by any one more than others, it is not punishable.

> "If ye do good and keep from evil, lo! Allah is Ever Forgiving, Merciful." (4: 129.)

'Abdul Majid Daryabadi has explained the meaning of justice in the matters over which one has control. He says: 'It is not necessary that the number of things provided to one wife should always correspond to those provided to the others. An African wife would be accustomed to things quite different from those of an American lady. The interests and desires of a young and an old woman are also bound to vary. The aim is not that all should be treated alike, but so far as possible amenities of life should be provided to each of them according to their taste and requirement. According to Jurists, justice among wives is an obligatory duty; but 'justice' means withholding one's hand from mal-treatment and oppression.'

'It is evident from the verse that justice among wives is an obligatory duty which implies that there should be no maltreatment or oppression: (Dur Mukhtar)

If there is fear of injustice only one marriage is permissible.

The verse quoted above and the following verse:

> "And if ye fear that ye cannot do justice then one only" (4:3)

Bear ample testimony to the fact that as a matter of principle only one marriage is allowed, but in case of inevitable need one can keep four wives at one time. This exception is made in Islam due to certain reasons. If a man is sexually strong and one wife cannot gratify his sexual desire, it is more appropriate that he should have a second wife than that he should commit adultery. Sometimes his first wife is childless and he cherishes the deepest longing to have a child. Sometimes his wife contracts some chronic disease and there is no hope of her recovery or she becomes extremely weak and disabled. In the above circumstances the approach of Islam is more realistic and reasonable as it does not permit illicit sexual relations in any case.

There is no denying the fact that even the sworn enemies of Islam cannot but acknowledge the advantages of polygamy in special circumstances. Wise and sagacious people must be aware of its advantages. Islam has allowed it with certain essential conditions. However, the usefulness of this system can hardly be disputed.

It is astonishing that the Western countries had made polygamy the subject of severe criticism In these countries there is open prostitution, flirtation and the love-making. Seeing this moral turpitude, some of the Western thinkers and intellectuals not only justify polygamy but also consider it as quite necessary for moral rectitude.

Miss Mary Smith, a lady teacher in a London school, has written in her book: 'The custom of polyandry which is in vogue in England is absolutely wrong. Men should be allowed second marriage.' In *Sunday Tribune* of the 24th November 1951, it is written about this book: 'I am sure that twenty five lac widows whose age is above twenty five will evince keen interest in this book and will purchase it like hotcakes.'

You can judge well from the above excerpts that polygamy which is permissible in Islam under extreme urgency is near to law of nature. The realistic approach to the problem has affirmed the truth of Islam.

Mary Smith writes in her book: 'Since the number of men is small, every woman is not successful in finding a husband.' She further observes: 'Polyandry has failed and this system is unscientific and unrealistic.'

As an effective means of guarding against sexual immorality, the polygamous way of life has begun to win growing popularity since the 17th century. In 1658 a person published a pamphlet which advocated polygamy as an effective means of checking adultery and the death rate of illegal newly born babies. A century after the publication of this pamphlet, a worthy and pious priest wrote a book in support of polygamy. A famous expert doctor of sex, James Hilton, prescribed polygamy as a remedy for checking adultery and prostitution.

Show Pinhar gave the following opinion about polygamy:

> 'Where are people depending upon one wife? I want to see them. Everyone of us is polygamous. Since every man is in need of a number of women, so there should be no such restriction on men.'

The famous doctor of sex, Mr. Kalechan, writes in his book:

> 'Although polygamy is generally practised in England, society and law do not recognise it. The society does not make any protest against the person who marries one wife but has kept two or three concubines or girl friends. If a person seeks permission to marry more than one wife the society begins to cry hoarse.'

'Allama 'Abdul 'Aziz Sadaish of Egypt has recorded an incident which is worth reading: 'I met with a Spanish person in London. We had an enlightened discussion on various topics on Islam. When we commenced discussion on polygamy that person remarked: 'Would that I were a Muslim and had a second wife.' I enquired the reason for it. He said: 'My wife has been mad for many years, I have, therefore, been compelled to develop sexual relations with other women because I cannot keep a second wife. Had I a legal second wife, I would have lawful children who would be the heirs of my large property. She would have been the cynosure of my eyes, my best friend and a source of comfort and consolation for me.'

The Outcome

Mrs. Birdsil, the President of the Young Men's Christian Association, said in a statement before the Booking Committee of Washington: 'The number of unmarried girls above fourteen years of age is one crore and twenty thousand. Against this number, the number of bachelors is ninety lac. According to this estimate, thirty lac girls are bound to go without marriage as the war has upset the numerical equilibrium between men and women.'

In the above situation, if polygamy is not practised, there is no force on earth which can protect the morals of the society. Even if we suppose that no harm is done to morality, would that not be sheer injustice to the thirty lac unmarried women? Someone has rightly observed: 'Some people may think that the comparison is between polygamy and polyandry; but this view is not correct; rather the topic which merits discussion is polygamy versus widespread adultery. Islam permits a little polygamy under some rigorous conditions to check immorality whereas those who believe in polyandry, find no remedy for widespread adultery and prostitution. They severely criticise polygamy; but raise no protest against a person who indulges in debauchery in order to gratify his sexual lust.

So far you have read about the views of the West concerning polygamy. Now let us examine the viewpoint of the eminent Hindus regarding this subject.

In a memorandum sent by the Madras Assembly to the Hindustan Committee, the necessity of the enforcement of polygamy in the Hindu society under special circumstances has been stressed. In other words, the Hindus have also begun to believe in the efficacy of a polygamous way of life.

What we really want to stress is that by acting upon the rules and regulations promulgated by Islam, one can guard one's chastity and morality more effectively. There is no other alternative except that a man should marry one, or in case of need two, three or four wives, provided he can do justice among them.

What are the things in respect of which justice and equity among wives is necessary? We shall discuss this topic in some detail while explaining the rights of women in the next pages. If there is a genuine need of more than one wife, one should marry more; but there is no room for adultery in Islam. The second marriage will be subject to the condition that a person does justice among his wives. Allah, the Exalted says:

> "And if ye fear that ye cannot do justice then one only." (4:3)

The Holy Prophet (peace and blessings of Allah be upon him) has said: 'If there are two wives of a person and he does not do justice between them, he will come on the Day of Resurrection with a paralysed portion of his body.'

Islam aims at dispensing justice and maintaining equity among all one's wives if he has a number of wives. He will be punished in the hereafter if he fails to do justice. His unjust treatment to his wife will be recognized by the paralysed portion of his body on the Day of Resurrection. He will thus be disgraced before all for breach of an essential condition of marriage.

Equity and justice can be maintained in things over which one has control. The details of such things have already been given above. But so far as human feelings and sentiments are concerned, these are beyond one's control. One should as far as possible try to maintain equity and justice in these things also and seek Allah's pardon for his lapses in this respect. The Holy Prophet (peace and blessings of Allah be upon him) used to deal with all his wives justly. He used to pray: 'O' Allah! This is a thing over which I have no power. So reproach me not in that over which Thou hast power but I have no power.' (Mishkat)

Hadrat 'A'isha (Allah be pleased with her) narrated her story to Hadrat 'Urwah (Allah be please with her) saying: 'O' 'light of the eyes of my sister! When the Holy Prophet (peace and blessings of Allah be upon him) fixed the turns of his wives, he did not give preference to any one among them; but he did justice. Although he met us all; but during the night he stayed in the house of the wife according to the appointed turn, and never stayed in the others' house.'

In the case of a second wife, if she is a virgin the husband should stay with her for the first seven days, after which equal turns will be fixed among the wives. If the newly-wedded wife is not a virgin, he should stay with her for the first three days and then appoint the turns among all his wives. These seven and three days should not be deducted from the appointed turns. Hadrat Anas (Allah be pleased with him) has reported that according to the Sunnah; 'If a person marries a virgin after marrying a widow or a divorced woman, he should stay with her for three days. Thereafter he should fix the turns.

The decision for taking a wife during journey should be made by casting lots so that there cannot be any injustice and the wives should think that fair dealing has been done with them. It has been stated in a Hadith; 'When the Holy Prophet (peace and blessings of Allah be upon him) intended to proceed on a journey, he cast a lot among his wives. He went with the wife in whose favour the lot was drawn out.' (Mishkat)

The wife has the right to transfer her turn, of her own accord, to her co-wife, and the husband will be bound to spend the time with that wife. In case she gives up her turn to the choice of her husband, he can spend his time with whom he likes.

There is no restriction on meeting and talking with any of the wives irrespective of her turn. One can also call all his wives and discuss with them; but he will have sexual intercourse with the wife according to her turn.

Is it necessary to maintain equity among wives in the matter of sex? The answer to this question is that sexual inclination depends upon the sentiment of love and affection, in which the maintenance of equity is difficult, but one should always try his best. If, however, despite one's efforts the heart is not inclined towards the sexual act, there is no offence; but it is not permissible to avoid sexual intercourse despite the urge, as it will be unjust.

Equity and justice should be done in the matter of providing food and clothing and other amenities of life to one's wives. One should do his best to please them.

You will be surprised to know that Islam does not tolerate the telling of lies. It is a great sin, but it is allowed in the case of wives if there be need of it. There is a Hadith narrated by Umm Kalthurn (Allah be pleased with her) 'I have never heard that the Holy Prophet (peace and blessings of Allah be upon him) had granted permission (in this respect), save three things: War, making peace among people and when a person talks with his wife or she converses with him.'

(Muatta Imam Malik)

It is not permissible even for a moment that a person should persecute his wife and injure her delicate feelings. Those who keep a number of wives at one time, but do not treat them humanely and justly make their home lives miserable. Instead of peace and harmony, their houses present scenes of constant wrangles and quarrels among wives. The husband loses his respect and honour in family and society, the same is the position of his wives.

The matter does not end here, one mother instigates her children against the others. The wives also try to create hatred against their father in the minds of their children with the result that a happy home turns into a veritable hell.

If equal treatment is not done to all the wives and the rights of one are overlooked due to the husband's inclination towards another wife, the other can commit such an indecent act as can never be imagined. You must be aware of the scandals and flirtations of the wives of the nawabs and kings. Islam cannot tolerate this wickedness.

The import of what we have said above is that Islam cannot, even for a moment, tolerate acts of immorality and debauchery. It strongly condemns moral delinquency and evil deeds and exhorts its followers to lead a pure, clean life. It permits sexual gratification' through lawful, natural means. If one wife cannot gratify him, and he is sure that he will be able to do justice, one can have two or more wives. But Islam does not at all permit recourse to adultery and the illegal gratification of sexual lust.

One is not allowed to keep more than four wives at one time. Those who do so, incur punishment by flouting this definite decision.

Hadrat 'Abdullah bin 'Umar (Allah be pleased with him) reported that when Ghaitan Thaqafi embraced Islam, he had nine wives who also embraced Islam. The Holy Prophet (blessings of Allah be upon him) said: 'keep four out of them.' (Ibn Majah)

Hadrat Qais bin Harith (Allah be pleased with him) said that when he became a Muslim, he had eight wives. He went to the Holy Prophet (peace and blessing of Allah be upon him) and stated that he had eight wives. Thereupon he (the Holy Prophet) said: 'Select any four of them.' (Ibn Majah)

Besides the above, there are many more Ahadith in which the Holy Prophet (peace and blessings of Allah be upon him) has forbidden the keeping of more than four wives. Those who possessed more than four wives were allowed by the Holy Prophet (peace and blessings of Allah be upon him) to keep four out of them and had to leave the rest.

Whereas Islam has allowed polygamy with certain conditions to guard one's modesty and chastity, it does not at all allow that the fair face of humanity should be besmeared with the filth of adultery and debauchery.

Piety Supreme

Islam protects the honour of people and their affinity, and that is why it limits the sexual urge. It does not give reins to the passion, nor does Islam mortify it. Islam does not allow people to become like beasts satisfying their lust moving from one person to another. It controls the sex urge under certain rules.

Man is the most superior creature on earth so he should have his own identity. He must control his sexual desire. Has he ever noticed some species of animals and birds that would never allow male intruders go to their females. They would chase any male intruder and fight with him. So why does he allow himself to be much inferior than those animals? Look at male lions and male crows as best examples.

If we really follow the teachings of Islam, we shall never find in our society any complexes such as the Id, libido or Oedipus complexes.

Islam forbids all such things as might arouse sexual urge in one way or another.

Islam has raised a woman from the swamps she ,was; and in the Neo Jahilia she still is; to the highest ranks, while the Neo Jahilia utilizes her innocence and beauty as to exhibit her at the counter of every big store house and trade place to attract vendors; or she becomes the private secretary of the big boss, and it is interesting to note that a beautiful young naive girl quickly becomes the private secretary of the boss. Allah knows what are .the results of the privacy and secrecy.

To stop people from many rumour and doubts about them, Islam has, a clear cut remedy. It forbids privacy between a man and a woman. If the nature of the work makes a woman go in and out of the office of the boss, then the door must be kept wide open when she is with him. It should be kept ajar.

Islam has taught her which parts of her body are to be seen by Ajaanib (singular Ajnabi-non-Mahram i.e. a man who can marry her legally if she is not married-to anyone else); and what parts can be seen by Mahaarim. (singular Mahram non-Ajnabi i.e. a man who can never lawfully marry her, because of consanguinity as father, uncle, etc.

The coming verse will mention them all); and husband is advised not to look at the sex organ of his wife as he might see something that lest he should hate her. To this Qur'an says

> "And tell the believing women to lower their gaze and be modest and to display of their adornment only that which is apparent, and to draw their veils, over their bossoms, and not to reveal their adornment save their own husbands or fathers or husbands' fathers, or -their sons, their husbands' sons, or their brothers, or their brothers' sons, or sisters' sons, or their women, or their slaves, or male attendants who lack vigour, or children who know naught of women's nakedness. And let them not stamp their feet so as to reveal what they hide of their adornment. And turn to Allah .."(Quran 24: 31)

(All the males mentioned in this verse with the exception of, slaves, children and attendants; are regarded as Maharim (Sing. Mahram mentioned before).

Islam has taught woman how to talk to *ajnabi* (a stranger-a non-Mahram) directly (although it does not much encourage the way of her talking to man face to face). Islam taught her, also to talk with him behind the curtain (and this way is much more preferable).

When a woman talks to an ajnabi, her voice should not be soft or have certain tone that could arouse sexual urge in whose heart is a disease.

Islam has told woman not to bedizen herself and not to show her *pudendum*.(1) She is to practise a strict pudency before all ajaanib (strangers). They should never see any part of her body except her palms and feet, while she may show her face as well according to some Muslim scholars.

The dress, a Muslim woman is allowed to wear, should cover the whole body with the exception of hands and face. (2) Should be loose enough so as not to show what she is covering. (3) Should be so thick that it does not describe the colour of the skin of the parts covered. (4) Should not attract man's attention or designed for show. (5) Should not be similar to male costume. (6) Should not be similar to the dress of unbelievers (kuffar) and (7) Should not be a drew of fame or pride.

Peaceful Attitude

Prevention is better than cure, goes parallel with the sound and healthy policy of Islam. Islam does not depend on punishment to build up its society, it tries to keep the society free from distractors. It does not combat the natural instincts; it arranges them and guides them to the proper channels. Islam prepares an appropriate and clean atmosphere, with no artificial stimulants. Under such an atmosphere the human desires develop naturally without any hindrance.

In the true Islamic religious curricula all the opportunities of going astray must be eliminated or at least minimized, and the means of sexual attractions must be removed. There should be no hindrance from, natural sexual satisfaction through legal means.

Islam asked both man and woman to lower their gaze, and told the woman not to reveal her adornment, lest the one in whose heart is a disease is affected.

Sayyid Qutub in his book: *Fi Dhilalil Qur'an* (under the shades of Qur'an) has the following to say (with slight adaptations):

> "No clean Muslim society will ever exist if sexual instincts are aroused every now and then and human flesh is exhibited all the time. This continued act of arousing sex urge leads to the kindling of sex fires that will never be extinguished."
>
> "The sexy look, the stimulating act, the nude, the bedizenment etc., etc. .... all those lead to no more than making that fire kindle more and more till one can no longer control oneself. The consequences are anarchy and there will be no

morale that control people. People have either to satisfy their sex urge and enjoy themselves to the brim, or there is frustration, neurotic cases, and a hundred and one complexes because of the inhibition after the sex drives were aroused. This is not less than a kind of torture.

"One of the means of Islam in building up a clean society is-to stop/such sexual excitement from happening and to preserve the deep natural desires between the two sexes and to remain safe and sound with its natural strength without any artificial excitement and to guide it to its proper safe and clean place.

"When people live with no morals, then the following things become common and ordinary things: a greedy gaze at the other sex, when the two sexes meet, each of them gives reins in his talk to the other sex, mixing up and co-mingling of the two sexes and some sort of privacy between a male and a female, lovely jesting between them, looking and touching parts of the body and these and even more become things that are taken for granted. Just because those who practise them and advertise them have a strong belief that this is the only solution, because in their opinion it prevents inhibition and it stops creation of complexes, and it reduce the pressure, and its repercussions (They are like the drowned man who clutches at a straw)."

Man is the vicegerent of Allah on the earth from the day Allah created our father Adam till when Allah inherits the Universe and who and what are on and in it.

Allah has created a natural attraction between the two sexes: One sex is un consciously attracted to the other. This natural attraction fluctuates from time to time.

Once such natural attraction is attractively exposed to artificial excitement, it certainly be purturbed and it will need satisfaction no matter whatever the cost. Otherwise the excited parts get tired and in the long run one might get psychological problems or nervous breakdown.

The means of the sexual excitement are many but the main ones are: a gaze, bedizenment, certain actions and motions, smile and laughter, flirtation and effeminate way of talk (voice).

Islam requires from its adherents to at least minimize, if not eliminate, these distractors for the common good of the society at large.

We are to strive in finding ways and means of legal and natural satisfaction of our sex urge.

There were times when people used to interpret everything as sexy. Even when they found a child suckling its fingers, they would say it depicts its sex behaviour. Have they ever thought that the world is full of things other than sex?

When this ideology was widespread, we found many a writer following the same line: whatever they wrote was sex centred. That was one of the reasons of beginning the downfall of our morals.

Honour for Fair Sex

Islam interdicts a man from derogating a woman. He is to respect her and help her honour herself. If he detracts her, he, is to be punished here in the world first, and then there, where neither wealth nor children will be of any avail or help, save only those who came to Allah with sound hearts.

Man is to lower his gaze before a woman and she is to lower hers as well. He is not to look at her with his purposeful continued gaze. The first unintentional glance, there is nothing in it, but not the succeeding ones with evil purpose. They are sinful.

Full Liberty

Islam has given people freedom with certain precautions and limits. It did not let them do whatsoever they liked. That would mean anarchy. People are not to transgress those limits, so that the human society could produce the expected natural products.

The following rights go side by side with the respected freedom: the right of property, the right of honour and respect, the right of marriage, the right of affinity, and the right of society.

Islam has taken much pains to arrange the problem of co-mingling between man and woman and tried to strike a balance betwixt the twain: positive and negative so that neither is to transgress the other or overpower it. This is where the principles of Islamic education must completely differ from other ideologies in education. Islamic society must have its own standards, peculiarities and identity. It should learn good things from the others and choose what do not contravene with Islam.

Practise what you preach is a good maxim. Take an example of education. Some people send their daughters to mixed schools. When those girls grow up they are prohibited from mingling with men. What a contradictory way of dealing with things?

In any good Muslim society there should be no co-education under whatever pretext. School boys, big or small, should under no circumstances ever mix with girls.

One might raise the following question, "Look here !" You said that women were taking part in different walks of life during the life of the Prophet and even during the early Caliphate. Why, then, do you say that she is not to mingle with men now? It is a new approach to Islam or what is it all about?

My answer to him is, "Yes, she was actually taking an active part in building up the Muslim society, and nobody can ever stop her from exercising her right to do so at any epoch of time, provided she follows strictly the teachings of Islam; she should never adorn herself before any *ajnabi* (stranger), she must wear the apparel covering all her body with the exception of hands, feet and (some scholars say) face as well. She should never wear tight, thin and transparent clothes. She ought always to wear underclothing. She is never to imitate men in their clothing.

> "She must be upright in her walk, there should never be a swing song way of walk. She must never do anything that might tempt or attract people. She ought to be shy as shyness is the best cloth for a Muslim chaste woman to put on."

> "There should never be a Khalwal' (privacy between a man and a woman i.e., co-mingling between the two sexes)."

It is *haraam*, (unlawful) in Islam for a Muslim woman to wear clothes that make her body become conspicuous. There is a Prophet (peace be upon him) saying which means: Two types of the people of the Hell I have not yet seen them (but are coming): People with whips just like the tails of cows with which they beat others (dictators and tyrants); and women dressed but naked (because their apparel expose their breasts, chests, necks, thighs etc. etc.) they are going astray (from the right path). They are misleading their followers and in whose hearts is a disease. Their heads (have become) as big as the humps of the biggest camels (their heads become so lofty because of the artificial hair-wig or anything else, and because of the new way of dressing the hair at coufeir or at a beauty parlour). They will never enter Paradise .

No Muslim virtuous woman is to wear man's drew or imitate him in his manly way of talk or walk. She should never try to make herself a man. She is not to be an Amazon. A man should never put on a woman's dress or copy her in any feminine way. He must not effeminate himself. He is not to be a Sissy boy.

It is narrated that the Prophet (peace be upon him) cursed the Sissies and the Amazons and told people to drive them out of their houses. He also cursed men who wear clothes like women and women who put on apparel like men.

It Is sinful to tattoo one's skin, sharpening teeth, and parting them (so as to have gaps in between) and joining the natural hair with any artificial hair (e.g., wig) but not plait.

The Messenger of Allah cursed the following:

> "The tattooer (doer) of the skin and the tattooed (the one done); the sharpener and shortener (doer) and whose teeth are sharpened or shortened; the parter of teeth and the one whose teeth are parted; the joiner of hair to the original one and to whose hair is joined new one; the thinner and penciler of the eyebrows and that whose eyebrows are thinned or pencilled; and the shortener of the hair at the forehead and whose hair is shortened."

The Prophet (peace be upon him) cursed all of them; the one who does any of the aforementioned things to others and those on whom such things are done.

Anyone who wants such things to be done, unto him, suffers a lot of pain unnecessarily. He wastes his time and money on luxury, instead of spending it on essential things. He tries to change his features, those features that were created by the All-Knowing Creator of the Universe. By doing so, he is as if telling Allah: "Look here ! You are wrong. You created me in this form. I am going to change myself to the way I like" (Allah Forbid). On and above all this, he is cursed by the Apostle of Allah (peace and blessings of Allah be upon him).

It is said that Mulaawiya was once talking to people on a pulpit at Medina and had a lock of hair in his hand he told them "Where are your Ulama'a (religious scholars). You join hair (before their eyes and they never do anything about it or reprimand you)? The Prophet forbade Muslims from using it as it is regarded as a counterfeit, because it deceives people and makes them think that it is the original hair of the person, while it is not. The Israelites (Jews) perished when their wives took to wig.

It is narrated that the Messenger of Allah prohibited Muslim from doing, the following:

> "Tattoo of the skin; sharpening; shortening and parting of the teeth; cutting short of forehead hair; a man should never be bedfellow to another man without clothes on; no woman is to be a bed-fellow with another woman with no apparel on; no man is to use silk (even) as underclothing or on his shoulders (more than four inches wide) as the non-Muslims do there must be no looting, no man is to ride on tiger back (a symbol of pride); no man is to wear a gold ring (only those in power may do so).

It is one of the ills of Neo Jahilia, that Muslim women go to beauty parlours and they prefer that massaging and their hair be done by men and not by women. Dear sisters have you forgotten that hair is among the taboo. It should never be seen by an *ajnabi* (a man who can legally marry her), let along be touched by him?.

There were times when thinning and pencilling of the eyebrows was done by prostitutes only. No chaste woman ever thought of it.

Well, sister in Islam; thank you very much for attentive listening to my whisper.

Now, may I ask my brothers in Islam to join hands with me and help our sister fulfil the teachings of her religion? Do you promise me that? Thank you so much. May Allah bless us and help us in our new task.

The Sins

During my reading of the Bible I came across a very interesting article about adultery. It is, as follows, after telling him to follow his parents instructions the, article goes on :

> "It can keep you away from bad women, from the seductive words of other man's wives. Do not be tempted by their beauty; don't be tempted by their flirting eyes. A man can hire a prostitute for the price of a loaf of bread, but adultery will cost him all he has. Can you carry fire against your cheat without burning your clothes? Can you walk on hot coals without burning your feet? It is just as dangerous to sleep with another man's wife.... But a man who commits adultery hasn't any sense. He is just destroying himself. He will be dishonoured and beaten up, he will be permanently disgraced ......"
>
> (Proverbs 6: 24 to 29 & 32 & 33)

We read the following from the Old Testament:

> "If a man seduces - a virgin who is not engaged, he must pay the bride-price for her and marry her. But if the father refuses to let him marry her, he must pay the father a sum of money equal to the bride price for a virgin."
>
> (Exodus 22: 16, 17)

> "The Lord gave the following regulations. Do not have sexual intercourse with any of your relatives. Do not disgrace your father by having intercourse with mother. Do not disgrace your father by having intercourse with any of his wives. Do not have intercourse with your sister or your step-sister, whether or not she was brought up in the same house with you. Do not have intercourse with your grand-daughter that will be a disgrace to you. Do not have intercourse with your aunt, whether she is your father's sister or your mother's sister. Do not have intercourse with your uncle's wife. She is

> too, your aunt. Do not have intercourse with your daughter-in-law or with your brother's wife. Do not have intercourse with the daughter or grand-daughter of a woman with whom you had intercourse, they may be related to you, and that would be incest. Do not take your wife's sister as one of your wives, as long as your wife is living. Do not have intercourse with a woman during her monthly period.... Do not have intercourse with another man's wife.
>
> (Leviticus 18: 6/20)
>
> "Do not commit adultery" (Exodus 19 : 20)

To protect the chaste woman and the family from any bad reputation, Islam is very strict about adultery and fornication. Islam regards anyone who commits Zinaa (adultery or fornication) as far from Islam the time he/she commits it.

Sexual intercourse in Islam is not a mere temporary satisfaction. It is the continuation of human life and human reproduction. Man being Allah's vicegerent on the earth, he is duty bound to build the world and develop it to the best of his advantage, he is to increase his number in multitude. Man (male and female) cannot fulfil any of these if he only satisfies his sex urge from one human body to another. Neither will he be able to build up a very good, healthy, problem free society.

Prostitution is the most serious disease in any society. The first thing a strumpet does is to discard her feminism, her humanity, morale and even manner, otherwise she will not make a good whore.

An adulteress (or fornicatress) causes a lot of social ills; to mention but a few examples: the affinity of the progeny is doubtful and becomes mixed (in Islam the child must be called after the name of his real father); she creates some sort of hatred between the parties concerned. The family tie of an adulteress, is at a stake; while the fornicatress seldom thinks of having, a family. To this Qur'an says

> "The woman and the man guilty of Zinaa (adultery and fornication) flog each of them a hundred stripes. Let not compassion move you in their case, in a matter prescribed by Allah if ye believe in Allah and the Last Day and let a party of believers witness their punishments."
>
> (Qur'an 24: 2)

The Arabic word Zinaa: means sexual intercourse between a man and woman not married to each other. The English word adultery applies to a married man or woman making love (sexual intercourse) with one who is not the legal husband or wife; while fornication means that both parties are unmarried. Zinaa means both, adultery and fornication.

Flogging a hundred stripes is applied to fornicators (unmarried committers of the act) whether one of the parties or both of them are unmarried. The unmarried is to be flogged a hundred stripes.

Those who commit adultery (married ones) are to be stoned till death.

If one of the parties is married while the other is unmarried; then the married member is to be stoned, and the unmarried one be flogged.

When either of the punishment takes place, there must be a party of Muslims witnessing so that it may serve as a lesson to them and it could make the wrong doers feel it much more painful.

If those who committed fornication do not repent, then they are not allowed to marry chaste people and believers. They are to marry people of their like (unchaste) or unbelievers. Qur'an has the following to say about this :

> "Let no man guilty of adultery or fornication marry any but a woman similarly guilty, or an unbeliever, nor let any but such a man or an unbeliever marry such a woman: To believers such a thing is forbidden." (Qur'an 24: 3)

Islam has taken very strict measures and precautions about the application of Hadd (Restrictive Ordinance of Allah) i.e., of flogging and stoning of unchaste men and women.

If anyone is accused of Zinaa, it ought to be provided by one of the four ways □Four eye witnesses. □Confessions ; the parties concerned to confess. □Circumstantial evidence e.g., an unmarried woman becomes pregnant. □Li'ann (each of the spouses curses himself/ herself in case his/her allegation of adultery is wrong and curses the other if the allegation against him/her is false).

There should be four eye witnesses who have seen the man and the woman committing Zinaa (adultery or fornication). They must have caught or seen them red handed with the actual act.

All the witnesses must be of full age, Muslims, sane, just and upright able to speak (not dumb or deaf), have good memory (can remember well what happened), have really seen the act (not just heard from others); the witnesses should not be near relatives of the accused, there must be no hatred between the witness and the accused; all the witness must be men; all the witnesses must give their evidence in one sitting. They must be impartial.

Failing this, the witnesses are to be flogged eighty stripes each. On and above that the slanderer or slanderers are to be deprived of one of their natural rights: Witness. They are not to give any further witness on any matter throughout their life, unless and until they reform and repent. Only then are they welcome back and given back their right of giving evidence, and allowed to act as witnesses.

This calumniation has been treated by Islam in such a way that no one ever thinks of putting forward any slanders or scandalous suggestions about any chaste woman.

Islam has been so strict with the slanderers so as the punishment for adultery and fornication may have its required effect.

Leaving everyone launching charges against everyone else without concrete evidence is the source of all anarchy. Anyone might put forward any scandalous accusation against an innocent person. The result of such acts is doubt. Every husband or wife becomes doubtful about the chastity of the spouse. He or she might even live in cloud of doubt about his or her own affinity.

In such a society where every male and female accuses everyone else of Zinaa, it is very much likely that those in whose heart is a disease or those who were, hesitant committing such scandalous things may do so, taking the advantage of the cloud of such allegations.

To protect the chastity of woman, the slanderer is given three types of punishments: □Corporal punishment: eighty stripes, □Moral punishment: deprived of witness, □Religious punishment: regarded as impious.

Qur'an elucidates this in the following way:

> "And those who launch a charge against chaste women, and produce not four witnesses (to support their allegations) flog them with eighty stripes, and reject their evidence ever after, for such men are wicked transgressors."
>
> "Unless they repent thereafter and mend (their conduct) for Allah is oft forgiving, most merciful." (Qur'an 24: 4 & 5)

In ordinary cases two witnesses suffice but for such allegations, there should not be less than four witnesses who have all really seen the man and the woman actually committing the act of Zinaa, and the four witnesses must have the qualifications mentioned before. If not, then the accused are given the benefit of doubt, so that they may reform and repent without being punished by others.

Sometimes the accused may confess that they committed adultery or fornication; then there is compassion. Each of them ought to be punished in accordance with his/her marital status. Flogging a hundred lashes to those who have never tasted married life, and stoning to death in a pit to those who have tasted married life.

It is related that Maaliz ibn Malik al-Aslamy came to the Prophet of Allah (peace be upon him) while he was in the mosque and confessed of his sin saying:

> "O Messenger of Allah, I have committed adultery, and I require of you to cleanse me of this abomination."

The Holy Prophet turned his face from him and sent him away. Next morning the man came and repeated his confession explicitly as before. The Prophet sent him away again, and sent someone else to go and ask Maaliz's kinsfolk whether there was something wrong with his mind. They all asserted that he was sane. Maaliz came again to the Prophet for the third time, and again the Messenger of Allah sent someone else to have more enquiries about Maaliz's sanity. They all affirmed that the man was perfectly sane. When Maaliz came for the fourth time, the Prophet asked him: "Are they immunised (by marriage against lust)?" Maaliz said, "Yes". Then the Prophet asked him, "Perhaps you have just ogled? Or you kissed the woman's mouth or touched her body?" Maaliz answered, "O Apostle of Allah, it was none of these things." The Prophet then asked him: "Did you have sexual intercourse with the woman?" Maaliz said, "Yes, I have done so." The Prophet said: "Did you do by her what happens when the Kohl stick goes into the Kohl jar?" Maaliz affirmed. Then the Prophet ordered that a pit be dug. Maaliz was to enter into the pit and be stoned till death.

Another good, example that we can cite now is that of the Ghamidia-a woman from the Ghamidi. She came to the Holy Prophet and said, "I have committed adultery. Cleanse me, then of this sin." The Messenger of Allah (peace be upon him) sent her away. On the next morning she was there again before him, telling him, "May be that you have wanted to turn me away as you have done with Maaliz. But by my faith and honour, I am pregnant."

The Prophet then ordered her to go and wait until delivery. After the birth of the, child she came back with her child wrapped in a rag. When he saw that, the Prophet told her to go back till the child was breast-fed and weaned it. When that happened she came back with her child toddling beside her saying "This is my child, O Prophet of Allah."

The Prophet then ordered that the child be given under care of a fellow Muslim, and the Ghamidi woman be stoned to death.

A drop of blood flew from her smashed head and, fell on Khaalid b. al-Walid's, face and he cursed her so loudly, that the Apostle of Allah heard him. Here the Envoy of Allah (peace be upon him) told Khalid within hearing distance of others: "Softly O Khaalid, this woman has repented with a repentance so true and deep that if it were offered by an extortionist, he would have been absorbed."

In another version of the Hadith (Prophet's saying) it is, related that the Prophet had said, "...Her repentance is so ample that if it were to be divided between seventy of the people of Medina it would be sufficient unto all of them."

The Prophet gave both Maal'iz and the Ghamidite woman 'a golden opportunity' to go back and think better of their situations and escape humiliation and death by repenting secretly and their repentance would be true. But, alas ! the divine influence has made them not to accept it, but to be cleansed in much an ample and true repentance.

We learn from the above Hadith (sayings of the Prophet) that the avowal of the sin should be four times, the same number as that of the witnesses and of the Li'aan. Both the parties concerned must be present.

If one of them admits and the other denies, the judge is to remind him/her of the act of punishment of the hereafter which is much more painful. The judgement will be: punishment for the one who admitted and the other is given the benefit of doubt and acquitted.

The following question might be raised: "Why is a married person who commits Zinaa' stoned to death while the unmarried is flogged a hundred stripes? Both of them committed the same thing."

Generally the person who has never tasted a married life is a naive, and more often than not he/she does not enjoy the act in the real sense and knows what he/she is doing. While the one who has tasted married life is more sexually mature and secure. When such a person does that act, he/she really enjoys it.

A man can marry upto four wives, provided he deals with them equally in all worldly matters. He can divorce his wife if the marriage proves a failure.

The wife can also divorce the husband if the nuptial contract permits that. She may go to the court to ask for a divorce. Islam is not like other religions and cultures which did not allow the divorce till very recently; and in some of the cultures, there should first be such allegations that make it a slur on the family life of the spouses, before any divorce is granted.

So why on earth do such married people commit Zinaa? It is a disease and a very bad and infectious one. There ought to be an amputation of such a disease before the public so as to be a lesson to all.

If an unmarried woman is found pregnant, then people are to investigate into the matter whether she committed Zinaa willingly or by force.

If a woman is married to a boy who has not come to age (not sexually mature) or married to a man whose male organ is excised, and she is found pregnant, then they are also to find out the causes of her pregnancy.

The same thing applies to a woman who was married and gave birth to a child within less than six months from the day her husband slept with her first.

After thorough investigation if it is found that the pregnant woman, from any of the above quoted cases or any similar cases, was forced or intimidated by someone, or someone slept with her mistakenly thinking that she was his wife, as she might have slept in his bed; or she was found still virgin because the male organ did not go into the female organ (the act could have taken place at the gate only and the semen only went into the body) or for some similar reasons. Here the woman is given the benefit of doubt if she did not confess that she did commit the act of Zinaa.

During the orthodox Caliphate the patrol saw a girl throwing something at the garbage. They found it to be a newly born girl. They followed her and saw her entering into the house of one of the greatest companions of the Prophet.

Next morning the companion was called before the Caliph and was told the story. He neither denied it nor affirmed it. He told them that he had only one daughter. They had better call her and ask her themselves.

When the girl was brought before the Caliph she admitted that it was her baby and she got it through Zinaa.

An unmarried young girl commits Zinaa and gives birth to a baby, how is it?

She asked to be patient until she finished what she was going to tell them. She went reminding them that a year before they must have found a dead body at the same garbage heap and they did not know the killer. It was she then who bad killed the man.

This is a third act, then. She killed a man and then confessed.

But, wait! She told them that, man was the illegal father of the baby.

They had a neighbour who told her parents that she was going on a journey and she wanted her daughter to stay with them till her return. The two girls slept together.

One day, in the middle of the night the daughter, of the neighbour happened to be a boy and not a girl. He threatened her and forced her to have sex at the point of a knife and raped her. She struggled very much and in the long run managed to get hold of the knife after he had completed the raping. She killed him with his own knife, dragged him and threw him at the garbage heap, before her house.

She was acquitted because she was forced to do the act.

If the judge has a complete proof or the woman admits, then there is no compassion. Drastic steps must be taken.

Suppose one of the married couple accuses the other of unchastity what steps are to be taken?

It is against human nature for one of the spouses who catches the other committing adultery to be able to live happily together afterwards. The accuser will be haunted by doubts day in and day out.

English courts never allow a married couple to give evidence against each other.

It is unfair to ask him to produce one eyewitness, let alone four because the accusation partly affects him as well. No sane man will ever dare charge his wife with such a degrading accusation if she had never done it; just because the accusation partly affects his reputation as well.

It is narrated that a companion., Hilaal bin Umayya, by name; came back home at night, and found his wife committing adultery with someone. He saw them both doing the act and heard them all, what they were talking about.

He went straight to the Messenger of Allah (peace be upon him) and told him what he had seen and heard.

By that time, Aya (verse) of the slanderers had already been revealed. The Prophet told Hilaal to bring evidence or he would be flogged eighty lashes as there was no other alternative.

Hilaal said that he had no evidence as he was alone. But Allah would have surely found him a way out.

The Apostle of Allah was about to order Hilaal to be stripped when a revelation came. He recited it to those present with Hilaal and sent for the wife.

When the wife came she was told of the accusation and the revelation was read over to her which was :

> "And for those who launch charges against their spouses, and have (in support) no evidence but their own. This solitary evidence (can be

> received) if they bear witness four times (with an oath) by Allah that they are solemnly telling the truth."
>
> "And the faith (oath should be) that they solemnly invoke the curse of Allah on themselves if they tell a lie."
>
> "But it would avert the punishment from the wife, if she bears witness four times (with an oath) by Allah that (her husband) is telling a lie."
>
> "And the fifth (oath should be) that she solemnly invokes the wrath of Allah on herself if (her accuser) is telling a truth."
>
> (Qur'an 24: 6-9)

They were then told: that if the husband is a slanderer he is to confess and face the punishment flogging eighty stripes; or if the wife had really committed adultery she is to admit and face the stoning to death.

Both Hilaal and his wife were sworn. He swore four times saying that he, was telling the truth. Then he was told to curse himself. He, swore cursing himself if he was telling a lie.

'Then it was the turn of the wife. She took the oath four times that he was telling a lie. When she was told to invoke the wrath of Allah on herself if her husband was telling the truth; she became bit hesitant at first, then she made up her mind saying that she would not be the cause of the shame of her parent. She swore the fifth oath cursing herself if her husband was telling the truth.

Here the Prophet punished neither of the two. He separated them for ever never to remarry.

We hear that in some societies they regard the scandalous accusations in courts between spouses as the easiest means of getting divorces. The worse of it, as it came to our ear, that most of these allegations are fabricated ones.

The case remains in courts for a period of upto two years before the judge rules out for the divorce, and the old couple remain separated during this period, each of them is free as a bird on a tree, doing whatever he or she wants waiting for the judgement. There is a security from the Welfare Department controlling with a hawk's eye for either to commit anything sexually during time of separation.

There are some of the things that are even worse than this in some other cultures.

In the Farewell Pilgrimage address the Prophet (peace be upon him) said, among what is said:

> "People! you have certain rights over your wives, and so your wives over you. They are the trust of God in your hands. So you must treat them with all kindness. You have taken them only as a trust from Allah, and you have the enjoyment of their person by the words of Allah.

Allaal al-Faasy in his book: *Naqd adh-Dhdti.* (Self Criticism) has written a full chapter on prostitution:

> "There is no worse danger to the family than the public and private types of prostitution. Prostitution is one of the oldest from times immemorial. It is one of the social caterpillars that absorb the backbone of the house and destroys its being."

> "Prostitution came in vogue because of (many) reasons; (some of) the reasons are lack of family sex satisfaction; lack of mutual love and some misunaerstanding between the couple and their integrity."

> "It is a pity that different social classes regard this problem as a trivial one, because they generally ignore it, thinking that it is one of the natural phenomena and it is very difficult to get, rid of. It is therefore taken for granted."
>
> "The only step taken by reformists was still to organise, the brothel taking periodical check and case of the places and the women so as to reduce the widespread of venereal diseases; thinking that it was a more physical illness. They took this step to help travellers getting quick sex satisfaction from those who are professionals rather than searching for it in decent societies."
>
> "The originator of this evil was Napoleon, the enemy of women, prostitution was one of the evils of the eighteenth century, regardless of the protest by Mouliere, Rousseau, Montesquieu, Voltaire, Diedroe and others....."

Here Allal al-Faasy means that prostitution in its present form was originated by Napoleon, as he said before that this evil is an old one.

Allal al-Faásy goes on discussing the problem in detail. He then gives us the following, remedy:

> "We shan't get rid of prostitution unless and until we rid ourselves of its main causes which are:
>
> ***Social Cause:*** Morals and belief play a major part in combating human behaviour and controlling it. We are, then, to educate our young to be virtuous, chaste and become the masters of their instincts. The nostalgia of this is that there is sublimation in fine and applied

arts and in social work. This could be done through youth organisations such as scouting, sports, etc."

Economic (Financial) Cause: "Some of the women, who take prostitution as a profession, do so, more often than not, because of hardship of life..."

"A woman might not be able to look after herself and feed the couple of mouths that she is responsible to feed. Circumstances force her to be a prostitute; because there is no such social security for her and the ones she is incharge of..."

Legal (Legislative) Cause: "If there is no authority to check people of what they do, it makes them do whatever they want. It is very difficult for anyone to control himself from each and everything if there is nothing to check his steps. Hence we had regulations and legislations. Laws are the best means of making people abide to morals and chastity."

"Societies should make rules and regulations to stop all types of prostitutions."

14

Significance of Veil

Seclusion by veiling is not synonymous with social and political segregation, it rather resolves the problem of interaction across gender boundaries. Veiling denotes the Afghani man's and woman's cultural pride, his or her self image, and allows for free social mobility across social spheres. Anderson, Wikan and Altorki all suggest that the veil may define a cultural definition of sexual seclusion, without necessarily implying segregation and oppression of Muslim women in everyday reality. The discourse to be assessed here is composed of a variety of situations, with social, religious and political as well as sexual connotations.

We use the term discourse not in a strictly linguistic sense, but rather in the broader meaning of Foucault's terminology. We seek to understand the metaphors and cultural idioms associated with religious modesty and veiling, by studying them within the more extensive political, social and religious context. A decade after the Iranian revolution, the discourse of veiling is not a question of to veil or not to veil; nor is it a question of being secular or religious, as was the case during the 1978 revolution and the following years. Rather, it is a question of how and where to veil and which veil to adopt.

The social and economic modernity in several Middle Eastern countries in the 1970s became synonymous with the unveiling of women. In the context of the social and economic modernity under the Pahlavi Iranian state, unveiling has often been associated with revolutionary acts, bravery, liberation, emancipation, and empowerment in the women's political and social movement. Two historical acts may illustrate such an image. (1) Upon the death of the famous mystic Mansur Hallaj in AD 922 his sister appeared in public unveiled to challenge men. (2) The story that a famous woman of the Bahai religion, Qurratu'l Ayn, in 1949 removed her veil to signal the equality of women and men. In Iran, the veil was negatively identified in the course of the economic modernity and social reforms that started with the Pahlavi regime and extended under the former Shah's regime in the early 1970s. This led to a compulsory unveiling law in 1936 and the importing of French-style clothes and hats for both men and women. The 1936 law meant a prohibition of wearing the veil at public places such as schools, the workplace, and outside on the street.

Kashfeh-hejab was one of the important socio-political reforms of the Reza-Shah (the father of the former king), who attacked whatever he considered to be the vestiges of backwardness, i.e. the *chador*. Chadori women of that period told they had to hide in corners when they were in the street, or their chador would be forcefully removed by the police. The Iranian tradition of wearing a chador (full-length veil) is customarily understood by the average people to symbolise cultural authenticity.

Recent historical studies of the veiling of Middle Eastern women support the idea that Islam did not invent the full-length veil and instead identify it with the urban lifestyle phenomenon of pre-Islamic Iran. However, the emergence of veiling as a 'true' tradition and a central aspect of the Muslim identity during the revolutionary movement, was associated with Islamic tradition. During the revolution, the wearing of a full-length veil by women became a symbolic weapon against the Shah's regime and his Western alliances. The full-length veil in post-revolutionary time-represents the victory of the Islamic state and the repression of other secular political ideologies.

The chador (full-length veil) covers the wearer from the top of her head to her wrists and ankles. During the Iranian revolution it has been correctly explained by many writers as a response to pre-revolutionary secular life experiences. As a revival of their identity many educated women, who previously only occasionally wore the full-length veil when visiting shrines, mosques or attending a funeral, began to wear a full-length veil in order to express solidarity with religious and lower-class women.

A full-length veil signals a cumulative identity of religious and social integrity and the authenticity of women's political protest. The practice of veiling in the ideology of the Islamic state and its local conservative agencies pertains to head and full-body cover, gender interaction and a range of bodily boundaries. The political ideology of the Islamic state views men as the weaker partner and in need of protection to control their sexual desire.

In other words, women tempt men, and thus endanger the social order and national political stability. The sexual danger of the woman in its invisible and visible forms is believed to be so powerful and impulsive that it can lead to the moral corruption of men and society. Hence, Muslim society such as Iran can remain socially ordered, harmonious, and healthy only if the women control themselves and avoid acts of exhibitionism. Many public notices put on the walls of shops, state offices and buildings warn women who do not comply with the ideal that they will not be served as proper customers. To receive proper service, women have to cover their heads completely, exhibiting no part of their forehead and wearing no make-up. Women's covering garment metaphorically produces political meaning, and failure to comply was often identified as an act of political protest and therefore a reason for punishment.

In post-revolutionary Iran, the full-length veil is not the only Islamic dress to receive public recognition. The common legitimate Islamic dress worn by the average urban woman consists of a long-sleeved, high-necked dress that stretches below the knees, a large head-scarf, trousers (not jeans) and thick dark-coloured stockings. Public control of women is dominated by hezbullahi men and women. There are new jobs for controllers in airports, offices, academic institutions and public places, and recruitment is on the basis of positive attitudes to the new social rules and Islamic knowledge. They function effectively and restrictively.

The wimple head-scarf was traditionally worn as a praying cloth by elderly religious women in private prayers, and represented a private marginalised code of piety. Since the revolution it has been transformed from being a private sign of piety into an ideal Islamic dress that must be worn by women in nurseries, schools, universities, workplaces and government buildings. It is recognised by the Islamic experts and the educational authorities as the ideal form of veiling and an 'appropriate' public Islamic symbol.

The wimple head-scarf should cover most of the hair on a woman's head, as well as the forehead, shoulders, neck and breast. Only an opening the size of the face should remain. At school trousers like American Lee jeans were prohibited, as being symbolic of the political and cultural influences of American Imperialism. At the age of nine girls are expected to start complying with a series of religious norms, and to make the transition from childhood to an adult.

Transforming the former secular educational system by means of religious knowledge, political consciousness and ideological forces has been one of the prime concerns of the Islamic Republic since the political turmoil in 1979. Today schoolgirls, university students and state employees are expected to practise full veiling and participate in the regular and obligatory prayers and fasts. Workplaces enforce the new restrictive head and body cover for women employees under the supervision of the Islamic association. In schools and at the workplace this control has sometimes developed into violation in the name of religious duty in directing others to what is lawful and to what is not lawful. In fulfilling this duty one is considered to be constructing the personal identity of a dutiful Muslim.

The familiar religious and cultural terms *amre-be-m'aruf* and *nahi-az-monker* have served as a platform for the process of censorship and social control in the post-revolutionary period. The new Islamic control at workplaces, universities and schools is part of the state administrative policy based on the new Islamic teachings and practices, and the enforcement system. The mode of regulation is through the religio-political reforms in workplaces and the recruitment criteria set up for government positions. Religious training and the acquisition of 'correct' prayer and correct Islamic appearance at school and at the workplace have become important elements in the Islamic education of girls and boys.

Educational institutions were threatened with prosecution and closure if they did not enforce full veiling on their female students and employees, and female teachers. School administrators and female students were threatened by the Minister of Education with dismissal if they did not oblige. The Islamic state mandate on veiling at schools and workplaces has created stress and feelings of distrust. For some, not to have a proper veiling involved dramatic consequences, such as physical attacks or a few hours in detention. This strict control of the full veil in particular led to violence against women during the period of war between Iran and Iraq. At that time women were defined as the vehicle of social disorder and political instability.

The less colourful and decorative appearance of women in public represented a strong image of solidarity, an expression of sorrow to families with casualties, and community solidarity. Public control of people's behaviour in the name of Islamic authority was not an uncommon practice in day-to-day interaction, particularly in 1989. The women's Islamic police could, for example, order a woman to fully cover her head and pull the scarf down to her forehead, and a religious oriented man passing by might remind you of your religious duty of being fully covered.

Conservative Muslim men and women have redefined the veil as 'true' Islamic norms that should be observed both in public and in private family gatherings. The family of hezbullahi's may adopt a stricter sexual segregation than the average urban family.

According to the conservative Islamic category a single hair may be as sinful as exposing all the hair. Strict religious women wear a full-length veil only exposing their eyes. Every single sexual interaction is considered important in itself for the record of one's behaviour on the day of judgment. The preacher Mostafi further discouraged women from shaking hands and instead encouraged them to call each other a religious 'sister' or 'brother'.

The preacher Zaki insisted that the youth were full of passion since economic conditions prevented them from getting married and having legitimate sexual relations. Hence, modest behaviour is considered desirable even in relations with male relatives, despite the fact that they are traditionally classified as mahram (legitimate kin). As such the idea of being a true Muslim woman, as instructed by conservative religious authorities, went beyond the common practice. The religious conservative men believe that the religious status of their women increases if they wear the traditional full-length veil.

There are different degrees of veiling, not only among women, but also among different Islamic categories. Both of the above cases reflect typical sources and patterns of family conflicts and the control of women for male Islamic ideological purposes. However, for some conservative Islamic authorities the public definition of what is a proper Islamic covering is more than simply wearing a full-length veil. Wearing trousers is also required.

In the post-revolutionary period, the Islamic political authorities encouraged the masses to watch over their family members, neighbours and relatives, in order to discourage them from committing non-Islamic acts. There are stories of the effects this had on the emotional relations and authoritative roles between family members. One party in a conflict could always claim the other was committing acts socially and politically endangering the stability of Islamic state. According to the view of the religious authorities, what constituted immodest behaviour of women refers not only to the public display of the female body, but uncontrolled social interactions. Religious modesty and veiling in its broader social context remain a pertinent ideology of Muslim women's femininity.

In 1989 the controversy surrounding the practice of womens' modesty and veiling was of concern for at least five categories of organisations. On the institutional level the following organisations were involved: the Islamic police, who seek to eliminate and punish 'incorrect' Islamic acts; the agencies of the moderate Rafsanjani government, who seek to moderate public rules by recognising different forms of covering garments; and the Islamic elite women's organisation, which is powerful in educational and work establishments, controlling behaviour in accordance with the new images of male and female roles as prescribed in the school text books.

The fourth group is represented in general by the female Islamic experts in the local area. The final category is the hezbullahi women, who like the Islamic elite utilise the wimple head-scarf, but in addition insist on the Iranian tradition of a full-length veil. The hezbullahi women's demonstration against poorly-veiled women was used by the Islamic police authority to tighten up the veiling rules. The pro-veiling slogans continued to be supportive of the revolutionary police in 1989. The street slogans in the post Iran-Iraq war period addressed whether bi-hejab (non-veiled) and bad-hejab (poorly-veiled) women should feel ashamed in the presence of mothers of martyrs.

By wearing dark colours and not wearing jewellery, particularly gold bracelets and necklaces that signify a higher socio-economic status, women express sympathy and solidarity towards the mothers of martyrs, both in the neighbourhood and the community at large. On one side of this controversy are the relatives of the martyrs who identify themselves as first-class Muslim citizens of the postwar Iran period, on the grounds of having sacrificed family members on behalf of the Islamic state and community.

On the other side of the controversy are the average urban middle- and higher-class women with very few martyrs in their families. They challenge the enforced Islamic dress by changing it to fashionable Islamic suits. In contrast, during the post-war period, the emphasis on the full-length veil has been maintained and manipulated locally by the hezbullahis, their argument being that it is the only 'true' form of veiling.

This kind of development strengthens the existing opinion between those directly or indirectly related to martyrs and those who are not. This duality has caused considerable confusion.

Negative Implications

The term bi-hejabi, with its negative implications, has been applied by the local preacher to women wearing the manto, although this is officially recognised by the state and is a dominant veil among upper- and middle-class urban women. Housewives busy with extra-domestic tasks such as purchasing household goods and attending to family matters associated with public life also find the Islamic suit more convenient than the full length veil. They are, for example, able to hold shopping bags in one hand and children in the other, something which is difficult when wearing the full-length veil.

Among thé middle-class women the tradition of veiling is impractical in their modern social and economic lifestyle, which includes a wide range of extra household activities. The fact that middle-class women distance themselves from the traditional religious garment of the full-length veil has given rise to numerous demonstrations in Tehran, where conservative forces demand a greater control over the implementation of the Islamic suit and scarf. For example, when president Rafsanjani recognized the loose fitting suit, the hezbullahi and the family of martyrs reacted immediately with a demonstration, condemning any act of bad veiling.

The participants in the July 1989 demonstrations opposed the wearing of colourful scarves and stylish Islamic suits, arguing that it dishonoured martyrs and undermined the attempts to sustain a revolutionary ideology against Western influences and the search for an Islamic authenticity. Hence, to the mothers of martyrs, the manto and the new style of thin stockings represent a pre-revolutionary women's clothing that indicates a lack of solidarity with their suffering. An example of a more liberal attitude of the post-war period in June 1989 was the resumption of the traditional marriage ceremony, characterised by public music and the custom of driving the bride and groom around the town while blowing the car horn. This custom had, like many other communal celebrations, been strictly forbidden during the war between Iran and Iraq, when the emphasis was on communal mourning and national expressions of grief and solidarity to families of martyrs.

Another sign of the return to normal life was the increased presence of tribal women in towns, the latter traditionally being less veiled than their urban counterparts. They come to town to sell their handiwork and crafts, including local musical instruments, at the market in Shiraz. Their colourful shirts strongly contrast with the dark colours and veils worn by the hezbullahi women.

The religious conservatives aim is to prohibit acts which they consider sexually provocative and socially destructive. Mary Douglas made a link between the rational behaviour of primitives and taboo-thinking. In her view taboo turns out not to be incomprehensible, but is an intelligible concern to protect society from behaviour that threatens its order. When conservative Islamists demand that both Muslim men and women should uphold community values through a series of restricted modesty and bodily boundaries, the aim is not only to moralise, but also to politicise Iranian society.

The official veiling on bodily boundaries includes both men and women, women often are most blamed for jeopardising revolutionary society. To look into the eyes, or touch the hand of a member of the opposite sex, whatever the relationship may be, is thought to lead to sexual temptation, and is therefore-outside of marriage considered a provocative act. The idea of having 'pure' eyes, a modest gaze and a plain voice, even in encounters between an adult brother and sister, is identical with hezbullahi: moralisation plan for Iranian society.

Preacher Mostafi, who is considered a hezbullahi and supporter of the Islamic regime, repeatedly warned her listeners at the fast month meetings against seductive body movement. She argued that not only would such behaviour devalue their prayers, but severe punishment would wait them on the day of judgment: 'One's body might be hanged by the breast, or by the single hair that has been displayed vulgarly in this world, and the offending part of the body might be burned.' She described the uncovered head and open-necked shirt as immodest and contradictory to 'true' Muslim morality.

The female breast and buttocks, the neck, foot and particularly the ankle, as well as the heel and arms are among the taboo parts of the body. They are often referred to with feelings of passion, and therefore are deemed seductive and detrimental to the maintenance of morality and political stability. High-heel shoes are blamed as a metaphor for seductive sexual behaviour. Such a negative view of women's clothing developed publicly and was adopted by the university Islamic 'sisters', who issued a long list of clothing rules for female students and private and state employees. Such an ideology is adopted by various categories such as schoolgirls, university students, religiously oriented women, ritual experts, students of religious schools, certified religious leaders, etc. They commonly moralise and politicise women's bodily movements in religious vocabulary and request official control.

Recognising male modesty as an important aspect of Muslim men's identity, it seems that the consequences of lack of modesty are more serious for women than for men. The Islamic state policy of sexual control of all its citizens does place some sanctions on male behaviour. Offensive remarks made by youths to women on the street have been discouraged by the Islamic police as being an insult to an Islamic sister. A man wearing a short-sleeved shirt with an open collar in public is also considered sinful.

In the post-revolutionary period there were several cases where youths were arrested if dressed in a Western teenage style, i.e. tight trousers and colourful patterned shirts. The fear of political repercussions, and of being arrested, has led many parents to increase their sanctions on the social activities of their children, and especially their daughters. The Islamic Republic was determined to moralise public social appearances by replacing whatever they believed to be an influence of Western culture. Hence, a T-shirt displaying a picture of a film star signified a careless identity of stereotyped manners, contrasting with the devoted Islamic youths, who were sent to fight against the Iraqi troops on the front line during 1981-82.

According to the conservative ideology men are considered the weaker part when it comes to controlling their sexual passion. Thus, when enforcing social rules, some of the forbidden acts of men may be easily forgiven, as these are believed to be caused by the sexual powers of women.

Despite a conservative ideological view on veiling, the veiling practice among women is far from uniform. Women have become more creative and fashion conscious, constantly attempting to subvert the blandness of the conventional veil. They have adopted various Islamic covering garments that play with colours, fabrics and design. Although a person's Muslim identity is defined according to the correct performance of daily prayers, veiling and modesty, women in everyday practice largely adopt a complex cultural and religious repertoire of behaviour, where a pure state of intention takes a priority over rigid appearance. To the majority, having faith is not necessarily a matter of adhering to the static norms, but a pure state of intention.

Using different forms of veil to fit different social situations is an important aspect of one's identity among middle-class women. Shazdeh's strategic veiling was once observed by the preacher Mumeni. Shazdeh replaced her full-length veil with a scarf while sitting in her car on her way back from a religious meeting. Seeing this, Mumeni warned her against this forbidden act, arguing that her fast would be broken due to her face and the backs of her hands being visible.

Shazdeh replied that the full-length veil disturbed her when driving and that it was too warm. These reasons were not accepted by Mumeni, who continued to warn her of the flames of hell and the day of judgment. This disappointed Shazdeh, and she told that she would no longer attend any of Mumeni's meetings. She did, however, continue to attend religious seminaries led by recent Islamic graduate preachers on the grounds that they were more liberal.

Despite being a devoted Muslim, the norms demanded by the preacher Mumeni were not compatible with everyday life. After all, she argued, on her two pilgrimages to Mecca, when the contact with God is especially strong, and when the seven times ritual walk between the holy places Safa and Marvah is performed by both men and women, it is not forbidden to display the oval face and the backs of the hands.

In the opinion of Shazdeh the norms advocated by Mumeni on the 'true' veil make religion static and difficult to practise on a daily basis, even for women like herself who strongly believe in women's modesty, the ritual of vow-making and the obligatory prayers, as well as in the importance of religious meetings. The decision of what veil to choose for a specific occasion is situational and reflects the realisation of a broader social and political relation. Some middle-class women use the full-length veil only at religious meetings as a shared code, and remove it once they are in the street and out of sight of other religious friends.

Ideally, a woman wearing a black full-length veil of heavy-quality cloth is identified by other religious friends as a woman deserving strong respect. The use of a thick quality full-length veil during religious gatherings reflects religious prestige and a strong moral identity. The religiously oriented middle class, in contrast to the religiously conservative women, may at smaller gatherings of friends from a Quranic course or at wedding parties, change from a thick-quality full-length veil to one thinner and lighter in colour. Such a change can often be explained as a matter of personal comfort, informality and pressure from other relatives.

The type of full-length veil worn may signify the degree of one's religious affiliation, personal strength and the religious occasion. For example, a full-length veil may be used at annual religious meetings by the more well-educated, modern working women, and a lighter, flowery one for happy occasions, such as the votive meal services where religious meetings develop into a feast. While women may dress elegantly at family visits and parties, the opposite may be the case at religious meetings where it is important to signify a pious identity.

Thus, a woman's good character is not only defined in terms of her relations with her male partner encountered in the public sphere, but also in terms of the moral identity sought in relations with other women.

Religious Meetings

The privacy of religious meetings does not mean that participants are less reserved in their veiling, and women are seldom poorly-veiled in the presence of each other at religious meetings, the possible exception being religious meal feasts such as *eftari* (the meal ending a fast), or when attending a less popular Quranic course with very close co-seminary friends.

Some women may use the dress as a religious device to signal special events by changing the colour and style of veil. For example, to mark celebrations such as the birth of the Prophet, or the death of the 'Umar," women may wear dresses that are more colourful and elegant under their full-length veil. Having a head-scarf under their full-length veil, women are more willing to lower their veil to their shoulders at the religious meetings since the wimple was officially defined as a proper and fully acceptable veil as it hung down to the shoulders, covering neck and chest.

Women who remove their head cover and/or display a golden necklace or bracelet may be criticised by others as exhibitionists. Such a display of a new style of dress or jewellery is often believed by female preachers to lead to jealousy and competition. The preacher Mostafi usually raised the theme of the veil in her speeches, whether in public religious halls or at private homes. Through story-telling she sought to illustrate the Islamic ideals and frameworks of meaning.

Mostafi repeatedly suggested that the importance of modesty today was connected to judgment in the after-life, and she asked if the women were taking seriously the responsibility of their own behaviour and that of others. She warned the women present of the possibility of committing a sinful act of incorrect prayers without being aware of it, despite being a religiously learned person. Furthermore, she listed the most sinful acts often committed by women, two of which were appearing poorly veiled and gossiping. Similar moral lessons were followed up by the preacher Zaki in another Ramazan meeting a few days later. She pointed out that some participants had been seen wearing the full-length veil at religious meetings, while dressing elegantly with colourful scarves on other occasions. Then she told the participants that to obtain the world of *akhirat* they must act with piety in spite of all the counter-forces.

The preacher Mumeni, like others in her rank, remained conventional when implementing the rules of Islamic modesty and veiling to her audience. A woman who has made the obligatory pilgrimage to Mecca is expected to display greater modesty and adopt a more restricted veil than before going to pilgrimage. Hajji women from middle-class families who have made the obligatory pilgrimage to Mecca do not always wear the full-length veil. In their eyes those who observe a restricted Islamic garment are old fashioned.

A full-length veil is seldom removed in the presence of a female preacher unless the women are wearing head-scarves and are fully covered underneath. This indicates the women's expectations towards each other, their identity of piety. A 'pious' veiling is valued as a means of ensuring merit in the life hereafter, and it symbolises the individual's strong belief and personality. As a religiously oriented woman put it to me, 'strict dress over worldly attraction'. Thus, she wears both head-scarf and a full-length veil, a double-Islamic dress for religious conservatism.

Changing one's traditional full-length veil to an Islamic suit has become a common practical solution among the old and the lower middle-class women. This has distorted the rigid ideology of the conservative hezbullahi Muslims, who argue that a full-length veil is important to one's cultural and religious authenticity. Being aware of the distorted practice and untraditional changes among women, the preacher Mostafi repeatedly warned her audience not to follow suit. Her remarks were directed at the strategic behaviour of the participants who changed their veil according to place and occasion. Such inconsistency in veiling is considered worldly (*donyavi*) and is associated with a kind of behaviour classified as 'dolly' (*arosaki*); i.e. behaviour considered artificial and Westernised, and that should be avoided even in the private sphere of family and friends.

According to the preacher Mostafi, women wearing a full-length veil, despite the heat and discomfort, display the firmness of their faith and their superiority in worldly matters. Although wearing a full veil might not seem attractive in the present, it will give rewards in the afterlife. Nezhat was among the elderly women who used to wear the new Islamic suit (manto) outside on the street, while carrying a full-length veil in her bag in case she wanted to enter a religious place. She was an active religious participant and played a conservative role vis-a-vis other religious friends, who identified her as a woman of strong faith. She was seen without a full-length veil several times by her Quranic colleagues and this left her with a feeling of embarrassment. In an attempt to avoid standardisation some girls change the wimple head-scarves of the school uniform, sewing an additional chin or forehead piece to make it resemble a hat. This is considered to be more attractive and makes the mandatory veil more tolerable.

Some prefer a black wimple head scarf on the grounds that it matches their black eyes, which they accentuate slightly with make-up. A fringe of curled or dyed hair displayed on the forehead was adopted along with the Islamic suit by middle-class urban women, who insisted on looking fashionable in their adopted Islamic suits. This signified opposition and seemed to be a form of resistance and political protest, since the women risked being stopped in the street and warned by Islamic police, and even fired from their jobs or arrested. These examples illustrate that the veil is not uniform and in practice it remains subject to identity management.

The Nature

One of the cultural peculiarities of the modern age is that it has created the trend of impudence and immodesty (informality and lack of feminine decorum in dress) among women. With the vehemence with which this trend was pushed forward in society, her scantiness of dress also took bold jumps ahead. Her exposure of body is a source of sensual pleasure to man. Therefore, he neither objected to it nor imposed any restrictions on it. Rather, he emboldened her and gave it a fillip. He deeply impressed on her mind that her beauty and elegance should be exposed to view for appreciation and applause. It is insulting to her charming personality that her physical charms be prudishly concealed. Her seclusion and concealment of charms in the presence of the opposite sex is unnatural. Her dress is not meant to keep hidden her elegance of form but to make it more attractive by artifice. So she should dress more to reveal her figure rather than conceal it from the view of admirers so as to make herself more attractive to them. His dormant passions may be excited and he may be drawn to her impatiently. The dress found lacking in this aspect of allurement is not befitting her graceful body. This resulted in such bold steps in brevity and peculiar revealing designs that hardly left anything to imagination where body curves and prominences were concerned. She began to expose shamelessly the one-time uncovering of which was considered most improper. The few remaining shreds may not take long to be boldly discarded. It appears even this burden is too much for her and she may get rid of them any day now. Propaganda in favour of perfect nudity is afoot and arguments are being sought in its support and it is being termed the true human nature (sullied by unnecessary items of dress). And the most powerful is the practical argument since she has already sufficiently advanced towards nudity. Perhaps never in man's recorded history human nature had been so insulted with temerity.

The modern age had made immodesty an art and created in its support an atmosphere that the woman cheerfully threw away her armament of modesty and started moving about half-clad. But the most strange happening is that there was no change observed in the dress of man. There was no move towards immodesty on his part. Rather he himself is taking to more and more formal dress with the passage of time and the so called advancement in culture. He himself dresses in keeping with the changes in the weather conditions, but does not allow the poor better half to cover her whole body even in chilly winters. His own dress is loose enough to be comfortable, but induces her to put on skin tight and troublesome dress which permit exact measurement of her physique. He himself puts on clothes of the extremely rough and thick textured fabrics and nobody seems to mind it. But the woman is offered by the designers and dress-makers clothes thin and almost transparent to reveal her skin. This is a strange contrast between the dresses of the two sexes and their attitude towards them. But the woman has failed to realize this contradiction yet. Whereas man is fully, if not over-clad, takes his partner out in the open market places and other public gatherings almost unclad. She ought to have rebelled against this attitude. She has, due to her simplicity and short sightedness, taken to it as a demand of the present day culture. And instead of hanging her head in remorse she raises it out of pride and a sense of superiority and with all her blandishments she corroborates, with him.

In this atmosphere of informality in the matter of dress, if a woman observes the Islamic limits and keeps her body concealed from the prying looks of strangers, she makes the blood of a lascivious person boil. She appears to him as a walking corpse which fails to provide his eagerly wandering gaze the morbid pleasure, he is after, every where.

No Restriction

An argument is put forth, which, truth to tell, has hardly any strength in it, that *hijab*, intervening between man and woman puts an unnecessary check on their passions, which remain suppressed and resulting in various psychological complications. And such checks on natural passions and the consequent suppression has violent reaction in the form of an outburst with dreadful consequences. But this absurd and meaningless philosophy is totally against human psychology. Experience has always confused it. The experiments performed in the West itself have convincingly proved that due to immodesty in dress and free mixing of sexes passions are inflamed and illicit sex becomes rife. So we find that free sex is becoming the unhealing sore of the Western society. The ruination of once happy families is common, moral values are down-trodden and physical, mental and nervous diseases are also becoming common due to this sex-anarchy. It has shaken the very foundations of Western culture. After witnessing these dreadful consequences no right-minded person should abstain from becoming supporter of hijab and supporting modesty and preaching this cult. If this Islamic Law of hijab had not existed, he would have found himself compelled to enact one and try to make men and women follow it.

It is usually asserted that hijab or purdah is a stumbling block in the way of women towards progress. This has left her weighted down by penury and she is a victim of decline and decay. She finds herself practically cut off from political and social life. Women who are free from this stricture have gone far on the road to progress.

But the difficulty is that this is not the one and only hurdle. So many other factors are stated to be our fetters where march on the road to progress is concerned. To some of them the entire familial system is a great drawback. It confines the poor woman to the four walls of the house. Some others regard the Islamic devotional acts barring the way of the Muslims towards progress. Salat or prayer interferes in the most suitable working hours. Fasting tells upon the health, and Hajj involves waste of time and money both. Poor Muslim ! He is at a loss to decide to whom he should listen and whose advice to overlook and ignore? Obviously he can please only one of them. Others are sure to be annoyed. Formality apart, many intellectuals consider Islam itself the greatest hindrance to the progress of Muslims. But it is the compulsion of a common Muslim that he, not withstanding his manifold infirmities and shortcomings, is not prepared to give up Islam.

Again, the progress of woman which is brought in question, if it alludes to that she has made in immodesty, dance and music and the like in the name of fine arts, her performance is certainly wonderful and she is at the "peak of glory and fame" in her own circle. But to attain these heights of progress and fame she had to sacrifice the high values like modesty, chastity, kindness, love, obedience and loyalty. For, without sacrifice of these exalted values, progress would have been impossible. Islam in this behalf has a particular viewpoint. To it, progress is that which creates in man human qualities of a high order. The progress that destroys those values is not progress at all. (It is abysmal degeneration).

It is an admitted fact that woman has, quite apart from this, made progress in various sciences and arts too, and has rendered valuable services in the field of learning and research. Some people labour under the erroneous notion that such progress is not possible with restrictions of hijab. But this misunderstanding is created by the pervading atmosphere where purdah and modesty are conspicuous by their absence. This , apparently glaring atmosphere intimidates the onlookers positively and it becomes difficult to understand as to how can woman make progress in a perfectly clean atmosphere. This other progress is not indebted to absence of purdah. There are other factors responsible for it.

Firstly, the women who have achieved great success in some field was the fruit of their untiring effort, constant struggle and their sincerity of purpose. Their merit must be appreciated. It is the divine law that those working with sincerity and devotion are rewarded with success.

Secondly, the present day culture is a shameless one. It provides facilities of sciences and arts only to such women as have the audacity to throwing away their purdah and taking their stand with the immodest lot. In this way the paths of progress have been practically barred to the women who stick to their hijab. Progress does not depend on hijab or absence of it but is closely associated with the facilities offered to the woman. The experience of the present age too bears testimony to the fact that the purdah observing women made progress in keeping with the facilities they received in their efforts and came out shoulder to shoulder with their sisters outside the purdah limits.

Again this generalization can be accepted as true only in case of women within the limits of hijab might have failed in making progress. It is an undeniable fact that the women discarding the limits prescribed for her by Islam, did not achieve any success worthy of pride for the Ummah. And nobody heard of any 'Ayeshah, Umm-e-Salmah, Asma' bint-e-Abu Bakr, Fatimah bint-e-Khattab or any Khansa' R.A.A. taking birth in the Muslim ummah today.

Within the Islamic limits for women on the one hand, they attained the highest position in knowledge and learning and on the other, were not totally dissociated from the political and social trends of the times. Rather they left their mark on them.

And along with all these remarkable endeavours such worthy sons and daughters emerged from their laps that proved to be the glory and pride of history, and such pillars of learning and knowledge and such leaders of arts received their training and upbringing at these (worthy mother's) hands, whose beneficence in the fields of learning and culture mankind can never fully acknowledge with gratitude. Was all this the performance of ignorant unlettered women?

The Sphere

In the face of the objections raised against purdah people in their bewilderment at once start with apologetic explanations, dragging the maulvis in their disputes as scape-goats and asserting that it is they who have in the name of purdah imposed all sorts of restrictions on women. Islam is against such impositions. Islam has exempted the face and hands of women from purdah, and she can expose them before strangers. Then they extend this exemption to the freedom of the modern woman.

There is only this much truth in it that the jurists have differed in the matter of exposure of woman's face and hands. Even if it is taken for granted that she can expose these two before aliens, no justification can be found in the Islamic Law for the freedom enjoyed by the women in the present day permissive atmosphere.

Islam looks at the relationship of woman and man from a peculiar view-point of which hijab is an important part. This view-point is diametrically opposed to the modern trend of thought and clashes with it at every step in life.

Islam has recommended to the woman to take her home as the real centre of her attention and activity. It does not like that she should step out of it without a pressing need. The modernists are not prepared to admit that her activities should be confined to the four walls of her home. Islam is dead against mixing of sexes whereas it is the essential element of the existing mode of living. Islam has ordained lowering of gaze against which the modern thought is totally devoid of any such concept of immediate lowering of gaze in case of accidental glimpse of an alien woman. It is possible this much regard of "purdah" (sudden reaction on his part) may be considered deprivation of a pleasure coming his way. Islam regards mixing of men and women during the courses of education and training, games and field events, etc., detrimental to their morality, when it is a fact that in the present set-up it all rests on free mixing of both sexes which is deemed a merit. Islam instructs the woman to keep to the side of the road (taking the foot-path if there is one) to avoid collision with men. Even in the performance of devotional acts she has been ordered to keep a safe distance between the two gatherings (of men and women in the mosque and Hajj pilgrimage), when it is a well known fact that the existing order cannot put up with this discriminatory treatment of women and wishes to see them shoulder to shoulder with men, on the roads, market places, offices and social gatherings. The fact is that it is not hijab alone that vexes her but without violating many definite ordainments of Islam, the Muslim woman cannot participate in the struggle of life with the freedom of modern woman.

The existing order invites the woman to a life free from all restrictions and hurdles, which Islam declares moral limits and observances essential (as a part of her belief and faith and not as mere sound advice). The destination and end of both is clearly before her and she can very easily decide her direction and her destination.

Under Cover

The purdah system among the Muslims has been the subject of fierce controversies between the old, conservative school of thought and the new, enlightened sections of Muslims brought up under the influence of Western education and culture. It has also come in for much abuse and mudslinging by the non-Muslim critics, writers and thinkers. Old-fashioned people, whose influence is still great, defend the existing purdah system as entirely in accordance with the teachings of Islam. They maintain that this system is not a post Islamic invention and a departure from the practices and customs that held sway during the period of the Prophet. On the other hand, the so-called advanced sections of the Muslims, who have taken every Western mode of thought and practice as an infallible truth, argue very much as if life and society in early Islam were patterned on that which is exhibited in Hollywood films and obtains in the fashionable circles of London and New York. The truth, as in many other cases, lies somewhere in the midway.

There is no doubt that the purdah system as it exists among middle-class Muslims has nothing Islamic about it. It is purely a non-religious social custom. Life in Islamic Arabia was set in a different pattern and the rigorous confinement of women within the four walls of their homes was a phenomenon not to be met with anywhere. This is not, however, to justify the standpoint of those Muslims who are anxious to prove that the wives and female relations of the Prophet and his companions enjoyed the same unrestricted freedom as the ordinary women in the Western countries, or freely intermingled with men without occasion and necessity. This had never been the case. Women in early Islam were not totally confined to their homes. They came out on occasions under the stress of economic, social and religious necessity, but when they did come out they dressed and moved in a particular way which did not make them objects of attraction and they remained very much apart from the society of men. Unnecessary intermixture of the sexes was never approved of by Islam and runs counter to the whole spirit of its teachings.

In discussing the question of purdah, these two aspects should be sharply distinguished, otherwise there will be much confusion of thought. The question whether women are free to go out of their homes and, if so, whether it is necessary to hide their faces completely under their veils, is different from the question whether they are permitted to mix freely with men on all occasions-in private gatherings, social and State functions and political assemblies. On the first issue, we are in agreement with the stand taken by our modernists; on the second issue, we unreservedly repudiate their conclusions. Let us analyse our arguments.

The defenders of the existing purdah system which means, in effect, close and complete confinement of women within their homes, build their case on the following verses of the Holy Qur'an:

> And stay in your homes and do not go about displaying yourselves like the display of the days of Ignorance. (xxxii 1 33)
>
> O Prophet, say to your wives and your daughters and the women of the believers that they let down over them their *jilbab* (over-garment); this will be more proper that they may be known, and thus they will not be molested. (xxxii 53)
>
> Say to the believing women that they cast down their looks and guard their private parts; that is purer for them; surely Allah is aware of what they do.
>
> And say to the believing women that they cast down their looks and guard their private parts and not display their ornaments except what appears thereof, and let them wear their head-coverings over their bosoms and not display their ornaments except to their husbands or...
> (xxiv. 30 31)

Purdah System

From the first verse, the defenders of the purdah system argue that Islam means to keep women closely and completely confined to their homes. This is a wrong interpretation. When the Qur'an says that women should stay in their homes and make no display of their charms, it is referring to the life in pre-Islamic Arabia, when women, despite the heavy social and legal disabilities from which they suffered, freely and frequently moved about and indulged in amorous talks with strangers or mixed with them on objectionably intimate terms. This is the kind of life which Islam wanted to replace by a life of decency and responsibility. So the Qur'an asked women to take more interest in the affairs of their homes and not wander about like butterflies to charm and attract members, of the male sex. The duty of remaining at home and the injunction prohibiting women from making a display of their charms are found together not without reason. The close proximity of these two items shows that women who are fond of displaying their beauty to outsiders cannot take the same interest in home affairs and family matters as others. If a woman, therefore, feels that her primary interest lies at home, she will naturally stay there and come out only in the face of a pressing necessity. This is all that the Qur'an means, and we are further supported in this interpretation by the next two verses of the Holy Qur'an which lay down some precautionary restrictions for women going out of their homes. If the Qur'an intended totally to prohibit the movement of women outside their homes, where was the necessity of laying down these restrictions on dress and movement? Moreover, as we have already explained in the previous chapter, the Holy Prophet expressly stated that women are permitted to go out for satisfying their legitimate wants when his companion, 'Umar objected to Sauda's coming out of her house.

Next comes the question whether women are required on coming out to hide their faces by means of a veil or *naqab*. The second verse quoted above directs women to put on a jilbab (over-garment) when they go outside their homes, and in the third verse it is stated that women should not exhibit any part of their body or ornament except 'what appears thereof'. Differences of opinion have arisen as to what the Qur'an exactly means by jilbab and what is the exact significance of 'what appears thereof.'

According to Alusi, the author of *Rub al-Ma'ani*, jilbab means an over-garment which a woman puts on over her ordinary clothes. Ibn 'Abbas, says Alusi, interpreted jilbab to mean a long and loose gown which covered a woman's body from her neck to feet. The author of *Fath al-Bayan*, a famous commentary of the Holy Qur'an, states that

"Ayeshah, the Prophet's wife, said: 'May God have mercy on the women of Ansar! When the Quranic verse relating to the wearing of jilbab was revealed to the Prophet, they tore off their big sheets of cloth and covered themselves with their torn parts (because, in those days, women did not use many clothes) and in this state offered their prayers behind the Prophet as silently as if crows were, seated on their heads.' These statements and interpretations read with that part of the Quranic verse which says that women should let down over them their jilbabs, because 'this will be more proper that they may be known, and thus they will not be given trouble,' give us the social and historical context to which the Quranic directions referred. It is clear from all this that: (a) the social behaviour of pre-Islamic Arabia was such that women moving out of their homes were interfered with and teased; (b) women in pre-Islamic Arabia did not properly dress themselves and used very few clothes moreover, they were fond of displaying their bodily charms, as testified by one of the above-quoted Quranic verses; (c) these conditions lasted, until Islam was completely successful; (d) Islam enjoined on women to put on a long overgarment, first, to serve as warning to the people that new standards of decency had come into force and Muslim women coming out of their homes observed these standards and should, therefore, be marked off from other women; secondly, to prevent the display of bodily features and charms. Now if the social morality of any country has advanced to the stage where women coming outside their homes are not interfered with or teased, the first ground on which women were ordered to wear a long overgarment disappears. But the second ground on which this injunction is based, namely, the need of preventing women from displaying and exhibiting their bodily charms, is not affected by any historical changes or development or social morality. As such there is no reason why this direction should not be observed by Muslim women even in advanced countries. Ordinary dress, even if it covers all parts of the body, can be such as to expose and bring into prominence the physical charms of women. It is, therefore, still necessary to put on a long over-garment over ordinary clothes.

But this does not solve the question whether women coming out of their homes are permitted to uncover their hands, feet and face, and whether a veil or naqab is necessary. It depends on the interpretation of the words 'except what appears thereof'. Let us see how the Prophet, his companions and the later authorities interpreted this phrase. Abu Dawud has related a tradition transmitted by 'Ayeshah, the Prophet's wife, wherein she says: Asma hint Abu Bakr came to the Prophet wearing thin clothes. The Prophet turned his face away and said: 'When a woman reaches puberty, it is not proper that any portion of her body should be seen by a man except these parts,' and he pointed towards his face and hands. 'Ayeshah also related that once her niece, Muzinah, came to her. On seeing her, the Prophet turned away his face. Ayeshah said that Muzinah was her niece and still a girl. The Prophet replied to her saying that when a girl comes of age, it is unlawful for her to display any part of her body except her face and two hands. Among the companions of the Prophet, according to Ibn Kathir, Sa'id and Ibn Mas'ud are of the opinion that 'what appears thereof' means clothes which a woman might be wearing. Ibn 'Abbas and Qatadah are of the opinion that it means eve-paint, signets and the hand-paint. Ibn 'Umar says 'what appears thereof' means face, hands and signet, because he is of the opinion that women are forced to uncover these parts. If they do not uncover their hands, they cannot buy or sell; if they do not expose their faces, they cannot act as witnesses, nor seek the hand of any man in marriage; if they do not uncover their feet, they can hardly go about for their necessities. Among the later authorities, 'Ata', Auza'i, Ibrahim Nakha'i, 'Ikramah and Dahhak agree that 'what appears thereof' has reference to hands, feet and face. Among the famous jurists of Islam, Imam Malik says that the entire body of a woman is included in *satr* (i.e. parts which should be kept fully covered), except the hands and face. Imani Shafi'i also makes an exception in favour of the face and hands. Imam Ahmad b. Hanbal says that the entire body of a woman should be kept fully covered except the face. Imam Abu Hanifah, the most widely accepted authority on Muslim jurisprudence, says that it is not lawful for a stranger to see any part of a woman's body, but he can see her face and hands. According to Imam Abu Yusuf, in addition to the face and the hands, the wrists of a woman may also be lawfully seen.

In his famous work, al-Muhalla, Ibn Hazm also expresses the same opinion. He says that the Quranic words 'they shall not display their ornaments except what appears thereof' expressly permit the uncovering of the face and the hands. Ibn Hazm further refers to an incident reported by Ibn 'Abbas who said that during the Farewell Pilgrimage of the Prophet a woman belonging to the tribe of Khasam came to see the Prophet. Ibn 'Abbas's brother, Fadl, was riding behind the Prophet on the same camel. The woman said to the Prophet: 'My father cannot perform the pilgrimage, which is a religious obligation, on account of old age. Is it permissible that I may perform the Hajj on his behalf?' The Prophet said, 'Yes.' The woman was very handsome and pretty. Fadl began to look at her. Thereupon the Prophet turned his face away. Ibn Hazm argues that if it were prohibited for a woman to uncover her face outside her home, how is it possible that the Prophet should have tolerated her to appear uncovered in public? Moreover, how could Ibn 'Abbas know whether she was ugly or pretty? Further, Fadl could not have looked at her. On these grounds Ibn Hazm declares that the uncovering of the face and hands in public is lawful for a woman.

From the opinions quoted above, it is clear that the vast majority of Muslim scholars, jurists and other religious authorities agree on this point: that a veil which totally covers the face of a woman is not necessary and that women have been permitted by Islam to come out with faces and hands uncovered in case of genuine need. But barring the face, the hands and the feet, all other parts, including the neck, should be completely covered and a long over-garment put on which leaves no part of the body exposed. Any kind of dress which, instead of hiding the bodily charms and features of women, brings them into greater prominence is definitely prohibited by Islam.

History and Tradition

The actual practice in the days of the Prophet, as evidenced by history and tradition, confirms the view that Muslim women came out of their homes frequently for satisfying their economic, intellectual and religious needs without putting on a veil but always dressed in full and wearing a loose over-garment which completely hid their bodily features and charms. Thus, 'Ayeshah, the Prophet's wife, reports that 'many believing women used to attend the prayers conducted by the Prophet wrapping themselves up in their long sheets. They then returned to their homes while it was still dark and nobody recognised them on account of darkness'. This report makes it clear that it was darkness and not the veil or any other face-covering which prevented people from recognising them. Another tradition states: 'Subiyyah Aslamiyyah - was married to Sa'd b Khaulah and he was one of those who were present at the battle of Badr. He died during the year of the Farewell Pilgrimage, leaving her pregnant. Sometime after the death of her husband, she delivered a child. When she became clean, she adorned herself to seek remarriage. Abu Sanabil Ba'kak of the family of 'Abd al-Dar passed by her and said to her: "Perhaps you intend to remarry as I see you fully adorned. By God, you cannot marry unless four months elapse on the death of your husband." Subiyah says, "On hearing this, I gathered upon me my clothes in the evening and came to the Prophet to ask him about this matter." The Prophet said that after childbirth, she could lawfully contract another marriage and allowed her to remarry.'

This incident, it is to be noted, happened after the last pilgrimage of the Prophet when the restrictions on the movement of women outside their homes had been enforced, and not in the earlier period, when Muslim women still enjoyed the untrammelled freedom of the days of Ignorance. It is clear that Subiyyah was not putting on a veil and her face was uncovered as otherwise she could not have been recognised. It is also clear that this uncovering of the face was not occasioned by her desire to remarry but it must have been her normal practice, as otherwise Abu Sanabil could not have identified her. It is also clear that Subiyyah did not go to the Prophet without putting on her full dress as she says, 'I gathered upon me my clothes,' which points to the use of many clothes including an over-garment. All this shows that women during the period of early Islam were not as closely confined to their homes as those of the Muslim middle classes now-a-days and that they enjoyed a fair amount of freedom of movement. But it is also clear from this that they observed all the restrictions on dress and movement enjoined by Islam. The picture which thus emerges is quite different from the traditional purdah observed by Muslim women and also from the untrammelled freedom of movement and dress enjoyed by women in Western countries. This is the point which our modernists forget when advocating the abolition of purdah.

That Islam has definitely prohibited the unnecessary intermingling of men and women and their joint participation in social and State-functions, is evident from the restrictions on the movement, dress and looks of men and women. Islam enjoins on both men and women to cast down their looks in the presence of each other. How is it possible for men and women to meet freely in dinners, tea-parties, social and State functions with looks cast down? There is not a single instance in the history of early Islam of men and women being allowed to meet each other freely in any social, political or religious gathering. Even in the mosques women had their separate rows at the time of prayers. They usually formed a separate group. The Prophet had enforced a rule that no man should stand shoulder to shoulder with a woman in the mosque, not even her husband or father. Bukhari relates a tradition on the authority of 'Ata' that during the days of the Prophet women performed their circumambulations round the Ka'bah but they were not allowed to mix with men. If this kind of segregation was enforced during religious worship and prayers, etc., which form the most essential duties of Muslim men and women, it is unthinkable that it was allowed to remain unobserved in other matters. Another example of this segregation of the sexes is found in the following tradition quoted by Abu Dawud in the chapter 'On the passage of women through streets'.

> Hamzah b. Abu Usaid Ansari transmits through his father that the Prophet was coming out of the mosque when he found that men and women had got mixed. He asked women to go behind and said: It is not proper for you to walk in the middle of the street. You should walk on the edge of the street. After this command, women walked so near the walls of the houses that their long sheets (over-garments) sometimes got stuck into the walls.

We have already discussed the point whether such segregation of the sexes would not exclude women from many public, social and industrial activities and we have shown that, barring emergencies, arrangements can be made in normal times for women to participate in all kinds of work in such a way that they do not mix with men. But where such intermingling becomes socially necessary and no method can be devised for preventing social intermixture, the needs of society must take precedence over legal command. Generally, however, men and women must work apart. If this leads to some deficiency in industrial or military strength, it must be put up for the sake of higher social values. In life one has sometimes to choose one evil from among many and it is always a rule that the greater evil should be avoided. It depends on the fundamental attitude of a civilisation whether it regards lack of industrial and technical efficiency as the more serious evil, or the breaking up of the family and the spread of sexual lavity with all its attendant consequences of jealousy, physical disease and weakness, etc., things which ultimately reduce and sometimes vitally impair the all-round efficiency of a nation and its capacity to put forth its most devoted and undivided efforts during a great social or political crisis.

15

Conclusion

First of all, prior to studying about the status of women in Islamic society and before dealing with the position of women under Islam, it would be well to examine how the question of women's rights and their claim for complete equality with men came to the forefront in modern times and what the underlying causes were which added strength to women's claim for freedom and equality. Such an analysis is called for in order to ascertain how far women's movement in modern history flourished out of a scientific and rational understanding of their powers, faculties and social functions and how far it represented merely a blind revolt against tradition, custom and artificial social restrictions and was prompted by desires untinged with altruism. It is necessary to make a dispassionate search for rational as well as non-rational factors in the modern women's movement, because otherwise our conclusions are likely to reflect the partisan spirit of one or the other side in the bitter controversy that has raged over women's demands.

An American writer, Mary R. Beard, sums up three divergent viewpoints on the subject of women's place in society in her book, *Woman as Force in History*. She says:

> One is the view that 'the women's problem,' a definition inspecting woman's place in society satisfactory to herself, can only be solved by

> complete equality with men, and that this equality can only be established under Communism. A second view is that woman must find her greatest happiness and contribute most to the state by limiting her ambitions to domesticity and still more narrowly to child-bearing, in order that the population rate may be high enough to keep a given nation secure against crowded societies on its borders, and strong enough within for aggressive action when desired against neighbours or more distant communities; this is the ideology of Fascism. The third view is that woman must have the right to choose her way of life even to the point of self centered interests; this is one among the ideologies of democracy.

Let us now see the actual historical circumstances which gave birth to these three viewpoints on the subject of women's place in society. We shall first deal with the democratic viewpoint which is historically prior to the ideology of fascism and communism.

The eighteenth century was a period of great social and intellectual unrest in Europe. The rising intelligentsia, and the middle classes of Western countries found themselves encumbered with a host of social barriers, economic restrictions and intellectual fetters which were blocking the path of progress in every direction. They were legacies of an age of feudalism which was already past. The feudal landlords, the Catholic Church with its vast power over men's bodies and souls and the Pope, headed the Church organisation, had a vested interest in perpetuating age-old customs and artificial social restrictions which the new spirit was seeking to break through. In these circumstances, it was not unnatural that, for the rising bourgeoisie of European countries, freedom and liberty should acquire a sanctity out of all proportion to their importance in the total scheme of human values. Thus, in the eighteenth and nineteenth-century Europe, liberty and freedom became exclusive sovereign values. The importance of all other ideals was lost sight of and the complementary values of order, discipline and responsibility, without which there could be no real liberty, were ignored and brushed aside as of no moment in the lives of-nations. History bears witness to the fact that when some powerful idea takes root in a civilisation, it permeates every sphere of human life and activity. The same thing happened with the notion of liberty which, extending from the domain of politics, invaded the social sphere and expressed itself in a demand for the readjustment of sex relations. Powerful voices were raised on behalf of the rights of the female sex which had long suffered from innumerable legal and social disabilities. Freedom and equality of, the sexes became accepted principles with the new social reformers.

In France, which was the centre of all revolutionary ideas, the Romantic school of literature and poetry first made an organised drive to popularise the ideal of sex equality. George Sand, who headed this school, was a woman of loose sexual morality. She proved unfaithful to her husband Who was driven to separation. Thereafter she led the life of a libertine forming promiscuous sexual relations with a number of men, among whom was Alfred Musse, a French poet of some renown. In her novels, *Lelia and Jacques*, she severely criticised the institution of marriage and advocated free love. George Sand was followed by another group of poets, novelists and dramatists among whom Alexander Dumas and Alfred Naquet stand out as the most prominent. These writers laid emphasis on the natural birthright of men and women to indulge in free sexual relations without the encumbrances of marriage. Mention must also be made of Mary Wollstencraft who wrote her book, *A Vindication of the Rights of Women*, in 1702. She reflected a more rational outlook which was coloured more, by the altruistic desire to serve the cause of women than open the floodgates of license. In this pioneer work she protested against the unjust and unequal treatment of women and condemned the whole system of law and custom that governed the relations of men and women. Her influence on the-women's movement in France was deep and widespread. These tendencies were reinforced by the Neo-Malthusian movement in England and France which sought to limit the growth of population by popularising the use of contraceptives. The Industrial Revolution in England, by throwing upon the crowded cities a vast army of peasants and rural craftsmen, unable to support their families, further accentuated this process and brought women into the economic field for the first time in history. The radicals and philanthropists of the 'fifties and 'sixties like Robert Owen, Ruskin, Bentham, and John Stuart Mill gave further impetus to the women's movement. In 1861 Mill wrote his famous book *Subjection of Women* in which he argued, with great precision and logic that the subjection of women was the product of age-long custom and did not testify to any inherent inferiority in the female sex. Mill contended that the distinctions between men and women which went to show the inferiority of women in the domains of mental and intellectual productions; were not natural but artificial, that is, a product of subjecting environment. The education and external circumstances in which women were being brought up were, according to him, responsible for their seeming inferiority; all other talk of her innate inferiority, he pointed out, was logical perversion and psychological misunderstanding. Under the stress of these social changes and intellectual movements, family ties loosened and domesticity lost its importance for women who were forced into the economic field by circumstances beyond their control. The ideal of sex equality came nearer, fulfilment than ever, though in ways which boded ill for the happiness, of individuals and the moral health of the community. In the Great War of 1914, a vast majority of the male population in European countries had to join the war services and many of non-military occupations, hitherto regarded as the closed preserve of the male sex, were thrown open to women who became more and more convinced of their ability to compete, with men on equal terms in all fields of life.

In 1941 when America entered the Second World War, millions of American women were taken into the armed forces, placed in uniform, disciplined by officers of their own sex working under naval and military authorities, accorded official ranking and honoured with decorations for bravery under fire; to relieve men for fighting, thousands of uniformed women worked as secretaries, clerks and officials. With skill and courage, women served as doctors and nurses in the battle areas and in war hospitals at home; and many were killed at the fronts while working near or under fire. In all the drives to raise money in aid of the armed services, American women assumed leadership and served in the ranks. They laboured to uphold the morale of the services at home and abroad. They toured the war areas and fronts as entertainers of the men under arms. They entered the war-production plants by millions and made possible the output of munitions and other war supplies on a scale that astounded the whole industrial world.

At the end of the war, American men and women alike in general hoped for a return to civilian life, and this meant a heated debate over public policies to be adopted with regard to 'equality of rights' in the distribution of employments, in the competition for places and rewards in economy and society. The old debate over women's place in society was reopened with added intensity. When in 1944 the War Department of United States issued its booklets for the education of soldiers at round table forums, it included one manual to invite a pointed argument: 'Do you want your wife to work after the war?' In this discussion one side argued that times have changed, that it is good and fitting for women to work that they are competent in any kind of job, hanker after economic independence, and are likely to hang on to a cash nexus for dear life. On the other side were those who argued that woman's place is in the home that her function is child-bearing and rearing and that men will not stand her competition with returned veterans.

So far we have examined the circumstances in which the democratic ideal of equality of sexes arose and gathered strength. Now let us turn to the Communist ideal. The leader of Communism in Russia, V.I. Lenin was ably supported and encouraged throughout his period of struggle by his wife, Krupskaya. When Lenin climbed to power in Russia, Krupskaya who had been a zealous champion of sex equality, helped to drive home, the issue of women's rights as one of the basic issues of the, revolution.

Lenin and his wife both knew very well that the Communist movement could have little prospect of success without the active support of women. And to win their full support, recognition of their right to full participation in the Communist regime was immediately given. In a speech delivered in September 1919 at the Fourth Moscow City Conference, Lenin declared: 'The Soviet Government has applied democracy to a greater extent than any other country, by the fact that in its laws not the slightest hint for any inferiority of women is left. I repeat, not a single state and no democratic legislation has done even half of what the Soviet Government did for women in the very first months of its existence.' In a conversation with Klara Zelkin, a prominent German socialist, Lenin elaborated the doctrine that 'real freedom for women is possible only through Communism.' Women must appreciate this and throw their energy into the Bolshevik Revolution,' he insisted.

'The Communist women's movement must itself be a mass movement, a part of the general mass movement. There can be no real mass movement without women. Unless millions of women are with us we cannot exercise the proletarian dictatorship, cannot construct on Communist lines. We must find out our way to them, we must study and try to find that way.' In Krupskaya's introduction to a Pamphlet by Lenin on Women and Society, the double power of women's revolutionary agitation and the Communist theory of its underlying importance were brought out. Krupskaya wrote, 'Ever since the beginning, of the Soviet rule, equal rights for women have been an object of interest, not only for women but for men as well.' As a result of these ideas, which impressed themselves on youthful minds, Russian women in great numbers agitated and organised at home and abroad for the realisation of their objects. They secured positions in Russia with the secret police and both judged and punished opponents of the Communist Party. After German troops invaded Russia, women who were not members of the Communist Party rushed like members of the party to defend their country. The Russian women, Communists as well as non-Communists, engaged in all phases of armed combat with the foe.

Like the Russian Soviet Revolution, the Fascist Revolution in Italy, Germany and Spain was also confronted with the necessity of winning women's support and their active co-operation in the struggle for Fascist ascendancy. The Fascist attitude to women was explained by Professor Maria Castellani in a volume on Italian Women, *Past and Present*, in which she said, 'Fascism recognises women as a part of the life-force of the country, laying down a division of duties between the two sexes, without putting obstacles in the way of those women who by their intellectual gifts can reach the highest positions.' Adolf Hitler, leader of the German Nazis, formulated the attitude of his movement towards women in a speech at Nuremburg on 15 September 1934, when he said, 'Woman has her battlefield. With each child that she brings to the nations, she fights her fights for the nation.' Such women as Sophic Rogge-Boemer, who called for the military training of women, were suppressed by Hitler and Goebbels in favour of women who devoted their strength and interest to child-bearing. Young women in large numbers responded enthusiastically to indoctrination on this point and entered the numerous maternity homes founded by the Nazis.

We have seen how the Democratic, Communist and Fascist viewpoints about the rights of women and their place in society were in part moulded by certain historical conditions and in part by political expediency designed to secure a larger following by enlisting the support of women. As far as the democratic viewpoint is concerned, it was free from the taint of political expediency but there was present in it from the very beginning a negative urge to sweep away age-long restrictions. Democracy failed, as in other fields, to develop a positive doctrine of women's rights and duties and continued itself to the removal of old abuses.

In contrast with the above-mentioned attitudes towards the problem of sex relations, Islamic teachings in regard to the position of women can be traced to neither of the sources. There was no political necessity for the Prophet of Islam to gain the favour of the fair sex, because the social conditions of Arabia were such that women's influence on the larger affairs of life was bound to be negligible. Nor was the Prophet of Islam confronted by the necessity of enlisting women for fighting a national war of defence or aggression against foreign countries. Therefore unlike Hitler and Mussolini, he had no motive to define women's rights and duties with an eye on the requirements of military defence or aggression. Again, in contrast to democracy, which was the outcome of a negative urge, to sweep away old restrictions that blocked the way to progress, Islam was more concerned with bringing some sort of discipline to a race of wild, freedom-loving Arabs who knew no respect for law and order and obeyed no central authority. The problem, therefore, for Islam was not so much the loosening of artificial bonds, as creating law, order and discipline among a people steeped in license and unacquainted with healthy social or moral restrictions. For all these reasons, Islam treated the question of sex equality and women's rights on its own merits and defined its attitude to sex relations on the basis of human nature rightly interpreted. Islamic teachings on this subject, therefore, spring from the ultimate facts of human nature in its social context. Military necessity, political expediency or merely blind revolt against the past did not in any way affect Islam's solution of the sex problem.

The question of the relationship between man and woman and their respective rights and duties is really a part of the larger socio-economic problem of man. Its solution depends on the way in which this larger problem is dealt with by a civilisation. It is wrong, therefore, to study the question of woman's rights and her place in society in isolation from the total context of human relationships in all their aspects. Before we pass any judgment on the particular way in which a civilisation deals with the sex problem, we should consider its total approach to human existence, so as, to, enable us to view its specific solution in their larger and total setting. But for this, we shall have to define the basic attitude of a civilisation towards life in general. In the next chapter, therefore, we shall attempt to define the basic approach of Islam towards human existence, in contrast with that of the Western civilisation, because this approach has decisive bearing on the way in which Islam grappled with the problem of sex equality and the rights of women.

Because of the pressure of many forces every country of the Moslem East, as we have seen, shows some trend of change in the relationship between religion and life. The control of Islam as an iron clad system of rules and traditions is giving way to a more individual interpretation of religion. Since this new spirit of religious liberalism deeply affects the life of women, one constantly feels the desire to know the personal attitude of Moslem women toward their religion, and their share in determining the new religious thought in Islam.

The older generation as a whole in every country tends to be conservative in all religions but this is especially true of Islam. This unquestioning adherence to the literal interpretation of the teaching of their religion is especially characteristic of women in the middle and lower levels of society, regardless of age, and also of the village women of Asia. This great majority of Moslem women, who have remained untouched by Western influence, have been little conscious of any changes in Islam, and have themselves undergone no change in their religious outlook. In fact, they constitute very often a distinct deterrent to change, opposing any deviation from established social customs, which are in their minds identified with religious sanctions. It is very often the orthodox wife or mother who maintains the rigid conservatism of the home, however lax men may become in their observance of religious customs outside the home.

The full meaning of Islam for the devoted Moslem woman is difficult for a mere outsider to understand. This is one veil of Moslem life which the Western observer cannot lift. Accustomed to a different form of religious experience, one from the West may easily draw a false conclusion regarding the relationship of Moslem women to their religion. The small number of women in the mosques in most countries — Turkey is an exception-which offers a striking contrast to the usual predominance of women in churches in the West, might be interpreted as a lack of worship of Moslem women, if one did not know that it is not the public prayers in the mosque but her private prayers at home which have primary significance for the Moslem woman. In her home the orthodox woman will pray, with her face turned towards Mecca, five times daily in the name of the Prophet to the one God, and will cherish the devout hope as a constant follower of Mohammed, that she may make the pilgrimage to the Holy City.

The keynote of the Moslem woman's religion is complete acquiescence to fate; to protest against a lack of privileges is quite foreign to her nature. Islam may have deprived her of privileges but not of responsibilities. Her primary obligation is to accept as the will of Allah, whatever is written on her forehead as her fate. This spirit of fatalism has insured the undisturbed control of Islam over the destiny of Moslem women through the centuries. Today, although the great majority of Moslem women have remained unchanged in their personal attitude toward their religion, a small minority of women has begun to question the relationship between the accepted teaching of Islam and the demands of their modern world. Education inevitably is undermining the characteristic attitude of fatalism toward religion and life. One begins to find in the different parts of the Islamic world Moslem women expressing an independent opinion of the interpretation of Islam, in order to bring religion into accord with modern needs.

Speaking on purdah in a public address, Lady Abdul Qadir, one of the outstanding Moslem leaders of India, said: "Purdah, as observed among certain classes of Indian Mohammedans, is far beyond anything enjoined by Islam and requires modification according to the needs of the day and the rapidly changing times." Another interesting illustration of the modern approach to Islam by a Moslem woman in India is the aggressive challenge to the Ulemas, the authorities of Islam, made by

Begum Habibullah, an enlightened Moslem leader in Lucknow in a newspaper article, in which she showed that the Koran does not teach educational inequality and segregation of women.

Indian women are deeply imbued with religion, but their religious devotion today does not cloud the vision of the educated minority, nor even of a larger number, so that they cannot discriminate between religious and social questions. The widespread testimony against child-marriage gathered from Indian women of all classes *by the Age of ass came as a great surprise Consent Commission,* doubtless to many in India and elsewhere who had not realized that there is a Growing spirit of religious freedom among Indian women. The All-India Women's Conference, representing as it does the inter-communal effort of women leaders to release social reform from the bonds of religious tradition, has repeatedly given utterance to the new religious liberalism. In India, more than in any other country of the East, women have been impelled to protest individually and collectively against social handicaps. The active promotion and support of the Child Marriage Act, and the repeated resolutions against polygamy passed by the All-India Women's Conference, are exerting a powerful force toward the freedom of Hindu and Moslem women from these and other social customs, hitherto regarded as determined by religious sanctions.

The fact that women have challenged the inviolability of these sanctions is perhaps no less important than the social reforms themselves. Some Indian leaders are especially concerned to keep their endorsement of social advance in harmony with religious teaching. In the discussion on polygamy at a recent 'All-India Conference, one of the Moslem delegates explained that she favoured the abolition of polygamy, but she wished to call attention to the fact that "it was permitted by their religion only in case of strictest necessity arising, as for example, in the event of there being no issue from the first marriage."

Syria offers an interesting example of an interpretation of the social teachings of the Koran, made by a young Druse girl Nazira Zein-el-Din, in her book, *As-Sufur-Weel-Hijab* (Unveiling and Veiling), which evoked much comment. This book was translated into several languages, widely circulated, and brought the author a trunkful of clippings from all over the world. The Islamic teaching concerning the veil was discussed also in an oratorical contest at the American University of

Beirut by Madame Ihsan Shakir El-Kousy, to whom reference has already been made. In her address, which received the second prize, she showed that the Koran does not prescribe the veil. Thus, incidentally she justified her own presence unveiled in a large university.

These two examples, however, are not typical of the .women of either Syria or Egypt as a whole but less so of Syria. There is very little evidence of any analysis of Islam and very little articulate expression on religion by women in Syria: a very small minority of Egyptian women is actively interested in the relation of religion to reform. The attitude of Madame Sharawi Pasha, to whom reference has already been made as the outstanding Moslem woman leader in Egypt, shows general conformity to the prevailing policy in Egypt as regards the promotion of social advance. She has carefully based her demands for social reform on the spirit of the Koran and has not promoted reforms which do not have Islamic sanction. For example, her claims for equality of education for girls have been based on the teaching of the Koran. She has urged a law prohibiting polygamy. Reference has been made to her very effective protest against polygamy in a public lecture at the American University in Cairo last year. But while protesting against polygamy she recognizes the exceptions for polygamy which are granted by the Koran (adultery, childlessness and incompatibility). One has the feeling that this policy of maintaining a careful balance between Islamic teaching and social reform, which is followed by Madame Sharawi and the Feminist Union, is dictated more by political expediency than by religious conservatism.

Among the women of Palestine no deviation from the conventional attitude toward Islam is evident. Moslem women simply reflect the prevailing religious conservatism. However, the interesting feature in the situation, to which reference has already been made in another connection, is that Moslem women pay the price for this conservatism, of which the veil is the symbol, willingly and with a sense of pride; since by retaining the characteristic Islamic customs they feel that they have a certain distinction in contrast to the Zionist community. It is worth recalling the incident showing the counter-influence of Arab national feeling in reference to the veil, when the, group of Arab women unveiled made a protest against Zionism. But as already explained, the veils were later resumed when the habitual spirit of conservatism reasserted itself. The great majority of Moslem women in Palestine, as elsewhere, are not aware of the new conflicting currents of thought.

The attitude of women in Iran and Iraq toward religion, as toward social advance, is one of passive acquiescence. Changes in Turkey have aroused much interest in both countries, and the Turkish method of drastic social and religious reforms has been little questioned in reference to its having an adverse effect on religion. The women of Iraq and Iran have been primarily interested in the achievement of Turkey. Very often in Iraq I heard the statement: "We need a Kamal Ataturk." In Iran the hope was frequently expressed at the time of my visit several years ago, that the Shah would follow Kamal Ataturk's example and issue an order to remove the *chaddur*. In Iran as elsewhere it was erroneously believed that unveiling in Turkey had been made compulsory. This hope has now been realized and, it is interesting to note, that the definite regulations against the chaddur have not apparently caused a widespread religious shock among the women of Iran. Even the conservatives are accepting the new freedom, I have been told, as they accepted the former social restrictions, in an attitude of acquiescence.

In marked contrast to the attitude of women in Iraq and Iran toward Turkey, Moslem women in India have repeatedly asked me with deep solicitude whether Turkey had cast aside Islam. "Have Turkish women lost their religion?" was the question that came alike from the student group and from conservative older women. The new freedom of Turkish women, if secured at the sacrifice of religion, would seem to Moslem women in India to have cost too high a price.

In Turkey women have regarded religious changes together with all other changes, as merely a natural part of the general transformation taking place in Turkish life. There has been remarkably little analysis of the new situation in reference to the effect on religion. During the first crucial years of change the conservatives retained the veil, which older women doubtless associated with religion. But by this time the veil has, I believe, for the great majority lost any religious significance it may have had. However, recent municipal legislation of Adana and some other cities, has doubtless brought a shock to those who still have the feeling of the relationship between the veil and Islam. But they will probably accept the enforced change philosophically, as did a conservative Turkish woman in Adana, whose comment on the new regulation was: "Well, the sin will be charged against those who issued such an order and not against us, because they are forcing us to do this against our wills." This idea that unveiling is an actual sin, is probably held by very few Turkish women today.

The viewpoint of these orthodox Turkish women can scarcely fail to be affected unconsciously by the modern atmosphere, which has become steadily more natural, even in the smaller towns of the Interior. The new type of preaching of the *hodjah* has also had its effect. As a simple Turkish woman in Talas told me several years ago, "They tell us different things about religion today. The hodjahs formerly taught that women must always be veiled and their voice never heard in public. But they say now that these things are not religion." Thus, the most orthodox women have been steadily exposed to the new idea, that social customs are not necessarily, identified with religion.

The educated Turkish woman has adopted such new ideas as a logical part of the modernization of Turkish life. Before the recent period of reform this educated minority was already progressive in religious thinking for, as has already been mentioned in the discussion of Turkish education, the social- religious revolution in Turkey was preceded by a gradual period of preparation. Today due to many forces there is said to be a decline in the formal practices of Islam. "Many people no longer pray five times a day. Everyone is too busy," was the comment of a young Turkish business woman. A young teacher explained why comparatively few young people go to the mosques. "We must make our worship more modern to suit our modern clothes and customs. Praying without shoes and with many genuflections was a good thing in the Prophet's day but does not suit our present kind of life."

Although the private prayers of the formal type are still continued by many Moslem women in the homes and to a lesser extent in the mosque, as has always been the case among women, the turning away from the ritualistic worship by the younger generation is undoubtedly a marked present-day tendency. However, this should not, as has been said before, be interpreted merely as a trend toward irreligion, but perhaps it may indicate the genuine urge for a reform in worship, so that it may be something more than a prescribed ceremonial. "We are beginning to recognize the difference between essentials and nonessentials," a thoughtful Turkish woman said. "The religious forms and social restrictions are not suitable today. These can be changed without destroying our fundamental belief".

Another Turkish leader, talking with a Moslem woman from Jerusalem, who had expressed the belief that Turkey had sacrificed Islam, said, "We have separated religion from externals and made it personal. Religicn is not a matter of clothes-the veil and the *fez*. It is not based on form but feeling. The repudiation of Islamic formalism therefore does not mean giving up Islam. The women of Palestine may be more outwardly religious in the orthodox sense of Islam but not necessarily more truly religious in the inner meaning of the term than are the women of Turkey."

In regard to this transfer of emphasis from the external to the more individual idea of religion, a young Turkish woman student in Istanbul University expressed the opinion that there is need now for a more positive interpretation of religion. "Most of the younger Turkish girls will grow up with very little idea of Islam," she said, "since nothing positive has taken the place of the old forms, which have lost their appeal, and since very little attention these days is paid to religion." The need for a more definite constructive idea of religion is probably not as yet generally recognized by the younger generation in Turkey, which associates religion merely with a peaceful existence of quiet contemplation in the shade of mosque walls and not with an intensely active modern life.

However, a number of thoughtful Turkish leaders, both men and women, but perhaps especially women, are beginning to realize the need of a new relationship between religion and life. It is, I believe, not too much to expect that Turkish women, who have gained so much from the social and religious reforms in Turkey, may now make some special contribution to the rethinking of religious values. Their voice, and the voice of Moslem women in other countries, which have been so little heard in shaping religious thought in the past, may help to answer the crucial question in the East today, as to whether the present spirit of religious liberalism in the Moslem world will mean the disintegration of Islam or the beginning of a new era of more vital faith.

Bibliography

Afifi Abu'l-'Ala, *The Mystical Philosophy of Muhiy'd Din lbnu'l 'Arabi*, Cambridge, 1939.

Ahmad, Zubaid, *The Contribution of Indo-Pakistan to Arabi Literature*, Lahore, 1968.

Arberry, A.J., *An Introduction to the History of Sufism*, London, 1942.

———, *The Mystical poems of Ibn al-Farid*, (ed.), Dublin, 1956.

———, (tr.), Discourses of Rumi, London, 1961.

———, *Muslim Saints and Mystics*, London 1964.

———, *Aspects of Islamic Civilization*, Ann Arbor,1963.

———, *Religion in the Middle East*, (ed.), Cambridge, 1969.

Arnold, Sir Thomas, *The Caliphate*, rev. edn., London, 1965.

Bagley, R.R.C., *Ghazali's Book of Cousel for King*, Oxford, 1964. .

Boyle, J. A. ed., *The Cambridge History'of Iran*. Cambridge, 1968.

Browne, E.G. *A Literary History of Persia,* Vols., reprint, Cambridge, 1957.

Burckhardit, Titus, *Introduction to Sufi Doctrines*, Lahore 1959.

Burton.Sir Richard, and Races that Inhabit the Valley of the Indus, London, 1851.

Corbin, H, Avicenna and the Visionary Recital, tr. *W. Trash*, New York and London, 1960.

Czaplicka, M.A., *The Turks of Central Asia in History and the Present Day*, Amsterdam, 1973.

Dawud, Rahbar, *God of Justice*, Leiden. 1960.

De Laet, *Description of India and Fragment of Indian History*, New York, 1963.

Divine Epiphany and Spiritual Rebirth in Ismailian Gnosis', *Man and Transformation,* New York and London, 1964.

Etude preliminaire pour le'Livre reunisiant les deux sagesses', *de Nasir-e Khosraw*, Tehran and Paris, 1953.

Faris, Nabith A., *The Foundations' of the Articles of Faith*, Lahore, 1963.

Faniqi, Bhrhan Ahmad, *The Mujaddid's Conception of Tauhid*, Lahore, 1940.

Faruqi, Ziya'u-i Hasan *The Deoband School and the Demand for Pakistan*, Bombay, 1963.

Field, Cland H., *Mystics of Saints of Islam*, London, 1910.

Fordon, S., *Preliminary Statement on a General Theory of the Islamization of the Malay-Indonesian Archipelago*, Kuala Lumpur, 1969.

Francois Bernier, *Travels in the Mogul Empire*, London, 1916.

Frykenberg, R.E. (ed.,) *Land Control and Social Structure in Indian History*, Wisconsin, 1969.

Gairdner, W.H. Temple, *The Niche for Lights*, London, 1915.

Gibb, H.A.R., *Islamic Society and the West*, London, 1960.

Gilsenan, Mechael, *Saint and Sufi in Modern Egypt*, Oxford, 1973.

Gonda, J., *History of Indian Literature*, Wiesbaden, 1973-75.

Haq. M. Anwaru'l *The Faith Movement of Mawlana Muhammad Ilyas*, London, 1972.

Haqq, En'amul, Muslim Bengali Literature, Karachi, 1957.

Hasan, Ibn, *The Central Structure of the Mughal Empire*, New Delhi, 1980.

Hasrat, B.J., *Dara Shikuh: Life and Works*, New Delhi, 1982.

Herklots, ed., by W. Crooke, Oxford, 1921, New Delhi, 1972.

Hodgson, G.S, *The Order of Assassin*, The Hague, 1955.

Holt, P.M. and Lambton, A.K.S., *The Cambridge History of Islam*, Cambridge, 1970.

Husain, Wahed, *Administration of Justice during the Muslim Rule in India*, Delhi, 1977.

Hussain, Yusuf, *L'Inde Mystique au Moyen Age*, Paris, 1929.

Husaini, S.A.Q., *The Pantheistic Monism of Ibn al-'Arabi*, Lahore, 1970.

Ikram, S.M., *The Cultural Heritage of Pakistan*, Karachi, 1955.

Iqbal 'Ali Shah, Sardar, *Islamic Sufism*, London, 1933.

Iqbal, Sir Muhammad, *Six Lectures on the Reconstruction of Religious Thought in Islam*, Lahore, 1930.

Irfan Habib, *The Agrarian System of Mughal India*, Bombay, 1963.

Irvine, W., *Later Mughals*, New Delhi, 1971.

Izutsu, Toshihdo, *Ethico-religous Concepts in the Quran*, 1966.

Ja'far Sharif, *Islam in India*, or *the Qamun-i Islam* tr., by G.A.

Jalbani,G. M, *Teachings of Shah Waliyullah* of Delhi, Lahore, 1973.

Khaja Khan, *Studies in Tasawwuf*, Madras, 1923.

Khushwant Singh, A History of the Sikhs, Princeton, 1963.

Landau, R., *The Philosophy of the Ibn'* Arabi, London, 1959.

Les Motifis *Zoroastriens dans la philosophie de Sohrawardi*, Tehran, 1946.

Lewis, Bernard, *Islam*, New York, 1974.

Lings, Martin, *A Sufi Saint of the Twentieth Century*, London, 1971.

L'ismaelisme et le symbole de la Croix', *La Table Ronde*, Paris, December, 1957.

Luckner, R.C., *The Bhagavad-Gita*, Oxford, 1969.

McCarthy, R.I. *The Theology of al-Ash'ari*, Beirut, 1953.

MacDonald, D.B., *The Religious Attitude and Life in Islam*, Beirut, 1965.

Manocci, N, *Storia do Mogor*, 1653-1708, tr. W. Irvine, London, 1907-8, reprint. New Delhi, 1980.

Massignon, L., *Essai sur les origines de lexique technique de la mystique musulmane*, Paris, 1928.

Mayne, P, *Saints of Sind*, London, 1965.

Meer Hassan Ali, *Observations on the Musulmauns of India*, London, 1832.

Melanges Louis, *Confessions Extatiques de Mir Damad*', Massing non, I, France 1965.

Mir Valiuddin, *Love of God*, Hyderabad-Deccan, 1968.

Mirza, Waheed, *The Life and Works of Amir Khusrau*, Calcutta, 1935.

Mohaghegh. Mahdi and Landolt. *Collected Papers on Islamic Philosophy and Mysticism*, Tehran, 1971.

Mohan Singh Diwana, *Sheikh Mysticism*, Amritsar, 1964.

Mohiuddin Ahmad, *Saiyid Ahmad Shahid*, Lucknow, 1975.

Mole Marigan, *Les Mystiques Musulmans*, Paris, 1965.

Monserrate, Fr. A., Commentary, tr. J.S. *Holyland and annotated* by S.N. Banerjee, Cuttack, 1922.

Moreland, W.H., *From Akbar to Aurangzeb*, London, 1923, New Delhi, 1972.

Mujeeb, M., *The Indian Muslims*, London, 1969.

Nageeb al-Attas, Syed, Raniri and the Wajudiyyah of 17th Century Acheh, Singapore, 1966.

Nasr, Seyyed H., *An Introduction to Islamic Cosmological Doctrines*, Cambridge, Mass., 1964.

Nicholson, R.A., *Studies in Islamic Mysticism*, 1921, Cambridge,1967.

Nyberg, H. S., *Kleinere Schrifteu des Iban 'Arabi,* Leiden, 1919.

Padwick, C.E., *Muslim Devotions*, London, 1960.

Palamer, E.H., Oriental Mysticism, London, 1969.

Petersen, E.L., *'Ali and Mu'awiya in early Arabic Traditions*, Copenhagen, 1964.

Philips, E.C.ed., *Politics and Society in India*, London, 1963.

Qanungo, K.R., *Dara Shikoh*, Calcutta, 1935.

Qureshi, I.H., *The Muslim Community of the Indo-Pakistan Subcontinent*, The Hague, 1962.

Rafiqi, A. Q. *Sufism in Kashmir*, Delhi, 1977.

Raverty, H. G. *Selections from the Poetry of the Afghans,* London, 1862.

Recherehes sur l'hermeneutique lutherienne' *Annuaire de l' Ecole des Hautes Etudfs Section des Sciences Religieuses,* Paris, 1939.

Richards, J.F. *Mughal Administration in Golkonda*, Oxford, 1975.

Riazu'l Islam, *Indo-Persian Relations*, Tehran/Lahore, 1970.

Rizvi, S.A.A., *Religious and Intellectual History of the Muslims in Akbar's Reign*, Delhi, 1975.

Rosenthal, E.I.J., *Political Thought in Medieval Islam*, Cambridge, 1962.

Russel, Ralph and Khurshidu'l Islam. *The Mughal Poets*, Cambridge, Mass., 1968.

Sadarangani, H.I., *Persian Poets of Sing*, Karachi, 1956.

Sadiq, M., *A History of Urdu Poetry*, London, 1964.

Saksena, B.P., *History of Shahjahan of Dihli*, Allahabad, 1958.

Saksena, R.B., *A History of Urdu Literature*, Allahabad, 1927.

Saran, P., *Studies in Medieval Indian History*, Delhi, 1952.

Schacht, J., *The Origin of Muhammadan Jurisprudence*, Oxford, 1950.

Schimmel, A., *Gobriel's Wing*, Leiden, 1963.

Sharif, M.M., *A History of Muslim Philosophy*, Wlesbaden.

Sharma, R.S. and Jha, V. ed., *Indian Society: Historical Probings*, Delhi, 1974.

Sharma, S.R., *The Religious Policy of the Mughal Emperors*, London, 1962.

Shehadi, F., Ghazali's *Unique Unknowable God*, Leiden, 1964.

Shejwalker, T.S., *Panipat: 1761*, Poona, 1946.

Shemesh, A.B., *Taxation in Islam*, Leiden, 1958, 1965.

Sherwani, H.K., *Muhammad Quli Qutb Shah*, Bombay, 1968.

Siddiqi, M.Z., *Hadith Literature*, Calcutta, 1961.

Smith, M., *An early Mystic of Baghdad*, Cambridge, 1920.

Sorley, H.T., *Shah 'Abdu' i Latif of Bhit: His Poetry, Life and Times*, 1940, Oxford, 1966.

Spear, P., *Twilight of the Mughals*, Cambridge, 1969, New Delhi, 1970.

Storey, C.A., *Persian Literature*, a Bibliographical Survey, London, 1927-58.

Subhan, J.A., *Sufism: Its Saints and Shrines*, Lucknow, 1960.

Sufi, G.M.D., *Kashmir*, Lahore, 1940-9.

Tarachand, *Society and State in the Mughal Period*, Delhi, 1961.

Tavernier, Jean-Baptiste, *Travels in India*, 1640-67, tr. V. Ball, ed. and revised by W. Crooke, London, 1925, reprinted, New Delhi, 1977.

Temple, R.C., *Legends of the Punjab*, London, 1893-1901.

Terre Celeste, *Histoire de la Philosophic Islamique*, Paris, 1964.

Thevenot, Jean de., Relation dei'Indostan, 1666-67, by Lovell, edn. by S.N. Sen, *The Indian Travels of Thevenat and Careri*, New Delhi, 1949.

Thomas, R.C., *Legends of the Punjab*, London, 1893-1901.

Thomas, W.F., *Mutual Influence of Muhammedans and Hindus in India*, Cambridge, 1892.

Titus, M., *Indian Islam*, Milford, 1930.

Tod, J., *Annals and Antiquities of Rajasthan*, Oxford, 1920.

Trimingham. J.S., *The Sufi Orders in Islam*, Oxford, 1920.

Tripathi, R.P., *Some aspects of Muslim Administration*, Allahabad, 1959.

Tritton, A.S., *The Caliphs and their non-Muslim Subjects*, Oxford, 1930.

Underhill, E., *Mysticism: A Study in the Nature and Development of Man's Spiritual Consciousness*, Paperback, New York, 1956.

Vaudeville, Charlotte, Kabir, Oxford, 1974.

Walker, B., *Hindu World*, London, 1968.

Wang Gungwu, ed., *Self and Biography*, Sydney, 1974.

Watanmal, L., *The Life of Shah' Abdul Latif*, Hyderabad, Sind, 1889.

Watt, M., *Muslim Intellectual: A Study of al-Ghazali*, Edinburgh, 1963.

Whitting, C.E.J., *Al-Fakhri*, London, 1947.

Wolfson, H.A., *Glimpses of Medieval Indian Culture*, Bombay, 1959.

Yusuf Iblish and Peter Lambron *Wilson Traditional Modes of Contemplation and Action*, Tehran, 1977.

Zaehner, R.C., *Hindu and Muslim Mysticism*, London, 1960.

Index

❑❑❑